Language, Migration and Social Inequalities

WITHDRAWN

MIX
Paper from
responsible sources
FSC
www.fsc.org   FSC® C014540

LANGUAGE, MOBILITY AND INSTITUTIONS
Series Editors: Celia Roberts (*King's College London, UK*) and Melissa Moyer (*Universitat Autònoma de Barcelona, Spain*)

This series focuses on language and new ways of looking at the challenges facing institutions as a result of the mobility and connectedness characteristic of present-day society. The relevant settings and practices encompass multilingualism, bilingualism and varieties of the majority language and discourse used in institutional settings. The series takes a wide-ranging view of mobility and also adopts a broad understanding of institutions that incorporates less studied sites as well as the social processes connected to issues of power, control and authority in established institutions.

Full details of all the books in this series and of all our other publications can be found on http://www.multilingual-matters.com, or by writing to Multilingual Matters, St Nicholas House, 31–34 High Street, Bristol BS1 2AW, UK.

Language, Migration and Social Inequalities

A Critical Sociolinguistic Perspective
on Institutions and Work

Edited by
**Alexandre Duchêne, Melissa Moyer
and Celia Roberts**

MULTILINGUAL MATTERS
Bristol • Buffalo • Toronto

Library of Congress Cataloging in Publication Data
Language, Migration and Social Inequalities: A Critical Sociolinguistic Perspective
on Institutions and Work/ Edited by Alexandre Duchêne, Melissa Moyer and Celia
Roberts.
Language, Mobility and Institutions: 2
Includes bibliographical references and index.
1. Sociolinguistics. 2. Linguistic minorities—Employment. 3. Immigrants—
Employment. 4. Immigrants—Language. I. Duchêne, Alexandre, editor of compila-
tion. II. Moyer, Melissa G. – editor of compilation. III. Roberts, Celia – editor of
compilation.
P40.L2977 2013
306.44–dc23 2013036521

British Library Cataloguing in Publication Data
A catalogue entry for this book is available from the British Library.

ISBN-13: 978-1-78309-100-3 (hbk)
ISBN-13: 978-1-78309-099-0 (pbk)

Multilingual Matters
UK: St Nicholas House, 31-34 High Street, Bristol BS1 2AW, UK.
USA: UTP, 2250 Military Road, Tonawanda, NY 14150, USA.
Canada: UTP, 5201 Dufferin Street, North York, Ontario M3H 5T8, Canada.

The policy of Multilingual Matters/Channel View Publications is to use papers that are
natural, renewable and recyclable products, made from wood grown in sustainable
forests. In the manufacturing process of our books, and to further support our policy,
preference is given to printers that have FSC and PEFC Chain of Custody certification.
The FSC and/or PEFC logos will appear on those books where full certification has been
granted to the printer concerned.

Typeset by Techset Composition India (P) Ltd., Bangalore and Chennai, India.
Printed and bound in Great Britain by Short Run Press Ltd.

Contents

Contributors

Kori Allan is a PhD candidate in Linguistic and Sociocultural Anthropology at the University of Toronto. She is currently completing her dissertation, entitled *Learning Flexible Labour: Citizenship and (Im)migrant Integration in Canada's Knowledge-Based Economy.* Her research interests are in language, labour and migration, and in neoliberalism, citizenship and governmentality.

Mike Baynham is Professor of Teaching English to Speakers of Other Languages (TESOL) at the University of Leeds, where he is Director of the Centre for Language Education Research. He has a long-standing interest in narrative and migration, exemplified in the volume co-edited with Anna de Fina, *Dislocations/Relocations: Narratives of Displacement* (2005, St Jerome). He has led a number of international research networks under the auspices of AILA, firstly on literacy with Mastin Prinsloo, and more recently on Language and Migration, co-convened with Stef Slembrouck. The activities of the Language and Migration Research Network included a seminar series with seminars held in Leeds, Limerick, Coimbra, Barcelona and Fribourg. With Jim Collins and Stef Slembrouck he co-edited a volume based on papers from earlier seminars entitled *Globalization and Language in Contact: Scale, Migration and Communicative Practices* (2009, Continuum). He is currently working with a research group developing a research agenda on lesbian, gay and bisexual issues in adult ESOL.

Eva Codó is Associate Professor of English and Linguistics at Universitat Autònoma de Barcelona, Spain. Her research explores issues of multilingualism and mobility from an ethnographic sociolinguistic perspective. She has carried out fieldwork in a number of institutional spaces in the Barcelona metropolitan region, most notably in state offices and NGOs. She has also participated in projects investigating language practices in educational establishments (secondary and post-secondary). Her research has been published internationally in journals such as *Discourse & Society, Discurso y Sociedad, Spanish in Context, Langage et société* and *Sociolinguistic Studies*. She is the author of *Immigration and Bureaucratic Control: Language Practices in Public Administration* (2008, Mouton de Gruyter).

Alexandre Duchêne is Professor of Sociology of Language at the University of Fribourg and Director of the Institute of Multilingualism of the University and HEP Fribourg (Switzerland). His research focuses on language and social inequalities, language and political economy and on linguistic minorities and international rights. Recent publications include *Ideologies Across Nations* (2008, Mouton de Gruyter), *Discourses of Endangerment* (with Monica Heller, 2007, Continuum), *Langage, genre et sexualité* (with Claudine Moïse, 2011, Nota Bene) and *Language in Late Capitalism: Pride and Profit* (with Monica Heller, 2011, Routledge).

Werner Holly was Professor of *Germanistische Sprachwissenschaft* at the TU Chemnitz, Germany. His main research areas are: pragmatics, linguistics of text and conversation, language in politics, language and the media, and audiovisuality. Major publications include *Imagearbeit in Gesprächen* (Tübingen, 1979), *Politikersprache* (Berlin, 1990), *Politische Fernsehdiskussionen* (with Peter Kühn and Ulrich Püschel, 1986, Tübingen), *Der sprechende Zuschauer* (edited with Ulrich Püschel and Jörg Bergmann, 2001, Wiesbaden), *Einführung in die Pragmalinguistik* (2001, Berlin), *Fernsehen* (2004, Tübingen), *Über Geld spricht man* (with Stephan Habscheid, Frank Kleemann, Ingo Matuschek and G. Günter Voß, 2006, Wiesbaden), and *Linguistische Hermeneutik* (edited with Fritz Hermanns, 2007, Tübingen).

Vally Lytra is Lecturer in Education at Goldsmiths, University of London. Her research interests include language, identity and social interaction in multiethnic urban contexts, language ideologies and discourses on multilingualism and faith literacies. She is the author of *Play Frames and Social Identities: Contact Encounters in a Greek Primary School* (2007, Benjamins) and has co-edited with the late Peter Martin *Sites of Multilingualism: Complementary Schools in Britain Today* (2010, Trentham). She is currently editing *'When Greek Meets Turk': Interdisciplinary Perspectives on the Relationship since 1923* (forthcoming, Ashgate).

Luisa Martín Rojo is Professor in Linguistics at the Universidad Autónoma (Madrid, Spain) and Member of the International Pragmatic Association Consultation Board (2006–2011; re-elected for the period 2012–2017). Since

2000, she has led a research group (MIRCO, http://www.ffil.uam.es/mirco/ index_eng.php), focused on studying the management of cultural and linguistic diversity in Madrid schools, applying a sociolinguistic and ethnographic perspective. Her publications in this field are numerous; the most significant could be *Constructing Inequality in Multilingual Classrooms* (2010).

Ulrike Hanna Meinhof is Professor of German and Cultural Studies and Director of the Centre for Transnational Studies at the University of Southampton. She has directed major research projects for the EU Framework programmes (*EU Border Discourse*, 2000–2003, *Changing City Spaces*, 2002–2005, *Sefone*, 2007–2010) and the AHRC's *Diaspora, Migration and Identity Programme* (*TNMundi*, 2006–2010). Key publications include *The Language of Belonging* (with Dariusz Galasinski, 2005), *Transcultural Europe* (co-edited with Anna Triandafyllidou, 2006), *Cultural Globalization and Music* (with Nadia Kiwan, 2011), *Music and Migration* (co-edited with Nadia Kiwan, 2011), and *Negotiating Multicultural Europe: Borders, Networks, Neighbourhoods* (co-edited with Heidi Armbruster, 2011).

Melissa G. Moyer is Professor of English Linguistics at the Universitat Autònoma de Barcelona where she leads the CIEN Research Team. She has carried out research on the management of multilingualism in public health institutions. Her current investigation is concerned with multilingualism and mobility in connection to linguistic practices and the construction of identity by persons who move around the globe and settle in new places for purposes of work and leisure. She is analyzing narratives of language and mobility trajectories of language tourists who travel to London to learn English. Among her recent publications are a chapter entitled 'Sociolinguistic perspectives on language and multilingualism in institutions' in M. Martin-Jones and S. Gardner (eds) *Multilingualism, Discourse and Ethnography* (2012, London: Routledge, pp. 34–47), 'What multilingualism? Agency and unintended consequences of multilingual practices in a Barcelona health clinic' (2011, *Journal of Pragmatics* 43/5, pp. 1209–1221) and 'The management of multilingualism in public, private and non-governmental institutions' (2010, *Sociolinguistic Studies* 4/2, pp. 267–296), as well as being editor of *The Blackwell Guide to Research Methods in Bilingualism and Multilingualism* (2008, Blackwell) in collaboration with Li Wei.

Ingrid Piller is Professor of Applied Linguistics at Macquarie University, Sydney, Australia. Her research interests are in intercultural communication, language learning and multilingualism, and how they intersect with social inclusion and global justice. Her most recent book, *Intercultural Communication*

(2011, Edinburgh University Press) provides a critical introduction to the field from a sociolinguistic and discourse-analytic perspective. Together with Kimie Takahashi she is the co-founder of the sociolinguistics portal *Language on the Move* at http://www.languageonthemove.org, where she also blogs about the sociolinguistics of multilingualism.

Celia Roberts is Professor of Applied Linguistics at King's College London in the Centre for Language, Discourse and Communication. Her publications in intercultural communication and second language socialisation include: *Language and Discrimination* (with Davies and Jupp, 1992, Longman) and *Achieving Understanding* (Bremer *et al.*, 1996, Longman); in the field of urban discourse, *Talk, Work and Institutional Order* (with Sarangi, 1999, Mouton); and in the field of language and cultural learning, *Language Learners as Ethnographers* (with Byram *et al.*, 2001, Multilingual Matters). Her main interest is in the practical relevance and application of sociolinguistics to real world problems.

Maria Sabaté i Dalmau (MA in Linguistic Anthropology, University of Toronto; PhD in English Studies, Universitat Autònoma de Barcelona) is postdoctoral fellow in the Department of English Studies at the Universitat Autònoma de Barcelona and consultant at the Universitat Oberta de Catalunya. Her research interests include intercultural communication and language practices and ideologies in bilingual, multilingual, migration and language minority contexts, within the field of critical ethnographic sociolinguistics.

Kimie Takahashi (PhD, Sydney University, 2006) is a Lecturer at the Graduate School of English at Assumption University of Thailand. Prior to moving to Bangkok in early 2011, she was a Postdoctoral Fellow at Macquarie University, Australia, where she was involved in a multi-site ethnography of the role of multilingualism and language learning in tourism between Australia and Japan. Her research interests include the inter-relationship between bilingualism, second language learning and gender, particularly in the contexts of study overseas, migration and employment. Her work has appeared in edited volumes and her first book, *Language Learning, Gender and Desire: Japanese Women on the Move*, was published by Multilingual Matters in 2012. With Ingrid Piller, Kimie is a co-founder of *Language on the Move*, a non-profit website dedicated to research on multilingualism, language learning and social inclusion (http://www.languageonthemove.org).

Cécile B. Vigouroux is Associate Professor of Sociolinguistics at Simon Fraser University, Vancouver, Canada. For the past 15 years, she has been exploring different ethnographic aspects of Francophone African migrations to Cape Town, South Africa. Among these are issues of transnational identity formation, reshaping of linguistic ideologies, and sociocultural transformations triggered by new forms of mobility. Her work aims at bridging sociolinguistics with other disciplines such as geography and, more recently, economy.

1 Introduction: Recasting Institutions and Work in Multilingual and Transnational Spaces

Alexandre Duchêne, Melissa Moyer and Celia Roberts

This volume on *Language, Migration and Social Inequalities: A Critical Sociolinguistic Perspective on Institutions and Work* appears at a time when linguists concerned with the social meaning of language are asking questions arising from its role in a changing social, economic and political context (Blommaert, 2005; Duchêne & Heller, 2012) and searching for new conceptual and explanatory frameworks to answer these questions (Coupland, 1998, 2010). The institutions and workplaces described here are all realms where the daily lives of migrants are regimented and controlled. They are also illustrative sites for looking at ways social inequality is (re)produced and challenged. Language in these contexts includes a focus on multilingualism and on normative modes of talking in the dominant language. Both sites play a central role in processes of categorisation and legitimation of migrant groups as well as in exercising agency in the organisation of and access to resources. Language, it is argued, is key in selection, social mobility and gate-keeping processes as well as being the object of organisational responses to these wider institutional processes. It is through language that the complex relationship between the material and symbolic capital of migrants is played out on a local scale, as power institutions of the nation-state interact with the globalised economic order.

Language in an Era of Globalisation

This book examines how social and political changes brought about by transnational migration and the new economic order, which are themselves the outcome of globalisation, produce new ways of regulating language and establishing what counts as 'linguistic capital' (Bourdieu, 1991). An explicitly critical ethnographic sociolinguistic stance provides an account of the overt and covert ways language and institutional practices address core questions concerning power and the place of migrants in various national contexts.

Specifically, the new conditions resulting from globalisation force us to reconsider the articulation between *language, migration* and *institutions*. In terms of *language*, the shift to the tertiary economy and so to the increased number of jobs in the area of services has made communication and language key. The chapters in this volume demonstrate how this actually works in various national, occupational and institutional contexts. Linguistic market-places are currently being shaped by global forces beyond the control of the individual. In many contexts and geographical spaces, there are new demands on competence in the dominant language. But in many other spaces, single language speakers no longer can get by in their local daily lives in the same way as they did in the past. Here, multilingualism and knowledge of more than one language have become almost a requirement.

Many of these changes affecting the heightened role of language are connected to *migration* and the manner in which people are mobile today. Migrants in the past tended to have limited connections with their country of origin, as travel was more expensive and contact was difficult to maintain. The internet, along with the inexpensive communication technology now available, has created improved means for migrants to communicate more frequently with family and friends all over the world almost instantaneously. Close-knit networks are facilitated and sustained because of the new ways migrants communicate and are in contact with each other through frequent travel. This in turn has led to the growth of new businesses and services to meet these new requirements.

The linguistic and cultural diversification of national populations in countries around the globe has led to the creation of a wide variety of services that target these new citizens as clients or receivers of welfare. *Institutions* such as those providing health, legal assistance, consumer goods and social services, to mention just a few, are facing new linguistic and communication challenges. These are also sites where control, selection and regimentation of these newcomers take place. Institutions are places where we can still encounter contradictory ideologies and practices concerning language. In some organisations, especially from public sector institutions, traditional ideologies connect a national language with institutional identity (see Allan, this volume). Here, social processes of exclusion are carried out on the basis of a person's competence and linguistic performance which can be identified and traced to localised micro-level social practices (see Codó *et al.*, this volume). However, in the private sector, multilingualism related, for example, to the marketing of consumer products constitutes an added value and contributes to the way private enterprises make a profit (Piller & Takahashi, this volume).

There is a constant and complex dialectic between what a host society considers to be regimented (language being one of the terrains on which control can be imposed) and the way migrants' linguistic resources can serve economic interests which benefit either large institutions or small-scale minority ethnic businesses. The regulation and the capitalisation of language work goes hand in hand with the blurring of boundaries between the state, the NGO and the private, or between the local and the ethnic businesses (see Sabaté on *locutorios*, this volume). This is a dynamic that invites us to constantly question the way language operates as an instrument of power across and beyond institutions. New conditions of language use and new forms of interests (re)produce new and old forms of inequalities and resistances to them. These are always based on the value that certain languages and varieties of language have over others – the hierarchisation of languages – which endows some with added value within particular domains of use. This critical stance can seem overly abstract, bleaching out the speakers from their speech. But inequalities of language are also embodied in speakers' experience of linguistic regulation and capitalisation. They are positioned by these processes but they also actively engage in resisting them. For this reason, in order to challenge the notion of migrants as victims and to focus on their active agency, we have included a separate section on resistance.

Sociolinguistics: Continuity and Change

The theme of this volume, *language* and *social inequality*, is not new to the field of sociolinguistics. This area of inquiry has always addressed, to different degrees, issues of linguistic inequality in examining the relationship between language and social life. Although taking different ontological and epistemological stances (Moyer, 2008), both variationist, language system-focussed sociolinguistics (Labov, 1963, 1966) and practice-based, culturally and ethnographically informed sociolinguistics (Gumperz & Hymes, 1972) are concerned with the way in which language indexes, or points out to, social phenomena and ideologies beyond their denotative meaning. Labovian correlational studies showed that variation and linguistic differences were regular and patterned and that stigmatised varieties served as stereotypes, identity markers or indicators of social group categorisations. While variationist sociolinguistics had shown the significance of the indexicality of the language system, Hymes and Gumperz started not with structuralist systems but with speakers and their communicative practices, drawing on the functional approach of Jakobson (1960) and Pierce (1977) and on the linguistic philosophy of Austin (1962), Searle (1969) and Grice (1989).

For Gumperz and Hymes, only an activity and practice-based view of language can account for linguistic diversity and multilingualism and any other approach, 'feeds into monoglot ideologies of language standardisation (. . .) and (. . .) into oppressive language and educational policies' (Gumperz & Cook-Gumperz, 2005: 271). Their concern with the linguistic production of social inequality stems from this approach of cultural difference in understanding, linking the fine-grained detail of the poetics (Hymes, 1981) and rhetorics (Gumperz, 1982a, 1999) of language use to social categories and powerful ideologies. Gumperz's interactional sociolinguistic theory (Gumperz, 1982a) explicitly focuses on the communicative dimension to racial and linguistic discrimination when interpretation or inferencing strategies in ongoing conversations are not shared by interlocutors from different sociocultural backgrounds. Interactions for Gumperz are, therefore, the substance of social relations of power and are where linguistic ideologies are played out (Eerdmans et al., 2003: vi; Gumperz, 1982b).

Hymes and Gumperz were laying down their pioneering theories at a time when the nation-state, communities and class and ethnic categorisations were treated as unified, integrated and fixed systems (for example, Gumperz's notion of 'speech community', which he has subsequently critiqued (Gumperz & Cook-Gumperz, 2005; Rampton, 2000). Relationships between language use and social labelling and processes of belonging and exclusion seemed more straightforward than they do today. The connection of language to theorisations of power and to a wider social, political and economic order were not a question of concern (Gal, 1998). Today, with the social and economic changes brought about by globalisation and the instabilities of late modernity, such concerns can no longer be ignored and require more wide-ranging ethnography as well as more detailed and nuanced understanding of interpretive processes.

During this period, the role of linguistic ideology in understanding the relationship between language and social stratification was also being developed, much of it linked to American linguistic anthropology and to the early work of Gumperz and Hymes. The central role of ideology in understanding language in the social world began with Silverstein's innovative paper (Silverstein, 1979) and his later assertion that language must be studied by looking at the interaction between form, use *and* ideology (Silverstein, 1985: 220). Globalisation and mobility in the late modern context gave the notion new urgency, as the rash of anthologies on linguistic ideology attest (Kroskrity, 2000; Schieffelin *et al.*, 1998).

Recent studies have drawn together some of the apparent dichotomies between a neutral notion of shared cultural knowledge and one of contestation, and between an explicit consciousness and articulation of language and one that sees linguistic ideology in embodied practices. For example, Kroskrity (2000) has disputed these dichotomies, arguing, with Giddens (1991), that speakers of a language will always have ideologies embedded in their relatively automatic conduct and that such apparently neutral concepts as shared cultural knowledge will always be derived from the interests of a group, whether it is the taken-for-granted knowledge of state policies on standards in language or of small communities of people struggling to have their voices heard and creating alternative modes of working and managing their lives.

So a balance needs to be struck between tracing the larger discourses about, for example, what constitutes acceptable language(s), and attending to the small-scale interactive moments within which both larger discourses lurk and also the resistances and alternatives to them. As Erickson (2004: 178–179) suggests, it is important not to 'reduce the local interaction order to the general social order'. Rather, as Gal points out:

> ... the notion of linguistic ideology allows for the integration of what, in more traditional terms, would seem to be different *levels* of social phenomena (e.g. macro-political and micro-interactional). To the degree that the implicit assumption of a micro/macro split has determined, in practice, the researcher's choice of field site and method [...] (it) puts aside the overly familiar separation of phenomena into levels and fruitfully suggests dissections of social life along different lines. (Gal, 1998: 318)

The critical perspective of this book draws on the sociolinguistic strands mentioned above, on linguistic ideology and on critical discourse analysis (Fairclough, 1992; Wodak, 1996). Language is considered a practice as well as a resource that can have both symbolic value and exchange value in a market economy (Bourdieu, 1991) and where knowing the right kind of language or variety can enable access to desired resources such as jobs or to public and private services provided by the state (i.e. airline businesses, health, education). This book also owes a debt to recent critical sociolingistic studies (Blommaert, 2008, 2012; Coupland, 2010; Heller, 2002; Jaffe, 2009; Scollon & Scollon, 2004) which argue, drawing on Giddens, that the sites we study are permeable and constantly influenced by other events, institutions, discourses and groups which flow across each other (Hannerz, 1996; Marcus, 2005). In contrast to studying a set of workplace or institutional interactions as relatively autonomous events with some background context added, the contributors attempt to make linkages across sites, activities and social actors, examining some of the ways in which discourses circulate and are recontextualised (Bauman & Briggs, 1990; Linell, 1998) and spatial, temporal and physical environments rework and reconnect social actors and their talk and text.

Migration

What distinguishes this volume is that the contributors are all grappling with similar questions about the economic and institutional regimentation of migrants and the manner in which this form of power, control and selection that goes on in the sites studied is carried out and resisted with language in its various modes and modalities (Kress, 2010). Migration and the mobility of citizens around the globe (Vertovec, 2009; Urry, 2007) pose important challenges to the linguistic and cultural homogeneity that nation-states still rely on for defining their physical boundaries, their language and identity as well as the rights and obligations of their citizens. Furthermore, the new social order resulting from neoliberal economic practices (Harvey, 2005), globalisation (Blommaert, 2012; Coupland, 2010) and outsourcing, as well as the dislocation of work and the expansion of marketplaces, is also challenging traditional ways the nation-state has organised its control over the people who have typically travelled to a new country looking for work or better life chances. These issues and the role of language are the linking threads of all the contributions that appear in this volume.

The focus on migrants, who are the protagonists of this book, requires a further caveat explaining to what category of people this term applies. The definition of *immigrant* has technically been used to refer to a person who enters or settles in a region or state to which he or she is not native, but the general understanding the word has acquired is more specific, namely, a person from the developing world settling in a more developed area, typically in the Western world. This act of essentialising that typically gets (re)produced by using the word *immigrant* or *immigration* is substituted here for the term *migrant* that we use to refer to any mobile citizen who migrates or is mobile for various reasons such as work, leisure, asylum or some other reason. Migrants, for our purposes, refer to air hostesses, clients at a call shop or a health clinic, undocumented citizens, highly qualified documented citizens, ethnic minorities who are second-generation migrants, children at school, as well as skilled and unskilled workers participating in an informal economy. The reasons and circumstances that have led those people to be migrants does not fit under the traditional *immigrant* label, which is imbued with such negative and stereotypical associations. Our emphasis is on understanding *migration* as a social process of mobility that stems from a wider and more global political and socio-economic order.

While migration has existed throughout history, there are certain new features that are important to understand in the lives of present-day migrants. Changing one's place in a physical or geographical space, whether it is just once, several times or on a regular basis, is only one dimension in which today's migrants are mobile. As Urry (2007: 47) points out, one can also be mobile along corporeal, geographical, virtual, imagined and communicative dimensions. For migrants arriving in a new place, knowledge of local language varieties as well as of the appropriate interactional and interpretative strategies is key for negotiating access to work as well as to social services and resources. However, the lack of valued linguistic resources does not render migrants as passive subjects under the control of powerful social agents. As Ahearn (2012: 278) notes, a socioculturally mediated capacity to act, along with strategies to contest and resist, as the chapters in Part 3 on *resistance* illustrate, is always an option open to migrants.

Institutions and Workplaces

Institutions and work site spaces are situated in locations where both the control of resources and the legitimisation of systems of regulation take place and hence are also spaces for the appropriation and subversion of the interactional and institutional order (Sarangi & Roberts, 1999). Institutions (public, private and NGOs) collaborate in the legitimation of the socio-economic order and they are the societal points of contact for transnational citizens migrating for purposes of leisure, labour or to flee from political repression. They are also discursive spaces where the classification and categorisation of migrants with scant material resources is carried out in order to meet and organise institutional goals.

The institutionalised workplace provides a look at language in the regulation of the labour market governed by a neoliberal economic model. A focus on work also shows the ways in which language operates as a means of social selection for migrants on the basis of language skills that are measured and evaluated in recruitment processes or job performance. This angle on language and migration also examines the capitalisation by employers of migrant language skills in the ways they manage multilingualism (Duchêne, 2011). This is carried out through the economic value and exchange or the commodification of language and identity, the hierarchisation of languages or the (non)-recognition of crucial multilingual practices. So, these environments can be called 'ideological sites' – 'institutional sites of social practice as both object and modality of ideological expression' (Silverstein, 1998: 136). In such sites, for example, the job selection interview, the talk and text is both ideologically framed and also functions to defend and (re)produce existing ideologies of power.

A Critical Sociolinguistic Contribution to Institutions and Work Sites

The aim of this book is to understand better how, in very different social and geographical contexts, linguistic inequality is (re)produced in the new economic order. The central theme threaded through the volume, and which draws it together, is the way new forms of interests value and regiment language in new ways, creating, in turn, new modes of resistance.

It brings together 11 original contributions to the field of language and migration from a range of institutional and workplace contexts, covering government and non-government organisations, workplaces, education, and also the informal sectors of the economy which are the product of larger institutional imperatives. They range over various geographical contexts (in Europe, Africa, North America and Australia).

This range and variety of contexts illustrate some of the phenomenon of 'superdiversity' (Vertovec, 2007) now present in large urbanised centres across the world and which encompass both elite and professional mobility and the forced migration of economic or political necessity. This volume is also designed to challenge other taken-for-granted divisions and to highlight relatively neglected areas in sociolinguistics. Migration studies in the social sciences rarely examine the central role of language and, similarly, socio- and applied linguistics have given much more time to education than to the workplace. A critical sociolinguistic perspective on these new sites refocuses the role of linguistic ideology in sustaining some of the paradoxes of current practices. For example, the regimentation and control of dominant national languages co-exists with a valuing of multilingualism to serve economic interests. This critical stance also drives the contributors' commitment to make the necessary links both across sites and activities and between macro circulating discourses and the micro-process of social interaction. The contributions show one of the central intersections between institutional regimentation and the new political economy by examining the way language is maintained as one of the distinctive criteria of selection.

The organisation of the volume in three parts, Sites of Control, Sites of Selection and Sites of Resistance, picks up different threads that illustrate: (i) the complex ways migrants must navigate the institutions of the state but also the new work conditions imposed by a neoliberal economic order; (ii) the processes of exclusion/inclusion experienced by migrants; and (iii) the varying opportunities migrants have to negotiate position, agency and resistance through language.

Sites of control

The two chapters in this section by Kori Allan and Eva Codó are concerned with the tensions that develop when control is exercised through the intersection between the labour market and state regulation. Allan's study of the English language classes offered to professional migrants in Canada examines how communication skills training depoliticises what is called the 'integration problem' and shifts the problem onto the migrants themselves and the requirement to develop an ideal worker-citizen. In this way, the control exercised by state institutions and employers is masked and the apparently neutral test of communication skills bleaches out the discursive and structural barriers that migrants face. Similarly, in Codó's chapter, NGOs and trade unions contribute to the shaping of migrants' personal and labour trajectories. Their chance of working in the formal economy and gaining or maintaining legal status is controlled by complex procedures which are mediated by both state and labour institutions. However, advisors can also hint at action which gives at least some measure of control to the undocumented migrants themselves.

The discourses of globalisation and neoliberalism are ones of 'mobility', 'flows', 'flexibility' and 'de-regulation' but many of the practices entailed in globalisation are of control and regimentation. The chapters in the section on control examine some of the practices that mediate between state policy on immigration and employment, and the local servicing 'industry' that has grown up to manage the migration process. These training, advisory and employment services hold within them the very contradictions which the state has to manage between openness and opportunity, on the one hand, and border patrol and limitations on the other. While borders control, both in bodily and symbolic ways, those who pass through or round them face new borders which, as these chapters show, fundamentally affect access to the labour market and their long-term futures. So this local industry, while projecting a public pro-migration face, masks its other work of governing those who come within its ambit. These services, in the act of supporting migrants, also shape them.

Both Allan's chapter on 'Skilling the Self' and Codó's chapter on advising on legal authorisation to work document the contradictions produced at local level when the standardisation of state bureaucracy meets individualisation (Heller, 2003, 2010). Allan discusses the contradiction migrant professionals face when their credentials and experience allow them through state border controls only to find that there are structural conditions which deny them jobs commensurate with their qualifications. The tension between state acceptance and employer refusal is then managed by offering advanced language training with the focus on individual self- improvement. Codó explores a related tension in the ways in which advisers act as both an arm of the state in gatekeeping migrant clients' applications and simultaneously find what Erickson (2004) has called 'wiggle room' – the ways around the system which enable individual applications to be bureaucratically processable (Iedema, 2003). Such small acts of resistance remind us that, while this book is divided into the three categories of control, selection and resistance, these categories are by no means watertight, and leak into one another as complex processes are managed at local level.

The theme of control, inevitably, lends itself to the theorisation of power and the methodological challenges that researchers with backgrounds in sociolinguistics and discourse face in tracking down its soft, invisible, capillary force, as Gramsci and Foucault describe it. Within this critical tradition, power is normalised so that it does not look like power but just order (Foucault, 1984) or authority (Blommaert, 2008). The Canadian training courses and Catalan legal advisory service appear as part of the order of things, a system which supports and shapes, fitting stories into boxes and sculpting subjectivities to meet dominant labour market discourses and processes. So, long before neoliberal ideologies exerted such influence, critical theorists had shown how pushing power down not to the people but to the local systems that governed them both masked and enhanced the centralising power either of the state or the organs of globalised capital.

Such soft power can only be identified through long periods of fieldwork and close micro-analysis, hallmarks of ethnography and sociolinguistics and what has come to be called linguistic ethnography (Maybin & Tusting, 2011; Rampton, 2007). This broad, interdisciplinary approach, combining holism with the fine detail of interaction, explores the capillary effects of power deeply embedded in the ordinary and the banal. Central to linguistic ethnography is a social constructionist notion of the self, often the moral self, and an understanding of language as thick with indexical and ideological values. Both these tropes underpin the Allan and Codó chapters.

The (moral) self

Both chapters draw on notions of the self and its regimentation and, underlying these, Foucault's theory of governmentality and Giddens' concept of the self as an ongoing project (Giddens, 1991). Foucault's notion of governmentality as the 'conduct of conduct' (Foucault, 1991) links together discipline and bureaucratisation through a series of 'technologies'. Most notably, here, are 'technologies of the self' (Burchell, 1996) and linguistic technologies such as the interview and language training and acculturation courses. Allan discusses the commodification of so-called soft skills which become the new cultural capital that migrant professionals are expected to acquire. Rather than the structural barriers that deny them access to the labour market, this group is taught to focus on the self as a project of improvement, an 'entrepreneurial self' (du Gay, 1996) that can only achieve through self-governance. Appropriate conduct in job interviews is presented as the only pathway to success. Moral regimentation is also an element of the gatekeeping processes of the Catalan advice and information centres. Applicants are expected to regulate their conduct and attitude according to the norms of the particular organisation and this regulation is part of its unspoken contract. But the data also show that the advisers perform their identities in alignment with these norms, negotiating a stance interactionally, which preserves their role as both gatekeepers and helpers.

Language always comes with values attached. The fact of migration and the linguistic differences that it brings insert individuals into particular symbolic spaces which reinforce and give legitimacy, or the opposite, to both forms of language and those who speak them. What counts as acceptability is controlled at both macro and micro levels. Using certain codes and minute language differences within these codes can have large interactional, cultural and material consequences. In both chapters, for example, multilingualism is firmly consigned to the backroom. Only English is used in the advice centres and the language training programmes in Canada where a certain kind of entrepreneurial English discourse is the only linguistic capital in town. Similarly, the expert English of the professional migrants does not travel well. The perceived foreignness of their self-presentations is a proxy for many other social and cultural differences which tag them as outside the mainstream in conduct and values. By contrast, the Catalan advice workers craft their advice so that it indexes a nuanced stance to their role, while applicants struggle with their piles of documents in an unfamiliar language. Again these language practices are normalised and taken for granted, not as instruments of power and control but as migrant-friendly resources for integration.

One of the connections made between globalisation and late modernity is that of the relative decline of institutions (Giddens, 1991; Harvey, 2005) and yet when we look at migration and the production of social and linguistic inequality, the role of institutions emerges as strong as ever. Institutional authority may be more dispersed and delegated, indeed more nuanced, and yet migrants' life chances and economic and social stability remain regimented in and by these sites of control. Bureaucratised institutions still decide what are the legitimate texts and the legitimate talk; migrants, whether professionals or undocumented workers, are still controlled and their identities and skills (de)constructed by normative and standardised categories.

Sites of selection

The contexts of *selection* that are discussed in Part 2 are carried out in job interviews for routine low-paid jobs (Roberts), in the hiring practices of a transnational airline (Piller & Takahashi), and in the educational programs of two types of educational settings: a secondary school (Martín Rojo) and a community heritage school (Lytra).

Keeping the gate

Selection here is understood in several ways. First and foremost, it is a form of gatekeeping or regulating the access to key societal resources which are both material and symbolic (Blommaert, 2005; Bourdieu & Passeron, 1991; Erickson & Shultz, 1982). Processes of selection are carried out by representatives of powerful institutions whose key goal it is to perpetuate themselves and their interests. But, there is a second, more subtle form of selection, and that is *self-selection*. In the production and reproduction of social inequality, Bourdieu (1977) points out that objective structures of society tend to produce subjective dispositions that again produce structured actions. Subjective dispositions, when they belong to migrants, such as in the cases presented in this book, can combine with selection processes carried out by institutional representatives and that end up leading to self-elimination in the context of schools but also with respect to an individual's job aspirations. Selection is also connected to power, as pointed out earlier – the power of institutions and certain individuals over others that results from the control exercised over valued resources. This is a power that is difficult for migrants to contest or resist, especially when access to institutional languages is an issue. It is often the case that the ideologically discriminatory selection practices underlying education, and job interviews involving mobile citizens are not questioned and hence they are accepted as legitimate forms of institutional practice.

Selection is tied to language, not only speaking the legitimate institutional language but also understanding and in most cases speaking the standard variety (Heller, 2010; Lippi-Green, 2011). The chapters in this section illustrate the subtle and implicit ways in which the exclusion of migrants is accomplished through detailed and localised analyses of how language accomplishes selection in both overt selection processes (Roberts, and Piller & Takahashi) as well as in more indirect educational contexts (Martín Rojo, and Lytra) which are intended to promote inclusion and end up producing inequalities by valuing certain kinds of knowledge and linguistic capital over others.

The logic of selection in the contexts analysed (i.e. workplaces as well as a state and a community-run school) must be embedded in a larger societal framework where we need to bear in mind that the people being selected are those who fit acceptable forms of speaking and understanding or behaving in a Foucauldian sense (Foucault, 1980). But where exactly do these accepted forms of speaking and behaving come from? How are they connected to power and why are they valued? The current political and neoliberal economic order are important keys to understanding how: for example, an Australian transnational airline interested in expanding its business to the Asian market recruits Japanese flight attendants whose personal aspirations happen to coincide with those of the airline (see chapter by Piller and Takahashi); or how acceptable ways of speaking and understanding are valued over a person's actual qualifications or job experience (see chapter by Roberts). State schools in Madrid are a terrain where the cultural and language resources brought in by migrant children are *decapitalised* by teachers' pedagogical practices (see chapter by Martín Rojo). The comparison with language classes of an academic and economically valued language like English that hinge on students' high academic performance illustrate just how exclusion is accomplished in this context. The second-generation migrants analysed in two Turkish heritage schools (see chapter by Lytra) show how migrants are competing among themselves through the promotion of discourses on the added value of being multilingual. The commodification discourse around knowing Turkish and English is connected to migrant agency and the development of a Turkish market niche in the United Kingdom. The meaning of Turkish in this case is changing in the community from a low-prestige migrant language to a language that is acquiring prestige through developing discourses about its new economic value. This is another illustration of how local ways of speaking are connected to a wider economic order based on the neoliberal idea of the free market (Harvey, 2005).

Levels of indexicality

In order to understand the way that micro-level interactional practices are analysed in Roberts' and Martín Rojo's chapters and how their localised meanings are related to wider processes of social selection on a more macro scale, the notion of *indexical order* is useful (Blommaert, 2012; Silverstein, 2003).[1] For example, the formal bureaucratic job interview discussed in Roberts' chapter is a normative instance of language use that is entextualised and can fit into a type of style as described by Agha (2007: 84–85) that has a stable and recognisable indexical meaning. The small but subtle non-normative interactional differences produced by applicants are interpreted, and have consequences and meanings in a higher indexical order which, according to Blommaert (2012: 38), is part of a general system of meaningful semiosis that is valid in groups at any particular time. The interactional practices observed in the classroom in Madrid presented by Martín Rojo also show simultaneous indexical orders. On one level, the interactions analysed show the subtle teaching style differences used in the monolingual class with migrant children and the bilingual class with more academic achieving children who are mostly Spanish. These differences amount to explicitly valuing and giving voice to certain children, views and pedagogical practices over others. The higher level indexical order of these micro-interactional processes that take place in the classroom is one of reinforcing social stratification and hence producing a wider scale social selection process where children will inherit the low social status of their migrant parents and end up filling the unskilled jobs reserved for them.

The notion of indexical orders is also relevant to processes of selection in the chapter by Piller and Takahashi. Meanings that Japanese women (as well as women of other nationalities) associate with being a flight attendant are ones of a glamorous and multilingual cosmopolitan identity. This idealised imagined identity is in stark contrast to the reality of the job, constituting another indexical order with meanings that are defined by the contractual and working conditions offered by the Australian airline company. A higher indexical order that can be identified connects with the neoliberal economic order and the way transnational business competes for making a profit in a globalised economy that employs skilled workers with low pay and strenuous working conditions (Duchêne & Heller, 2012). This contradiction is lived on an individual and personal level by flight attendants who develop new ways of justifying the reason for holding on to such a dead-end job with limited possibilities for advancement.

The chapter by Lytra on new discourses about the commodification of Turkish that is circulating in local heritage schools in the UK can really only be understood by taking into account the meanings that are assigned to the Turkish language in the British context. On a wider social scale or indexical order in the UK, Turkish is associated with a language of an ethnic minority that is not valued in mainstream society.[2] The reaction of the Turkish community observed in the language classes taught in the heritage schools is one of assigning a positive meaning to knowing Turkish, but Turkish along with English. The discourses concerning the knowledge of Turkish as added value is a different indexical order which is in the process of developing but which at the same time indexes a higher scale indexical order where the value of knowing Turkish is associated with the neoliberal economic order where multilingual language skills can be used for earning money by developing an ethnic business niche.

Sites of resistance

The chapters in Part 3 all question the ways in which power dominates spaces and institutions and how manifestations of resistance are linked to processes of regulation and regimentation. These issues are explored on a variety of terrains: the discourses on immigration produced by social actors in a neighbourhood in Germany (Meinhof & Holly), heath services in Spain (Moyer), the informal economy in South Africa (Vigouroux) and on the telecommunication sector and *locutorios* in Barcelona (Sabate).

Resistance and domination

Resistance in these studies is linked to various aspects where language operates as a means of creating domination. Domination in the case of Meinhof and Holly's study, for instance, highlights the reaction and the contestation to dominant discourses of integration that are highly present in political and public spaces in Germany. These discourses on integration are becoming the object of positioning for migrant communities that often distance themselves by criticising it and contesting its ideological foundation, but also they tend to adopt some more subtle stance taking which embraces the dominant discourse. Resistance in that sense occurs in a form of counterdiscourses which nuance and reconfigure the official and dominant discourse on integration. What Meinhof and Holly also show is that those reactions and contestations are far from being ideologically homogeneous. On the contrary, they are complex and often ambivalent. It is not just a question of opposing a counter-discourse to the dominant one; it entails more subtle strategies which range from banalisation and interiorisation of the discourse to self-empowerment. In all the strategies described by the authors in Part 3, there is a dominant discourse that constitutes the central element of 'positioning' and as a consequence the central support which immigrants have to deal with.

In the chapter by Moyer, structures of domination linked to a health clinic setting illustrate a prototypical site for the ways access to health are achieved. In her study, Moyer shows how institutional order is strongly intertwined with language as a resource and how key information needed for the delivery of healthcare is negotiated. Although the institutions are aware of the importance of language in order to circulate medical knowledge, they do not always provide the necessary means to guarantee the exchange of information needed to carry out the medical diagnostic and to deliver treatment. The health institution reproduces power through the ways it regulates language practices (such as the use of cultural mediators as interpreters) which in return creates reactions and forms of resistance towards the manner in which health information and language are managed and regulated.

Vigouroux offers another perspective on resistance as a reaction to power. In her chapter on the informal economy in South Africa, she shows that the linguistic order of the official economy tends to accentuate the exclusion processes of francophone African migrants in South Africa. In contestation to this, mobile Africans are taking up agency and creating new economic structures with their own organisational process and a linguistic order defined by themselves. What Vigouroux eloquently emphasises is that those informal structures are not completely disconnected from dominant economic organisations in South Africa. On the contrary, they also exist as an ethnic niche which produces profits for the official recognised economy.

In a similar vein, the chapter by Sabaté also questions the dominant structuration of the Spanish economy. By focusing on the ways in which *locutorios* emerge as parallel sites to the official telecommunication sectors in Spain, she is able to show that their existence is intrinsically interrelated to the regulation of access to the telecommunication sector for migrants living in Spain. Telecommunication, as she notes, constitutes a central instrument for migrants which enables them to maintain links with their home country. However, undocumented migrants who wish to avoid state control do not seek access through the official telecommunication companies. *Locutorios* are ethnic businesses that are a reaction to state control exercised in the telecommunication sector. If reaction and contestation can be seen as a form of resistance to established social orders, the chapters all strongly insist on the importance of seeing resistance not only as a reaction but also as action, which entails its own structuration and which engages in new forms of organisational order.

Resistance as action on and through language

Resistance as action appears in the chapters as a productive way of understanding the role of language in relation to migration, institution and work. In Meinhof and Holly's chapter, the action can be seen in discursive terms. Speaking out, taking a stance with regard to the notion of integration is one way of resisting political correctness. It is also a way of exercising one's own agency by positioning oneself and creating new forms of allegiance. In Moyer's chapter, patient agency in challenging established interactional practices is also a way of resisting institutional regulation. The action is then located in the ongoing interactional order (Cicourel, 1992) that occurs in the flow of the conversation in the medical setting.

Moyer convincingly argues that the role of the mediator and his positioning with respect to the institution is instrumental in the way patients are deprived of their agency. The particular interactions studied in this chapter also shed light on the potentiality of the action of the mediator in the distribution of health resources. If the mediator can deprive the patient of his or her own agency through selective entextualisation processes, one could also legitimately argue that through this action it also could be, under certain circumstances, instrumental in providing the condition under which the patients could be heard and be an active actor within the institutional structure and within the interactional order.

Vigouroux also offers a productive way of understanding resistance as action. The thorough analysis she carries out of both the ways in which language operates as a gatekeeping mechanism to access the formal economy (this is true for both national citizens and migrants) and the existence of the informal economy (which is also intimately linked with language issues, in this case Lingala) constitute a terrain of actions which allows resistance to forms of regulation imposed by the states in the matter of immigration and which in the end allows other forms of integration of migrants in the South African context. In the case of the *locutorios* documented by Sabaté, migrants can be seen as taking concrete action. The Pakistani entrepreneur in her study has set up a business that employs other migrants as well as catering to the specific needs of other migrant populations in the area. Those migrant economic initiatives are in many ways also regulated (in a similar way to the informal economy described by Vigouroux). They are sites of resistance to a larger national-economic order and subversive ways of dealing with regimentation.

Resistance and the reproduction of social inequalities

If resistance as reaction and as action tends to shed light on ways in which language becomes instrumental in challenging power issues based on language regimentation, the chapters also interrogate the negative and the social inequality-creating side of resistance and question the ways in which resistance can be productive in reversing power issues. In fact what the chapters also pinpoint is that resistance cannot completely avoid its own power logic and finally it tends to reproduce power relations in many ways instead of erasing them. If the *locutorios* provide access to telecommunications, they are also sites in which social hierarchy and exploitive conditions are reproduced. The internal organisation of *locutorios* also regulates migrant access, reproducing racialised and linguistic hierarchised categories. If they are sites of resistance which allow the migrants to survive, they are also workplaces where the linguistic skills of the workers are exploited and commodified, benefiting the managerial entrepreneurial owners more than the producer of the linguistic resources themselves.

In the South African case, the informal economy also exists because it provides profits for the state. An inside look at the informal economy shows that it is also mired with power struggles. For example, the basis upon which language competences are allowed to confer a certain value of distinction on some (e.g. the Lingala speakers), tends to deprive other migrants of access to this arena and a way to earn their livelihood. A dynamic of social structuration exists where middle-class migrants, who do not have access to the formal economy (often due to their lack of English competence) tend also to be excluded from the informal economy.

Inequalities on the basis of language are at stake again here. In the Meinhof and Holly chapter the question of the consequence on some of the discourses produced by migrants is raised in order to challenge immigration discourses. Some positioning of those actors tends subtly to adapt and adopt the dominant discourse and as such to reproduce the social order. Social distinction among migrants is observed in the health clinic analysed by Moyer where the cultural mediator with his professional training and knowledge of institutional languages manages to distinguish himself over his compatriot in the clinic setting. In sum, what those chapters definitely oblige us to ask is: (a) under which circumstances certain forms of resistance emerge and why it takes the forms it takes; (b) who centrally profits from these acts of resistance and who is excluded from their potential benefits; and (c) what are the consequences that can emerge from the various forms of resistance we observe. The chapters in this section do not provide definitive answers to these questions; however, they invite further research in this domain.

Acknowledgements

Most of the contributions to this volume were first presented at the AILA Research Network on Language and Migration seminars held in

Barcelona, Spain in 2009 and in Fribourg, Switzerland in 2010. The contributions by Melissa Moyer were in part funded by the research project FFI2011-26962 from the Spanish *Ministerio de Economía y Competividad* and by the mobility grants Salvador de Madariaga PR2011-0574 from the Spanish Ministry of Education and the AGAUR mobility grant 2011 BE1 00986 from the Catalan Research Council.

Notes

(1) Relating to Foucault's (1984) ideas on orders of indexicality.
(2) See Blommaert (2012: 32–37) for the relatedness of scale and indexical order.

References

Agha, A. (2007) *Language and Social Relations*. Cambridge: Cambridge University Press.
Ahearn, L. (2012) *Living Language. An Introduction to Linguistic Anthropology*. Oxford: Wiley.
Austin, J. (1962) *How to Do Things with Words*. Oxford: Oxford University Press.
Bauman, R. and Briggs, C. (1990) Poetics and performance as critical perspectives on language and social life. *Annual Review of Anthropology* 19, 59–88.
Blommaert, J. (2005) *Discourse*. Cambridge: Cambridge University Press.
Blommaert, J. (2008) Notes on power. Working Papers in Language Diversity. University of Jyväskylä, Jyväskylä.
Blommaert, J. (2012) *The Sociolinguistics of Globalization*. Cambridge: Cambridge University Press.
Bourdieu, P. (1991[1982]) *Language and Symbolic Power*. Oxford: Polity Press.
Bourdieu, P. and Passeron, J.C. (1977[1970]) *Reproduction: In Education, Society and Culture*. Beverly Hills: Sage.
Burchell G. (1996) *Liberal Government and Techniques of the Self*. In A. Barry, T. Osborne and N. Rose (eds) *Foucault and Political Reason* (pp. 267–282). London: UCL Press.
Cicourel, A. (1992) The interpenetration of communicative contexts: Examples from medical encounters. In A. Duranti and C. Goodwin (eds) *Rethinking Context: Language as an Interactive Phenomenon* (pp. 291–310). Cambridge: Cambridge University Press.
Coupland, N. (1998) What is sociolinguistic theory? *Journal of Sociolinguistics* 2 (1), 110–117.
Coupland, N. (ed.) (2010) *Handbook of Language and Globalization*. Malden, MA and Oxford: Wiley-Blackwell.
Duchêne, A. (2011) Néolibéralisme, inégalités sociales et plurilinguismes : l'exploitation des ressources langagières et des locuteurs. *Langage & Société* 136, 81–106.
Duchêne, A. and Heller, M. (eds) (2012) *Language in Late Capitalism. Pride and Profit*. London: Routledge.
du Gay, P. (1996) *Consumption and Identity at Work*. London: Sage.
Eerdmans, S.L., Prevignano, C.L. and Thibault, P.J. (2003) *Language and Interaction. Discussions with John Gumperz*. Amsterdam: John Benjamins.
Erickson, F. (2004) *Talk and Social Theory: Ecologies of Speaking and Listening in Everyday Life*. Cambridge: Polity Press.
Erickson, F. and Shultz, J. (1982) *The Counselor as Gatekeeper: Social Interaction in Interviews*. New York: Academic Press.

Fairclough, N. (1992) *Discourse and Social Change*. Cambridge: Polity Press.

Foucault, M. (1980) *The Power/Knowledge. Selected Interviews and Other Writings 1972–1977*. New York: Pantheon.

Foucault, M. (1984) The order of discourse. In M. Shapiro (ed.) *Language and Politics* (pp. 108–138). London: Blackwell.

Foucault, M. (1991) Governmentality. In G. Burchell, C. Gordon and P. Miller (eds) *The Foucault Effect: Studies in Governmentality* (pp. 73–86). Hemel Hempstead: Harvester Wheatsheaf.

Gal, S. (1998) Multiplicity and contention among language ideologies: A commentary. In B. Schieffelen, K. Woolard and P. Kroskrity (eds) *Language Ideologies. Practice and Theory* (pp. 317–332). Oxford: Oxford University Press.

Giddens, A. (1991) *Modernity and Self-Identity. Self and Society in the Late Modern Age*. Cambridge: Polity Press.

Grice, P. (1989) *Studies in the Ways with Words*. Cambridge: Harvard University Press.

Gumperz, J. (1982a) *Discourse Strategies*. Cambridge: Cambridge University Press.

Gumperz, J. (ed.) (1982b) *Language and Social Identity*. Cambridge: Cambridge University Press.

Gumperz, J. (1999) On interactional sociolinguistic method. In S. Sarangi and C. Roberts (eds) *Talk, Work and Institutional Order: Discourse in Medical, Mediation and Management Settings* (pp. 453–472). Berlin: Mouton de Gruyter.

Gumperz, J. and Cook-Gumperz, J. (2005) Language standardization and the complexities of communicative practice. In S. McKinnon and S. Silverman (eds) *Complexities: Beyond Nature & Nurture* (pp. 268–286). Chicago: University of Chicago Press.

Gumperz, J. and Hymes, D. (eds) ([1972]1986) *Directions in Sociolinguistics: The Ethnography of Communication* (pp. 35–71; Reprint pp, 52–66). Oxford: Basil Blackwell.

Hannerz, U. (1996) *Transnational Connections: Culture, People, Places*. London: Routledge.

Harvey, D. (2005) *Neoliberalism*. Oxford: Oxford University Press.

Heller, M. (2002) *Eléments d'une Sociolinguistique Critique*. Paris: Didier.

Heller, M. (2003) Globalisation, the new economy and the commodification of language and identity. *Journal of Sociolinguistics* 7 (4), 473–492.

Heller, M. (2010) *Paths to Post-nationalism*. Oxford: Oxford University Press.

Hymes, D. (1981) *'In vain I tried to tell you'. Essays in Native American Ethnopoetics*. Lincoln: University of Nebraska Press.

Iedema, R. (2003) *Discourses of Post-Bureaucracy*. Amsterdam: John Benjamin.

Jaffe, A. (2009) *Stance. A Sociolinguistic Perspective*. Oxford: Oxford University Press.

Jakobson, R. (1960) Linguistics and poetics. In T. Sebeok (ed.) *Style in Language* (pp. 350–377). Cambridge: MIT Press.

Kress, G. (2010) *Multimodality. A Social Semiotic Approach to Communication*. London: Routledge.

Kroskrity, P. (ed.) (2000) *Regimes of Language*. Santa Fe, NM: School of American Research Press.

Labov, W. (1963) The social motivation of sound change. *Word* 19, 273–309.

Labov, W. (1966) *The Social Stratification of English in New York City*. Philadelphia: University of Pennsylvania Press.

Linell, P. (1998) *Approaching Dialogue*. Amsterdam: John Benjamins.

Lippi-Green, R. (2011) *English with an Accent*. London: Routledge.

Marcus, G. (2005) Ethnography in/of the world system: The emergence of multi-site ethnography. *Annual Review of Anthropology* 24, 95–117.

Maybin, J. and Tusting, K. (2011) Linguistic ethnography. In J. Simpson (ed.) *Routledge Handbook of Applied Linguistics* (pp. 515–528). London: Routledge.

Moyer, M. (2008) Researching as practice: Linking theory, method and data. In Li Wei and M. Moyer (eds) *The Blackwell Handbook of Research. Methods in Bilingualism and Multilingualism* (pp. 21–41). Oxford: Blackwell.

Pierce, C.S. (1977) *Semiotics and Significs*. Bloomington: Indiana University Press.

Rampton, B. (2000) Speech community. In J. Verschueren, J. Ostaman, J. Blommaert and C. Bulcaen (eds) *Handbook of Pragmatics*. Amsterdam: John Benjamins.

Rampton, B. (2007) Neo-Hymesian linguistic ethnography in the United Kingdom. *Journal of Sociolinguistics* 11 (5), 584–607.

Sarangi, S. and Roberts, C. (eds) (1999) *Talk, Work and Institutional Order: Discourse in Medical, Mediation and Management Settings*. Berlin: Mouton de Gruyter.

Schieffelen, B., Woolard, K. and Kroskrity, P. (eds) (1998) *Language Ideologies. Practice and Theory*. Oxford: Oxford University Press.

Scollon, R. and Scollon, S.W. (2004) *Discourse in Place. Language in the Material World*. London: Routledge.

Searle, J. (1969) *Speech Acts. An Essay in the Philosophy of Language*. Cambridge: Cambridge University Press.

Silverstein, M. (1979) Language structure and linguistic ideology. In P.R. Clyne, W.F. Hanks and C.F. Hofbauer (eds) *The Elements: A Parasession on Linguistic Units and Levels* (pp. 193–247). Chicago: Chicago Linguistic Society.

Silverstein, M. (1985) Language and the culture of gender: At the intersection of structure, usage and ideology. In E. Mertz and R.J. Parmentier (eds) *Semiotic Mediation: Sociocultural and Psychological Perspectives* (pp. 219–259). Orlando: Academic Press.

Silverstein, M. (1998) The uses and utility of ideology: A commentary. In B. Schieffelin, K. Woolard and P. Kroskrity (eds) *Language Ideologies: Practice and Theory* (pp. 123–145). Oxford: Oxford University Press.

Silverstein, M. (2003) Indexical order and the dialectics of sociolinguistic life. *Language and Communication* 23, 193–229.

Urry, J. (2007) *Mobilities*. Oxford: Polity Press.

Vertovec, S. (2007) Super-diversity and its implications. *Ethnic and Racial Studies* 30 (6), 1024–1054.

Vertovec, S. (2009) *Transnationalism*. London: Routledge.

Wodak, R. (1996) *Disorders of Discourse*. London: Longman.

Part 1

Sites of Control

2 Trade Unions and NGOs Under Neoliberalism: Between Regimenting Migrants and Subverting the State

Eva Codó

Introduction

A number of scholars have pointed out that generalised mobility is the defining social process in the constitution of contemporary social life (Urry, 2000). However, a simple zooming in on today's forms of mobility reveals not only that not everyone travels with the same ease, but also that opportunities for mobility are severely constrained by issues of power and inequality (Gogia, 2006). A case in point is labour migration to the developed regions of the world. Although a necessary building component of the economic prosperity of receiving regions, this form of mobility is increasingly seen as problematic by politicians, the media and popular discourse in Europe and other parts of the world. Consequently, over the last decade the legal mechanisms for regular entry into the privileged North have tightened substantially for individuals arriving from the developing South.

This chapter historicises the evolution of services of legal advice and application assistance for migrants seeking legal authorisation to work in Spain.[1] Taking an ethnographic perspective, it analyses the major shifts that have taken place in the organisation and delivery of immigration advice over the last decade, and explores some of the contradictions that emerge in daily counselling practice.[2] It argues that, in keeping with neoliberal rationality, the Spanish state has offloaded immigration information to civil society organisations, in particular, trade unions and non-governmental organisations (NGOs). However, rather than retreating from social governing, the neoliberal Spanish state continues to enforce its regulatory function through its partnership with labour and civic forces. These organisations willingly subscribe to a state subsidiary function as a means of pursuing their specific institutional agendas, i.e. protecting the national labour market through the documentation of illegal aliens in the case of unions, and caring for the underprivileged in the case of NGOs. In practice, both organisations exert a great deal of bureaucratic, linguistic and moral control over migrant advice seekers, yet they also find themselves having to cope with a number of contradictions connected to the restrictive nature of Spanish immigration laws. In order to accomplish their respective institutional goals (and, thus, get as many individuals documented as possible), unions and NGOs must subvert the state. They do that by alerting migrants to the existence of 'loopholes' in the documentation procedure and providing them with insider specialist knowledge to gain authorisation. While the practical results are similar, the two organisations, because of their different values and missions, legitimise their practices on different grounds and resort to different interactional strategies for handling sensitive but crucial pieces of information for many applicants.

This analysis of the field of immigration information in Spain builds on the findings of a previous ethnography (2000–2002) carried out in a state immigration office. That piece of critical sociolinguistic research examined in detail the process of information exchange between state employees and undocumented migrants seeking proper authorisation to reside in the country (see Codó, 2008 for further details). At the time, I documented incipient shifts in the organisation of the field of immigration advice, which have in fact consolidated over the last decade. I analyse their implications in this chapter and link them to the sociopolitical, organisational and epistemological changes (Song, 2009) that neoliberal technologies of governance have brought about in advanced capitalist societies in recent decades.

This chapter is organised as follows. First, I discuss the different nature of labour unions and NGOs, the multiple ways in which their work is becoming articulated with that of the state and the challenges they face. Second, I present the general relevance of Spain as a case study and, more specifically, of the field of immigration advice. Third, I zoom in on the major stakeholders in the field and explain the shifts that have taken place in recent years. Fourth, I present the ethnographic data studied. Fifth, I analyse the ways in which unions and NGOs exert bureaucratic, moral and linguistic control over the migrant population they serve. Sixth, I consider the dilemmas they face in relation to the restrictive nature of the documentation procedure, the ways in which they manage to subvert the state and their different legitimating discourses and practices. Finally, I discuss the wider implications of this piece of work for understanding the neoliberal governing of societies and for reconsidering some prevalent dichotomies in discourses about migration.

Trade Unions and NGOs in a Neoliberal Sociopolitical Order

As I mentioned above, this is a study of a partnership between the state, trade unions and NGOs in a key socio-administrative field connected to processes of migrant mobility, i.e. immigration law advice. It is an illuminating case study for understanding the ways in which traditional state services are being outsourced to social organisations in late (neoliberal) capitalism, and the consequences and contradictions associated with this process. In this section, I outline the agendas, legitimising ideologies and current challenges both types of organisations face, to lay the ground for the subsequent parts of this chapter.

Currently, trade unions are in decline in the industrialised nations of the world, not just in terms of union density (the percentage of the workforce who are union members) but in terms of sociopolitical power. The reasons are varied. We can enumerate the major ones linked to economic neoliberalisation here: the outsourcing of industrial production to developing countries; the casualisation and flexibilisation of work and thus the growing importance of the informal economy; the expansion of the service sector where unionisation has traditionally been weak, and so on. The second set of reasons is connected to the globalisation of labour. As Penninx and Roosblad (2000) point out, the modern, organised union movement is closely linked not just to industrialisation but to the consolidation of the nation-state in the 19th century. The internationalisation of the world's economies has opened up a totally new scenario that challenges the traditional national framing of labour relations. In the global labour market, workers in different nation-states compete with each other, with huge wage differences between countries and regions, a situation which national unions have yet to find ways of dealing with. In addition, in many countries, unions have come under attack for being too bureaucratic, and even for their close links to the political powers (Porta Perales, 2009).

Unions' reaction to their increased social weakness has been twofold. On the one hand, they seem to be turning into progressive social movements of a general kind, and thus, increasingly, they play down their 'core' mission (i.e. labour protection). They orient their work and actions towards the defence of general social values like tolerance, democracy and human rights. For example, the defence of workers' rights is now often framed within the general protection of human rights (Gallin, 2000) or, in the case of this chapter, the labour organisation studied strives to present itself as a pro-migrant organisation working for migrants' social insertion (beyond labour concerns) and fighting racism and xenophobia in general (not just in the workplace). On the other hand, and as means for revitalisation, unions have sought to establish partnerships with governments and employers' associations. A case in point is workplace training in the UK, which is currently in the hands of unions (McIlroy, 2008). While there are serious doubts about the effects of these partnerships on union revitalisation, scholars seem to agree on the fact that unions are increasingly taking up service delivery and public administration roles, as I also claim in this chapter. This, it is argued, pushes unions away from employment regulation (Ewing, 2005) and clears the way for the state and employers to implement deregulated labour policies which, in fact, weakens unions still further.

NGOs, in turn, are social organisations invested in the ideologies of volunteerism and altruism, and in the principles of ethics and social solidarity. Their mission is founded on the values of universalism and equal rights. They are inheritors of 19th-century charity and philanthropy culture, associated to the work undertaken by bourgeois female reformers among the poor and the most destitute. However, as Agustín (2007) shows, behind the overtly supportive mission of those reformers lay a desire to control and morally regulate the populations identified as in need. This is still observable in the practices of many social welfare NGOs.

NGOs construe themselves as key social actors in the industrialised countries of the West that provide an alternative to, replace or complement the work of the state (see Herranz Bascones, 2005 for an example of that type of rhetoric). Despite being seen in largely favourable terms by the citizenry, scholars have cast a critical light on their work and social function, arguing that they are often caught between resistance and accommodation (Gallin, 2000). Although they strive to present themselves as offering an alternative to the state, in fact, many of them function as service contractors for the state (Garrido, 2010a; Gilbert, 2004; Gómez Gil, 2005). Some authors have even claimed that they are fundamental actors in neoliberalism and indispensable partners to the economic and political powers, which rely on NGOs to mitigate or correct forms of exclusion and inequalities produced by the new economic and work orders (Ryfman, 2009).

Increasingly, social welfare NGOs are supplying services that were previously state run, and although they continue to be state funded, these services are considerably cheaper, as many NGOs rely on volunteers to undertake a substantial amount of the work they do. Another piece of criticism that has been levelled against NGOs is that, often, despite their discourses of solidarity and social change, their practices work to reproduce an unequal social order, and to manage and regulate populations on behalf of the state (Inda, 2006).

The ethos of volunteerism underpins the ways in which NGOs operate. The 'commodification of solidarity', as Gómez Gil (2005) puts it, attracts many a social activist, enables NGOs to be cheaper contractors than private for-profit organisations, and constitutes them as powerful actors in the economic scene. Finally, it is the same volunteer ethos which, in the discourse of NGO staff, backgrounds the negative features of their work order (instability, underpayment and overwork, among others) and foregrounds the social good of working for these organisations.

In this section, I have discussed how, currently, despite the amount of discursive production devoted to either legitimising or simply masking it, the work of NGOs and labour unions cannot be disentangled from the work of the state. In different areas, i.e. social welfare and workplace training, these institutions have come to take on public administration and service delivery roles. One such social area in Spain is immigration law advice. Often, non-state organisations operating in this field are described as 'intermediary' or 'mediating' institutions that assist migrants with navigating the complexities of the legal framework. Frequently, a sharp contrast (and even opposition) is established between the 'welcoming' stance of these organisations towards migrant citizens and the 'non-welcoming' logic of the state (Subirós, 2010). However, as I will show in this chapter, the picture is a lot more complex than this.

Immigration, Legal Advice and Migrants' Trajectories in Spain

This chapter examines ethnographic data on free immigration advice gathered in Spain between 2009 and 2010. Two specific services are studied, one run by a trade union and another one by an NGO, both located in the Barcelona metropolitan area, in Catalonia.

Spain has a fairly decentralised political structure. It is organised into 17 regions (*comunidades autónomas*), of which Catalonia is one. Both Spanish and Catalan are official languages in Catalonia. Providing a quick picture of the two languages' distribution is unfeasible, as their use depends on a combination of geographical, social class, institutional and interpersonal considerations (see the articles contained in the volume edited by Woolard & Frekko, 2013, for an instructive presentation of issues in the current sociolinguistic debate in Catalonia).

Whereas areas like education and health, for example, have long been the sole responsibility of the Catalan regional government, the regulation of migrant flows was exclusively in the hands of the central government until mid-2011, after the data presented here were collected. In 2011, the Catalan government was authorised to decide on initial work permit applications, but not on the rest of the procedures (family reunion, work permit renewals, legalisation through proof of settlement [arraigo], etc.). In each province (there are four in Catalonia), there is an *oficina de extranjería* (foreigners' office) which is dependent on the central government and whose head is the *subdelegado del gobierno* (the provincial Spanish government representative).

No other country in the world has recently experienced as sharp an increase in the number of resident aliens as Spain. The figures illustrate this. While the percentage of foreign population was officially 2% in 1999, it had risen to 12% in 2009[3] (according to data from the Spanish statistics office).[4] In 2005, Spain was the third country in the world – after the United States and Germany – to have received the highest number of migrants since 1990 in absolute terms, and the first one in relative terms (Colectivo IOÉ, 2010).

The fact that these demographic and social changes have occurred in such a short time span facilitates the analysis of the ways in which the state, institutions and social agents are adjusting to the emerging new realities of Spanish society. Another crucial characteristic of the Spanish case is that the mass arrival of migrants has taken place in a period of time defined by neo-liberally inspired adjustments in public services, and thus reconfigurations of the links between the public and the private. For these reasons, I claim that the examination of the shifts that have occurred in the field of immigration advice constitutes a privileged window from which to capture some of the transformations of contemporary capitalism.

In Spain, legal advice interactions are central to the labour and personal trajectories of many migrants. This is due to the specific characteristics of migration trends to the country, which are largely shared with other southern European societies (Arango Vila-Belda, 2002). In Spain, migration flows are characterised by the sustained presence in time of a large proportion of undocumented workers, that is, foreigners residing in the country without proper work authorisation (Kostova Karaboytcheva, 2006). In fact, the vast majority of foreign labourers have legalised their status after a period of unauthorised residence in the country (hence the importance of immigration consultation services) and only a small percentage have crossed the border having been granted a work permit beforehand (González Enríquez, 2008).

Some authors attribute the pervasiveness of workers' unauthorised entry to the inefficient and rather inflexible nature of Spanish immigration policies (Kostova Karaboytcheva, 2006). For others, however, it is tied to the loosely regulated nature of the labour market (Arango Vila-Belda, 2002), but also to the fact that some important sectors of the Spanish economy (mainly agriculture and construction but also so-called 'personal services', that is, domestic work) depend on their capacity to mobilise the cheap and intensive labour that undocumented immigration provides (Giménez Romero, 2003).

The state has responded by attempting to document the large number of undocumented labourers through mass legalisation campaigns (up to three between 2000 and 2005). However, as the data show, these campaigns have not helped to diminish the number of undocumented labourers since new ones continue to arrive (Kostova Karaboytcheva, 2006).

In the current context of economic crisis, undocumented migrants' work opportunities in the informal economy have diminished. In the years of the Spanish economic boom (late 1990s and the early years of the 21st century), it was relatively easy for male migrants to find informal jobs in the ever-expanding building sector and for female labourers to be employed without a contract in low-paid (and highly exploitative) jobs in the service industry (including domestic work). In the face of increasing competition for jobs, since 2009, legal status has become, more than ever, a pressing need to access the Spanish labour market, as I will discuss later.

The immigration law: Policy and reality

In 1997, the yearly quota (*contingente*) was established as the means to organise the arrival of foreign labour in Spain. The *contingente* determined not only how many people would be allowed to legally enter the country but also for which professions (supposedly only those where there was shortage of national workers). Since 2009, this legal entry way has been virtually closed, as the list of professions where there is worker demand is very short and highly specialised.[5]

Currently, the only way for migrant workers to obtain legal authorisation to work in Spain is through the *arraigo* procedure. This procedure entails that foreign labourers enter the country either illegally or legally (on tourist or student visas which they then overstay), and then reside in the country without proper authorisation for a minimum of three years for the *arraigo social* (only two years are required if they can prove a sustained period of work in the informal economy, which implies reporting one's employer).

After that period of uninterrupted unauthorised residence (which they must prove by means of their registration with the local municipality), and provided they can (1) show they have community and/or family ties and (2) furnish a job offer, they are legally authorised to work and live in the country. In practical terms, this means that the Spanish state condones the existence of a regular pool of undocumented labourers that live off the ever-expanding informal economy. The official discourse is that facilitating migrants' documentation processes would have a magnet effect and encourage the arrival of more undocumented labourers. Yet, the fact that the government has needed to open up regular mass authorisation campaigns over the last decade questions the deterrent effect of such policies.

Over the last decade, trade unions and NGOs have increasingly played a major role in counselling migrants and organising their documentation processes. In the following section, I will explain how and why that has happened, and I will discuss these institutions' relationship to the state.

The Field of Immigration Advice[6]

Currently, there is a neat division of labour as regards migration-connected bureaucratic procedures between the state on the one hand, and unions, NGOs and other agencies (mainly law firms) on the other. Basically, the state is in charge of decision making,[7] while the rest of the stakeholders are responsible for supplying information and providing practical help with the application process. This division has not always been so clear. Ten years ago, during my earlier fieldwork, I visited a number of state offices where information to the general public was provided, for example on requirements for documentation processes. By contrast, over the last decade, there has been a process of gradual shutting down of state-run immigration information desks.[8] This has run parallel to the opening up of city immigration legal advisory services, which local municipalities have begun to supply as part of their welfare programmes. Given their specialist nature, however, the provision of these municipal services has been largely outsourced to trade unions. This process has strengthened the position of these organisations in the field. I shall explain the origin of union legal advisory services in what follows.

After the passing of the first foreigners' law in 1985, one of the two major Spanish trade unions (the one analysed in this chapter) was a pioneer (Solé & Parella, 2003) in offering immigration advice for what were at the time labelled 'foreign workers'. Their first office in Spain was opened in Catalonia (where my study was conducted) in 1988 (Bertran i Bruguera, 2007). Initially, this trade union's main concern was with migrant workers' labour rights. Immigration law information was, thus, conceived as another union service. In the early days, discourses about the need for an 'open door' policy in solidarity with fellow workers abounded. However, as foreign labourers increased in numbers (around the mid-1990s), trade unions started to worry about what they saw as the negative effects of undocumented labourers on indigenous workers' wages and work conditions. As González Enríquez (2008)[9] claims, unions moved from a service to a regulatory stance in relation to migrant labour. For example, they began to demand stricter government control on informal economy activities which they viewed as directly related to the growth of undocumented labour.

In fact, immigration advisory services have not had an easy fit within unions. At the union analysed here, there was for a long time talk about the need to 'unionise' the service (Bertran i Bruguera, 2007), which in fact meant two different things. On the one hand, it referred to the need to integrate migrant workers' issues as part of core union policy and not just as some peripheral information service (which was not achieved, at least not formally, until 2004, when the union's Immigration Secretariat was created). On the other hand, unionisation was connected to the need to recruit new (migrant) members and change migrants' perceptions of unions (as organisations that provide services to them, most notably legal advice; Solé & Parella, 2003). In many ways, the drive to unionise the service was a response to the risk, in the words of union leaders, that it might 'subconsciously replace the role of public administrations or of other civic organisations' (Bertran i Bruguera, 2007: 363). However, since 1996, when those words were uttered, both things have happened.

As I mentioned above, funding for trade unions' free legal consultation is public and, to a large extent, comes from agreements with local municipalities that provide free legal advice as part of the welfare services they offer to their populations. Currently, union immigration advice services form a real network of information-provision desks (the union analysed has 45 such desks in the Catalonia region), with information resources, tips and assistance travelling constantly among the different offices/advisors. This union is, in fact, one of the major organisations serving migrant citizens in Catalonia (Bertran i Bruguera, 2007). Although there are other agencies that also work in this field, as I will explain later, they are less prominent both in terms of the numbers of clients served and of its ease of contact with state authorities. For example, only the union (not the NGO analysed in this chapter) has weekly meetings with the state's representative in the province in charge of immigration policy delivery (the *subdelegado/a del gobierno*). At these regular meetings, the union is informed about amendments to the law or changes in decision-making rationalities.[10] They also get the

chance of discussing 'problematic' cases with high-ranking immigration officers in the Barcelona area. In addition, the union can give appointments for
the submission of applications on behalf of the state.

By and large, the few NGOs that work in this area tend to be local (unlike
the union, which has offices nationwide in Spain) and, thus, be less up to date
with regard to changes in bureaucratic practice.[11] There are various civil and
religious associations that furnish free-of-charge legal advice for authorisation
applications (although in some cases, only the information might be free,
while assistance with paperwork may be fee paying).[12] Some of the NGOs
might be migrant associations with culture-maintenance and/or religious
objectives; others might be organisations set up and run by members of the
indigenous population. Some might be staffed by volunteers; others may not.
However, since knowledge in this area is highly specialised, volunteer-based
organisations[13] might in fact redirect legal advice seekers towards larger NGOs
or some of the union services described earlier for precise information.

The NGO analysed in this chapter is a highly institutionalised organisation which has operated in a post-industrial city near Barcelona since 1994.
It was created and is still run by members of the local middle classes. It is
structured as a cluster of organisations providing services to migrants (assistance with asylum seeking, welfare resources, CV-writing advice, psychological help, language classes, etc.), although the most prominent in terms of
clients served is immigration law advice. This service is staffed by NGO
employees (not volunteers). Like the union service, this NGO is subsidised
mainly by the local municipality with some economic assistance from private foundations and a couple of savings banks.[14]

Migrants who do not know about union or NGO free legal consultation
desks often require the services of private law firms. Unfortunately, I cannot
ascertain what percentage of the migrant population they serve, although
they seem to be rather peripheral in the field. What is interesting, and
emerges from interviews and service interactions, is that law professionals,
as players in this field, are not welcome, either by the state or by the other
organisations. In their discourses, NGOs and trade union advisors accuse
lawyers of being misinformed, not caring about the consequences for
migrants of taking certain legal actions, and even of ripping them off (that
is, by encouraging migrants to apply for legal status even if they know that
they do not fulfil the state's requirements).

To sum up, the Spanish state has, over the last decade, consolidated a
strong (although not explicitly avowed) partnership with trade unions and,
to a lesser extent, NGOs in this field. This process has turned these organisations into quasi-public institutions which govern migrant populations on
behalf of the state.

Ethnographic Data

The analysis presented in this chapter is based on ethnographic data collected in 2009–2010 in the context of a broader research project investigating multilingual policies and practices in institutional contexts in Catalonia and, more specifically, in non-governmental and social organisations. Regular observations of practices were carried out in the two desks analysed between 2009 and 2010. Each desk was visited regularly for five/six months each year (January to July 2009 and December 2009 to May 2010). In 2009 I focused more on the NGO service, although I also visited the union service occasionally, whereas in 2010 my main objective was the union service. Informal conversations were held with advisors throughout and email correspondence was maintained after fieldwork was finished. This was important for me, as the complexity and changing nature of the Spanish immigration framework meant I had to go back to them on several occasions. Advisors were formally interviewed in 2010. My ethnographic understanding of the two contexts was also shaped by my participation in group consultation sessions and various information activities organised by the two organisations, and by the larger ethnographic endeavour of which the data analysed here is but a part. My co-researcher M. Rosa Garrido filled me in with numerous ethnographic details about the two organisations, since her involvement with them had been longer than mine. Her work also facilitated my access to both services.

In the recorded consultation sessions, migrant clients were told about the project and the purpose of the recordings, and were asked for informed consent. Except in a couple of cases, they did not object to being recorded. Advisors made a point of making it clear to clients that my recording was not connected to their chances of being served appropriately. Yet, despite our efforts, the power imbalance of the situation was difficult to even out, and certainly weighed in their decision to grant me permission.

The union advisors felt somewhat uncomfortable in having me observe their information practices, let alone record them. In fact, in 2009 I only observed Elena, the union advisor at the time, but did not record her consultation interactions. In 2010 I had greater familiarity with the institution and the advisors, and that eased the process of recording. Nevertheless, the sensitive nature of the context surfaced twice, when Anna, the advisor then, asked me to stop recording in the middle of her service interactions with immigration advice seekers, which, as I will discuss later, was revealing of her awareness of the contradictions of their service practices.

My focus on the institutional side of the service, coupled with the fairly large numbers of clients served daily and the fact that these desks were not located in community organisations where migrants could socialise with one another afterwards, made it difficult for me to establish close relationships with clients. This would have enabled me to obtain their perspective on the two services investigated and could have thrown light on different aspects of the relationship of the state with social organisations/unions. Notwithstanding, the data presented are rich enough to illuminate the changing nature of that relationship, and the dilemmas that it engenders for the advisors in real consultations.

Regimenting Populations: How and Why

There are three dimensions of regulation in unions' and NGOs' advisory practice: bureaucratic, moral and linguistic. By bureaucratic regulation, I refer to the fact that, beyond informing, counselling and assisting migrants with paperwork, trade unions and NGOs act as gatekeepers of the legalisation process (in lieu of the state). It is they who decide who is a legitimate applicant – that is, who meets the requirements, and who does not – and therefore, it is in that sense that they (rather than the state) regulate the bodies that get a chance of being allowed into the country.

Although decision making is the sole responsibility of the state, in the excerpts below we shall see how migrant applicants' selection process is de facto carried out by the labour and non-governmental agencies that assist them. This is so because these advice agencies refuse to file those applications that do not fulfil the requirements set by the government. Although one could think that efficacy/success criteria would explain this policy, the data reveal how these organisations' strict control over who gets to apply for legalisation is connected to the specific arrangements they have with state authorities. Excerpt (1) below, taken from an interview with one of the NGO advisors (Maria), bears witness to the trade-off nature of the agreement between the state, NGOs and unions.[15]

(1)
*MAR: [...] els sindicats sí que tenien una via directa perquè clar és un organisme que té molta més força que una oenagé local però a nivell d'oenagé no teníem cites directes havíem de demanar el fax i ara cada quinze dies tenim una taula en la que tenim unes cites assignades que **nosaltres ens hem de comprometre que realment les persones que apuntem en aquella cita nosaltres els haguem revisat tota la documentació i que realment està tot correcte.**

%tra: *[...] the unions did have a direct channel because of course it's an organisation which is a lot more powerful than a local NGO but as an NGO we did not have direct appointments we had to send a fax and now every fortnight we have a desk were we have some appointments allocated and **we must commit ourselves to making sure that the people that we have for that appointment we have reviewed their documentation and everything is correct.**

*EVA: ah vale això hi ha un compromís per part de la oenagé de.
%tra: *oh okay so there is a commitment on the part of the NGO.*

*MAR: clar no pots i si hi envies algú que realment no compleix et diuen ey a ve::r que la persona vingui amb els **amb la documentació més o menys ordenada** o sigui que ells saben que ve aquella persona ja saben que **són persones que realment compleixen tots els requisits** i **tenen una certa urgència a presentar el tràmit.**
%tra: *of course you cannot and if you send someone who does not fulfil [the requirements] they tell you, hey make sure that the person comes **with all his/her documents orderly arranged** I mean then they know that **those people meet all the requirements and need to submit the application rather urgently.***

One of the noticeable aspects in (1) is that different organisations appear to have different prerogatives with application submission, and that these prerogatives seem related to their size and position within the field. All 'privileges' are dependent on satisfying the state's requirements. So, in this case, in exchange for having a fixed number of applications allowed every fortnight, NGO advisors have to 'commit' themselves to 'making sure everything is correct' in the applications that are filed, which means making sure that migrants fulfil the legal requirements and that they have included all the necessary documents, but also that their documents are properly arranged and that their cases are urgent.

Advisors put a lot of effort into arranging documents 'properly' (basically, the way state officers want to find them). For example, Anna, the union advisor, reviews each file more than once and frequently makes the state's requirement explicit to migrants (*'ahora lo pongo en el orden que ellos quieren'*, now I am arranging this the way they want). As regards assessing the urgency of a file, the government demands that unions and NGOs prioritise applications, a rather thorny issue, which illustrates the opportunities for control that are put in the hands of these organisations.

Not only does the state demand selection, close monitoring and hierarchisation of applications in exchange for favourable submission conditions, but it also appears to encourage competition among its subsidiaries, which at least some of these organisations seem happy to take part in. This is what transpires from (2) if we attend to the advisor's display of pride in her union having been congratulated by immigration officers.

(2)
*ANN: ens donen cita:: prèvia abans que si ho demanen per altres advocats que hi ha uns interessos econòmics [...] **llavors el que sí ens demanen és que els expedients estiguin bé** i la veritat és que en una última reunió ens van felicitar on hi havia altres entitats i altres sindicats **ens van felicitar no -¿** dient que la veritat és que els expedients quan veuen que vénen del nostre sindicat pues pts estan contents **perquè saben que hi ha una mínima garantia d'ordre** eh -¿ sí.

%tra: *we are given earlier appointments than lawyers because there is a profit side to it [...] then **what they ask us to do is to make sure that the files are okay** and the truth is at the last meeting **we were congratulated** there were other organisations and other unions and we were congratulated right -¿ they said that when files when they see that files come from our union they're happy **because they know there is a minimum guarantee of order** right -¿ yes.*

Interesting in this excerpt is the way the state's expectation of reciprocity is encapsulated by Anna's use of the expression *'el que sí (que) ens demanen és que...'* (as opposed to plain *'el que ens demanen és que...'*), which in Catalan indicates that the commitment expected of the other party (in this case, the trade union) is of a binding (almost moral) nature.

As we said earlier, not all representative agents receive such 'favourable' treatment by the state. Private law firms, for example, are made to wait longer to file their cases, as Anna explains (and seems to legitimise) in (3) below.

(3)
*ANN: a més la delegació del govern ens ha donat la possibilitat de tenir u:n ara no o sigui ara estem en canvis ja veurem com acabarà però tenim una taula on nosaltres com a sindicat portem i el que sí ens han demanat és que per exemple **ens donen cita:: prèvia abans que si ho demanen per altres advocats que hi ha uns interessos econòmics** no o sigui com que som una entitat sense ànim de lucre [...].

%tra: *in addition the immigration services have given us the possibility of*
          having a: I mean now we are in a process of change we'll see how it all
          ends but we have a desk where we as a union take [applications] but
          what they've really asked for is ok for example **we are given earlier**
          appointments than lawyers because there is a profit side to it,
          I mean because we are a non-profit [...].

Drawing on paternalistic discourses, the for-profits and private businesses that work in this area are problematised by the state. As a consequence, those migrants who pay for professional counsel are penalised by a
state machinery which, as a bureaucratic organisation, should be driven by
the principles of rationality, fairness and equality (Weber, 1948). My claim is
that, despite official rhetoric, what really seems to be at stake here is the
interest of the state in using unions and NGOs as its arms, that is, as bodies
through which to serve the state, in this case in facilitating the process of
decision making.

There are a number of ways in which the state benefits from its partnership with civil society organisations. First, the fact that unions and NGOs
are in charge of information services helps cuts down on public expenditure.
Secondly, the documentation process becomes more 'orderly'. Instead of
having to communicate with a high number of individual applicants (as it
did in the past; see Codó, 2008), now the state only deals with a handful of
social organisations which either act as representative agents for migrants or
review each application carefully before submission. The 'messiness' of interacting with a highly diverse clientele is thus avoided. Further, the state is
ideologically not seen as investing (too many) resources on newly arrived and
undocumented foreign labour.

Unions and NGOs, in turn, also take advantage of these established
arrangements. By agreeing to exert strict control over who gets to apply for
authorisation, both agencies manage to offer a better service to the applicants they assist. This is because, on the one hand, these agencies have
precise insider information and can provide insightful advice. On the other
hand, the documentation process is faster if assisted by either of these two
organisations. This helps to raise the profile of unions and NGOs in the
field of immigration advice (probably at the expense of law firms) and to
dispel some applicants' doubts (as I observed) about the quality of a non-
paying service. In the medium run this also means more clients, and therefore more grounds on which to justify the public funding these organisations
receive.

It could be argued that migrants also benefit from this arrangement (if
we exclude those that resort to law professionals, that is). Generally, the

information exchange process runs more smoothly than at the state offices I observed in my previous work (Codó, 2008), and the advisors have a real commitment to help. However, there is more than meets the eye and, as I shall explain in what follows, migrants are also subjected to various forms of moral regimentation in these services. By moral regimentation I refer to the regulation of attitude and conduct which I observed in both NGO and union services. I claim it is moral in nature because it is bound up with notions of 'good' and 'bad' clienthood.

The regulation of attitude is not explicitly demanded by the state, as happens with bureaucratic control. By and large, it takes a different shape at each service. While at the union it is connected to clients' displaying attentiveness, responsibility and cooperation (not missing out on documents, bringing properly arranged files, etc.), at the NGO it is linked to issues of gratefulness and appreciation. I connect these differences to the distinct values of each organisation.

At the union, assessment of proper attitude is linked to migrants' facilitating the advisor's bureaucratic tasks, as can be seen in (4) below. Regulation is carried out both negatively (although usually through ironic comments such as *'lo traéis todo bien ordenadito eh?'*, literally, 'you are bringing everything properly arranged, right?' rather than through overt reprimands), and positively, as happens in the excerpt below, through the explicit praising of clients' cooperation.

(4)

01	***ANN:**	dime.
	%tra:	*how can I help you?*
02	***CLI:**	es para e:l le: # l'arraigo.
	%tra:	*we came about an arraigo [documentation application].*
03	***ANN:**	< vale ##> [>] déjame ver todo lo que tienes ##
04		de prue::bas y de todo eh?
	%tra:	*< okay ##> [>] I'd like to see everything you have ##*
		evidence and everything right?
05	***CLI:**	<para presentar las cosas>[<]
	%tra:	*<to submit the things>[<].*
	%act:	client hands documents over to the advisor.
06	***ANN:**	a ver tenemos aquí informe social: 1 # contrato de traba:jo
07		# cuarenta horas # un año #4 muy bien.
	%tra:	*let's see we have here the social repo:rt # the job co:ntract*
		# forty hours # one year #4 very good.

08 ***UUU:** #11.

09 ***ANN:** octubre del 2006 # hasta febrero 2008 # y entonces
10 tenemos <[nom ciutat] [>] febrero.
    %tra: *October 2006 # until February 2008 # and then we have*
    <[city name] [>] February.

11 ***CLI:** < sí> [<].
    %tra: *<yes> [<].*

12 ***ANN:** que bien # que viene alguien <con todo> [>]!
    %tra: *so good to have somebody come with everything [>]!*
    %act: Anna gazes at researcher and pulls a face indicating
    tiredness.

13 ***EVA:** < [=!laughs]> [<].

14 ***CLI:** < no ya::> [<] porque <ha
15 preguntado y sabemos> qué hace falta.
    %tra: *< ri::ght> [<] because we*
    have enquired and we know what's needed.

16 ***ANN:** < de verdad # o::h! >
    %tra: *<frankly # kkhh! >*

[...]

Anna revises the documents handed over to her by the clients who are
applying for legal status through the *arraigo* procedure. She reviews their file
thoroughly (note the use of the verb 'see', a regular choice in this context,
which sheds light on the advisor's personal examination of every single document), and then in line 12 suddenly praises the clients' organised file, raising
her gaze and looking at me (I was sitting behind the clients facing her). Her
use of *'alguien'* (somebody) reveals how rare the situation is for her. The face
she pulls while she utters those comments indicates her tiredness at having
to spend so much time sorting out documents from the pile that is usually
given to her. This is reinforced by her comments in line 16, where *'o:h'*
expresses her frustration at her frequent inability to make clients act as professionally as this one has done (lines 14–15). The way attitude regimentation is carried out at the union is related to this organisation's notions of
good clienthood. In my conversations with union advisors, they defined
'bad' clients as those that may question their expertise. This indicates to
what extent cooperating with the advisor (in its multiple forms, including
respect for his/her expertise) is the value that defines relationships at this

service. Yet expertise plays a larger role. Union advisors' deep knowledge of immigration laws is also the element that is repeatedly drawn upon to justify the key role of these organisations in the field and as a guarantee of service quality.

At the NGO, however, relationships are constructed on different terms, which means that the moral regulation of conduct takes different forms. It surfaces in the ways in which those clients that do not 'appreciate' the work that is done for them are problematised. This type of discourse (which I never heard among union advisors) can be observed in (5) below. Although expecting appreciation in return for one's work is part of being human, in the NGO context, comments of this type are made repeatedly, and are the criteria for distinguishing 'good' from 'bad' clients at this institution. For this reason I argue that non-appreciation connects up, more broadly, with key NGO values, like the ethos of volunteerism. Although these advisors are not volunteers, it is true that they work long hours, as somewhat part of the general understanding that working for an NGO is different from working for a private company and that it involves a deep commitment to one's job. Hence, the need for appreciation. Thus, Maria's complaint (*'no saben el que costa mantenir el servei'*) is both personal and institutional, as she is referring to her personal efforts to provide a good service and to the paperwork that obtaining public funding regularly involves for the organisation.

(5)
*MAR: i el fet de que sigui gratuït moltes vegades és **no valorar el servei** o sigui no saben lo que realment hi ha al darrere el que costa mantenir el servei i tot.

%tra: *and the fact that it is for free many time it's like* **they don't appreciate the service** *I mean they don't know what's behind it what it takes to maintain a service like this.*

Clients' 'non-appreciation' of the service has practical consequences for them, as advisors link it to a lack of understanding of what the service is about (this is construed as a form of non-appreciation). For example, advisors refuse to simply furnish application forms to those clients who claim to have the information on requirements and bureaucratic procedures. Advisors construct this (that is, the mere handing over of forms) as running counter to their assumption of what constitutes good service, which involves engaging in long (often rather personal) service interactions with clients, in which they produce checklists, highlight important information, write clarifications or synonyms for certain terms, and such like.

Finally, another pervasive form of regulation is, as I have explained else-where (Codó & Garrido, 2010), the unproblematic imposition of Spanish as the 'commonsensical' language of communication with clients, and, related to this, advisors' reproduction of the we/they, frontstage/backstage distinction drawing on Catalan/Spanish bilingualism which I also documented in the government office previously studied (Codó, 2008). In a bilingual community like Catalonia, it is illuminating to observe that language choice is not open but fixed, as encounters are routinely opened in Spanish by advisors. Further, these practices, which practically efface Catalan from service talk, contradict the official stance of both the union and the NGO with respect to the public status and use of Catalan with migrants (see Garrido, 2010b, for more information on the numerous tensions observed at this NGO).

The naturalisation of Spanish as the lingua franca at both the NGO and the union services examined is so pervasive that this language becomes, in fact, a prerequisite for accessing information and advice. This is both the result and the cause of constructing multilingualism as exceptional and rather unnecessary, which reproduces the ideological grounds on which belonging is constructed by the nation-state (Moyer & Martín Rojo, 2007).

Dilemmas and Contradictions

The adoption of an unquestioned subsidiary role (in relation to the state) is not without tensions for trade unions and NGOs. One of these tensions is linked to the ways in which these organisations handle the supply of information on 'loopholes' in the immigration law. Obviously, these tensions are more acute for trade unions than for NGOs because, practically, they involve clients engaging in irregular contracting practices, which unions oppose. However, information on these loopholes is crucial advice for a lot of migrants as, often, they constitute the only way to obtain legal status, given the currently restrictive nature of the Spanish documentation process. Facilitating this type of information also seems crucial for both NGOs and unions in order for them to be able to pursue their specific institutional agendas.

The 'loopholes' I alluded to earlier are tied to what most authors call 'fictitious contracts' (see, for example, Parella Rubio, 2003). These are job offers (a necessary requirement for documentation), which are in fact not offers for 'real' jobs. In fact, migrants arrange with their employers that they will not receive any wages for the duration of the contract and that they will pay for their own social security contributions while they actually continue to work in the informal economy.

These fictitious contracts are most frequent in the domestic work sector for a number of reasons. First of all, there are fewer requirements for employers, who must only prove that they earn the minimum established by the government. Secondly, they are less risky, as inspections in households are rare (Kostova Karaboytcheva, 2006). Third, they are easier to obtain (would-be residents can ask acquaintances, fellow countrymen, neighbours, etc.). For example, in the case of women who work part time as cleaners or caregivers without a contract, they can ask the families they work for to give them a (fictitious) full-time contract, but in fact continue working part time. In those cases, the arrangement is usually that the migrant pays for her own social security contributions.[16]

Throughout my two-year fieldwork, I documented how pervasive this practice was, especially in the later period because of the country's economic downturn. In fact, migrants were trapped in a sort of 'vicious circle' where legal status was dependent on work and work was dependent on legal status. For many, obtaining a fictitious contract was the only way out. As explained earlier, however, offering one of those contracts is, often, a personal 'favour' that employers do for migrants. Obviously, this makes them highly vulnerable to last-minute changes of mind of would-be 'employers', as I also attested in a number of cases.

One key question is what stance NGOs and trade unions take (as institutions) in relation to these practices. As would be expected, unions and NGOs provide dissimilar legitimising grounds and experience their engagement with these practices differently. To begin with, Anna, the union advisor, presents the situation as 'contradictory' for them in (6) below, whereas Maria, the NGO advisor, whose opinion we shall see in (7), does not.[17]

(6)
*ANN: primer, el tema amb la relació amb el sindicat molt bé [...] el que sí és cert és **que hi ha vegades vivim situacions de contradicció** quan ve una persona i no porta el temps reglamentari per poder demanar papers però a més et diu no no vull denunciar perquè realment estic bé o sigui em tracten com a qualsevol altre treballador [...] com a sindicalistes hauríem de dir no no això no es pot suportar i hem de denunciar però o sigui no aconseguim res perquè l'objectiu per mi i jo penso per tots els assessors i assessores **és que les persones que estan aquí tinguin papers** # sigui, ja estan aquí una altra cosa són les polítiques d'immigració eh:: [...] **el que sí tenim clar és que quan estan aquí han de tenir papers** o sigui no -¿ aleshores amb el sindicat en aquest sentit no ens hem sentit mai pressionats evidentment.

%tra: *first, concerning the relationship with the union, it's good [...]*
            however it's true that **sometimes we live contradictory**
            situations *when a person comes and he or she has not been in the*
            country long enough for legalisation and in addition he or she says
            I don't want to report my employer because I am okay I mean I get
            treated as any other worker [...] as union members we should say
            no this is not correct and we should report the employer but I mean
            it's no good because the goal is for me and I think for all the
            advisors that **those people that are here get documented # I**
            mean they are here already the immigration policies are another
            matter right [...] **for us it's clear that once they are here they**
            must get papers right -¿ *so in that sense we've obviously never*
            felt pressured by the union.

In her comments, Anna establishes a distinction between (macro) immigration policies and daily (micro) practice, which is, however, not unproblematic, as advisory practice is also part of union policy. The way Anna constructs her arguments provides evidence for this. First, she presents her views from a group rather than from an individual perspective (as opposed to Maria in (7), who speaks in individual terms), which means there is a collective understanding that documentation should be made easier for migrants already in Spain (although, strategically, Anna does not mention how). Thus, Anna's position towards helping migrants get documented is phrased as a general claim towards irregular immigration ('*el que sí tenim clar és que quan estan aquí han de tenir papers*', for us it's clear that once they are here they must get papers right¿). In other words, Anna's position is political (not personal), as it would correspond with a trade union representative. Her defence of the need to legalise undocumented labour is in accordance with the union's agenda (that is, fighting work in the informal economy through getting as many workers documented as possible). In a nutshell, accomplishing this goal seems to legitimise the overlooking of illegal or semi-legal contracting practices, the rationale being that in the medium term labourers who get documented through fictitious contracts will effectively enter the formal economy.

As I mentioned earlier, Maria, the NGO advisor, takes a fairly different stance. She frames her actions in individual terms and as legitimised by her commitment towards helping individual clients better their life conditions. She also explicitly voices her lack of interest in knowing whether migrants work in the informal economy or not (note the dissimilar backgrounding of the issue of work in the two advisors' accounts, as would be expected). Another interesting contrast with Anna is that the only possible source of tension Maria envisages is not in relation to NGO values, but in connection with the illegal nature of fictitious contracts, that is, in relation to the state. Maria justifies her practices on the grounds that fictitious contracts are not instances of big fraud, and prioritises helping clients, that is, pursuing the NGO agenda, to abide by the law, even if this implies subverting the state.

(7)

*MAR: jo penso que si no és una cosa jo penso que sí és una cosa realment # que: és això no? que és una trampeta petita que no necessàriament és una cosa que perjudiqui a una altra persona i que no suposa cap gra::n # frau ni res i que això **per a aquella persona li pot suposar de a tenir papers a no tenir papers o de poder tenir una feina a no poder tenir una feina no li diré fes això però bueno hi ha aquestes possibilitats** i:.

%tra: *my opinion is that as long as it's not something really # I mean if it's only cheating a bit but it's not like something that goes against somebody else or it's not like a big fraud and thanks to that **a person may have papers instead of not being undocumented or may have job instead of being unemployed of course I will not tell them to do that but at least say there are these possibilities** a:nd.*

*Eva: clar dir-li les possibilitats.

%tra: *of course tell them about the possibilities.*

*MAR: clar si realment hi ha una altra via per la que se'n pugui sortir pues no val la pena ni comentar-li però si realment és una persona que no té cap altra solució i penses que amb això se'n podria sortir pues donar-li la possibilitat de 'realment si hi hagués algú que et signés com que treballes a casa seva' **sense entrar si treballes o no treballes**.

%tra: *of course if there is some other way for him to get documented then it's not even worth mentioning if but if there is no other solution and you think this could solve the problem then give them the possibility like tell them 'if there were someone who could sign like you work at their place' **independently of whether they work or not.***

In the previous paragraphs we analysed advisors' discourse and observed that, despite their different arguments for legitimising this practice, both the NGO and the union immigration advisor agreed that offering information on fictitious contracts was justified. So, in fact, they took the same practical stance. But what happens in situated talk? Do advisors belonging to the union and those belonging to the NGO disclose those pieces of sensitive information differently? If so, why?

What the data show is that practice is a lot messier than official discourse, and that we need to go beyond broad institutional affiliation to understand individual strategies. I begin by focusing on the union immigration advice service first. That service was staffed by two different employees, Elena (until late 2009) and Anna, who took over from her. Anna was an immigration advisor and a core union member (*sindicalista*), while Elena only had an employment relationship to the union, and thus felt less committed to core union values.[18] Despite the fact that they belong to the same organisation, in practical terms they act differently.

While Elena would resort to implicits and often voice her concerns about the fictitious contracts through comments like '*no es correcto, pero bueno*' (it's not correct, but anyway),[19] Anna would not hesitate to encourage migrants to get one (as in the reconstructed interaction below). However, she would always make sure my recording device was off (or tell me to switch it off), aware as she was that, as a representative of the union, she was not 'allowed' to say that.

(8)

01	*ANN:	y no hay nadie que te pueda hacer un contrato?
	%tra:	*and isn't there anyone who can give you a contract?*
02	*CLI:	estoy haciendo unas horas cuidando unos yayos pero él
03		quiere saber las responsabilidades que van sobre él.
	%tra:	*I'm working part-time taking care of an elderly couple but he*
		says he wants to know what he'd be responsible for.
04	*ANN:	nada esto no graba ni desgraba ni nadie le va a pedir
05		cuentas de por qué tiene una empleada de hogar.
	%tra:	*nothing this does not pay or deduct taxes and no one is ever*
		going to ask him why he's got a domestic worker.

By contrast, Maria, the NGO advisor, who in (7) legitimised the supplying of information on how to bypass the requirements of the immigration law on account of her willingness to help individual migrants, was less explicit in her interactions with clients. In that sense, her practice was more similar to Elena's. Her way of approaching the topic was a lot more indirect and detached than Anna's, as can be observed in (9) below. In this interaction, the client is trying to find out how to get his permit renewed. As it turns out, one of the requirements for the renewal is that he is employed, and thus paying social security contributions, which he is not, because he is only receiving a family allowance at the moment. The only solution for him seems, again, obtaining a fictitious contract as a domestic worker.

(9)

93	*MAR:	ten muy en cuenta que es en base que cotice # si eso
94		no cotiza ya no: hay que hacerlo por otra vía total-
95		mente diferente que habría que ver <cuál> [>].

%tra: *you need to take into account that it's on the basis of your paying contributions # if that's not the case then it must be done through other means and we would have to see <what>.*

96	*CLI:	< cuál es esa vía> [<]
97		porque claro si me encuentro que no:.

%tra: *<what those means are>* [<] *because of course if I find myself no:t.*

98	*MAR:	sería o::

%tra: *it'd be either::r*

99	*CLI:	yo no me voy a ir tengo dos niños aquí o sea.

%tra: *I'm not going to leave I have two kids here.*

100	*MAR:	[=! laughs] no no hay otras vías pero entonces la cosa
101		se complica un poco más # la: siguiente sería # tener
102		la posibilidad de que te puedas dar de alta en algún
103		régimen # o bien porque alguien te pueda contratar o
104		te puedas dar como de alta como empleado del
105		hoga::r.

%tra: *[=! laughs] no no there are other ways but then it gets more complicated # the next one would be # having the possibility of somehow being registered with social security # either because somebody gives you a contract or because you can get registered as domestic wo:rker.*

There are several telling features in the way Maria approaches the issue. First, her use of the vague expression *'otra vía totalmente diferente'* (through other means) to introduce the topic, followed by *'habría que ver cuál'* (we would have to see what means), which is a way of announcing a solution without revealing much. Also interesting is her use of the impersonal *'hay que hacerlo'* (lit. it must be done) in line 94 instead of a second-person appeal to act. When she is asked to clarify what that other 'means', she prefaces her explanation with 'but then it gets more complicated'. Her *'tener la posibilidad de'* (lit. having the possibility of) in lines 101–102 is also fairly impersonal, though her use of *'te puedas dar de alta'* (lit. your registering yourself) subtly indicates that what she has in mind is not a 'regular' contract (as employees are usually registered with social security by employers and not by themselves). Her turn finishes with very few details. In her *'o te puedas dar como de alta como empleado del hoga::r'*, she is a bit more specific about the contract type she has in mind, but she does not reveal how the client should do it or what the requirements would be. Although the interaction continues for a few minutes, she never reveals the practicalities of the arrangement she suggests. The advisor seems to assume (and this is a recurrent pattern) that the client already has the information (through his/her personal network). If this is the case, s/he will probably know what to do (and the advisor will not have to explain). If s/he does not, then s/he will request further details. It is only in these cases that Maria will volunteer the necessary information.

What I am trying to say is that Maria, the NGO advisor, deploys interactional practices which would be more similar to Elena's, one of the union advisors, than to Anna's, the other union advisor observed. However, rather than being contradictory, these observations would make sense if factors that transcend institutional belonging are taken into consideration. As was remarked earlier, Anna was a *sindicalista* (a trade unionist), and in that sense, more combative and outspoken than Elena in defending workers' rights. This would explain why she would not hesitate to help undocumented foreign labourers get documented (that, incidentally, also contributed to helping indigenous workers). Her *sindicalista*, and thus fairly politicised position, would also explain why she was careful not to be recorded. In addition, she was also more experienced than Elena, and thus probably less concerned about the consequences of encouraging migrants to engage in fictitious contract practices. In short, for Anna her union values clouded possible worries about the legal nature of such contracting practices, which, as I have suggested earlier, would have positive medium-run effects on both individual workers and the national labour market. The less politicised views of Maria and Elena, by contrast, may explain their more subtle, less forthright interactional stances.

Discussion and Conclusions

Until recently, there has been little research on *how* individuals migrate, as Agustín (2007) claims but, as border controls tighten, research is on the increase. The study presented here fits squarely into that growing body of studies which seek to understand the many 'whens' and 'hows' of individuals' migration trajectories. In this chapter I have suggested that, to do that, we must look at language, and most specifically at verbal interaction in a key discursive space – immigration advice. When one tries to do that ethnographically, one of the first questions that one must puzzle out is why that activity is taking place in that particular context, and how it connects up with the political and social transformations of late capitalism.

I have framed my analysis within an understanding of two key interconnected processes, i.e. globalisation and the neoliberal offloading of public services to civil society organisations. These processes pose a number of challenges for trade unions and NGOs. Currently, both types of institutions seem to have adopted a public administration role as service contractors for the state. One of their challenges is, thus, how to discursively and practically reconcile that public service status with their institutional values and mission agendas.

Rather than a simple transfer of responsibilities and control from the state to social and labour organisations, I have shown in this chapter that the state retains its capacity to control and regulate the social body. It does so differently from the past; it now uses social agents, like unions or NGOs, to achieve its regulatory goals. Relations among public, private and non-governmental organisations have changed; in fact, they have become more complex and entangled than ever.

In spite of their genuine commitment to helping undocumented migrants, I have illuminated different ways in which labour unions and NGOs act as instruments of regulation. One of my main claims has been to present these institutions as the real gatekeepers of migrants' processes of documentation in Spain. The acceptance of this role grants them certain prerogatives from the state, and this aids the case of the migrant applicants they assist. The interactions I witnessed were a lot more informative than most of the encounters I had observed at the state immigration office 10 years earlier. The facility of application submission and the numerous success stories that circulate raises the profile of these institutions among the undocumented population. All these elements, together with the free nature of the service, keep client numbers high, and should thus ensure the survival of the service. This explains why advisors unproblematically accept the gatekeeping regime that is imposed on them. However, I have also shed light on the inequality that is built into the partnership with the state by showing how it puts those applicants who may apply for documentation individually or through a law firm at a disadvantage.

The second dimension of regulation I have explored is moral. Advisors' regulatory practices approve of certain client attitudes and disapprove of others. They are connected to the terms under which relationships between advisors and clients are constructed in each context. Whereas at the union service, cooperation, self-responsibility and respect for advisors' expertise are foregrounded, at the NGO, clients' attitudes are evaluated with regard to their gratefulness and appreciation of advisors' personal and institutional efforts. Although I have not explored it in detail here, I have also mentioned that language choice is a terrain of regulation as well, where Spanish is the only legitimate language of interaction.

Acting as subsidiaries to the state means that NGOs and unions face a number of contradictions. The main contradiction I have explored in this chapter is related to their commitment towards assisting migrant clients and facilitating their documentation process in the face of the restrictiveness of the legal mechanisms for documentation in Spain. This means that, while they are the state's service contractors and thus regulate populations on its behalf, they also decide to subvert the state by informing clients of the existence of loopholes in the documentation procedure. Facilitating this information benefits migrants' cases but also contravenes the law.

The personal and institutional tensions around the issue of the fictitious domestic service contracts have helped to throw light on advisors' different legitimising position, and on the ambivalence of interactional practice. It is Anna, the most politicised advisor, who has fewest reservations about speaking openly of those contracts, both to me and to her clients. However, she is also the most careful about not being recorded speaking about them. While one could think that her *sindicalista* status would make her less prone to disclose information on fictitious contracts, I have explained why I think it is actually the other way round. By contrast, Maria and Elena, although belonging to different institutions, are more cautious in interactional practice. They tend to use rather indirect strategies to provide the information and wait for the clients to demand further details, which I have attributed to their less politicised stances.

To finish off, this chapter has brought to light the problematic nature of some prevalent dichotomies in the field of immigration studies. One of them is the welcoming versus non-welcoming logic of institutions that operate in this field, which often leads researchers to classify them as belonging to one or the other category. While the romantic myth of non-profits as institutionalised sites of caring and giving within a community persists (Joseph, 2002), I have shown that, within the conditions of contemporary capitalism, the strict division between welcoming and non-welcoming bodies is difficult to uphold. The second dichotomy my data have questioned is the difference between legal and illegal aliens as a major categorising device. The boundaries are less clear cut than one might think. A legal foreign worker may actually be working 'illegally' because of the nature of the contracting agreement s/he has been forced to reach to meet the requirements of the documentation process. If s/he then does not work legally long enough, s/he may not be able to renew his/her permit and go back to illegality (unless s/he finds a way to cheat the government once again). But what is the status of those contractual arrangements? The contracts are not forged, so they are not illegal; it is the inexistence of a labour relationship that makes them irregular. But what about part-time domestic workers who are employed full time? Are they not in a labour relationship with their employers? These issues illustrate not just that reality is too messy to be categorised, but also that the keys that open the gates of our industrialised societies have become commodities which, in themselves, epitomise the numerous avenues of inequality and social injustice.

Transcription conventions

The excerpts analysed in this chapter have been transcribed following the procedures established in the *LIDES Coding Manual* (LIPPS Group, 2000). When the main tier is not in English, a free English translation is provided on a dependent tier (*%tra*) located just below. The dependent tier %act provides information on participants' actions as talk is produced. Other conventions employed are presented below:

*UUU	Undecidable speaker
##	Longer pause (shorter than 1 second)
#1	Length of pause in seconds
[=! text]	Paralinguistics, prosody
:	Lengthened vowel
[>]	Overlap follows
[<]	Overlap precedes
< >	Scope symbols

Acknowledgements

The author would like to give thanks for the feedback received from Celia Roberts and Melissa Moyer to the earlier drafts of this chapter. She would also like to acknowledge the financial support of the Spanish *Ministerio de Ciencia e Innovación* through funded research project HUM 2010-26964 (*Multilingüismo y movilidad: Prácticas lingüísticas y la construcción de identidad*).

Notes

(1) This refers, specifically, to citizens of countries not belonging to the European Union (and Switzerland) or the European Economic Area (including Iceland, Liechtenstein and Norway), who are subject to practically no restrictions to work and live in Spain.

(2) Although my impression is that the changes examined in this chapter have occurred everywhere in Spain (albeit perhaps with different intensity), my claims here will be limited to Catalonia, as this is the Spanish region where I conducted my fieldwork.

(3) Given the large number of irregulars, these figures can only be approximate.

(4) See http://www.ine.es.

(5) The list for the second term 2013 is available from: http://www.sepe.es/contenido/empleo_formacion/catalogo_ocupaciones_dc/pdf/CatalogoOcupacionesDificilCobertura.pdf

(6) The details provided in this section were valid in 2011 when this chapter was first submitted. Changes in policy and practice may have occurred since then of which I may not be aware. I apologise for any inconsistencies in that regard.

(7) Under the term 'state', I include both the Spanish state and regional administrations (for example, the Catalan government).

(8) This evolution became apparent to me during my ethnographic engagement with the union and NGO services investigated, when I was told repeatedly that that was the case. In 2011, when this chapter was written, there was no face-to-face consultation desk (as there used to be in 2000) for individual queries; detailed information seemed only available through email or a phone information service which was always engaged. The standard way in which information on requirements and procedures was provided was through standard information sheets (for which there is a special desk). I could not ascertain to what extent clients could, informally, solicit further information from that desk. However, my knowledge of the logics of that particular institution (and of the Barcelona branch in particular) leads me to figure out that deviations from the established role of the desk were at best limited.

(9) This author claims that there are still visible tensions within the organisation between trade unionists and representatives of its immigration advice services with regard to their take on migrant issues.

(10) During my fieldwork I frequently observed NGO advisors asking union advisors for updated information on administrative procedures.

(11) Surprising as it may seem, the way the Spanish immigration laws are bureaucratically handled by the different state-run provincial offices (in charge of decision making) can vary enormously. An example I got to know during my fieldwork was the requirement in Barcelona to submit a full-time job offer to gain legal authorisation under the *arraigo* procedure. In the nearby Girona province (only 100 km away from Barcelona), two part-time contracts served the same purpose, but in Barcelona this arrangement was not accepted.

(12) I thank Safae Jabri for this piece of information. She conducted ethnographic fieldwork at a Moroccan association in Barcelona.

(13) Migrants' social networks also carry out a great deal of the informing and counselling that migrants require as part of their documentation process, as Sabaté (2010) shows.

(14) In Spain, there is a special kind of savings bank (called *cajas de ahorros*) in which it is required by law to invest part of their profits on welfare programmes.

(15) All the names that appear in this chapter are fictitious to preserve the anonymity of participants as well as of the organisations they work for.
(16) At the time the data were collected, this was around €160 per month.
(17) Although Anna does not directly refer to the issue of fictitious contracts in this extract, her comment about getting those already in the country documented is an allusion to that practice.
(18) This became evident to me through her comments, as when she complained that she was expected to join the demonstration organised by the union on 1 May (Labour Day in Spain).
(19) Taken from my fieldnotes, 2 April 2009.

References

Agustín, L.M. (2007) *Sex at the Margins: Migration, Labour Markets and the Rescue Industry.* London and New York: Zed Books.

Arango Vila-Belda, J. (2002) La inmigración en España a comienzos del siglo XXI: Un intento de caracterización. In F.J. García Castaño and C. Muriel López (eds) *La inmigración en España: contextos y alternativas* (pp. 57–70). Granada: Laboratorio de Estudios Interculturales.

Bertran i Bruguera, C. (2007) Anàlisi de les pràctiques comunicatives que s'estableixen en una oficina sindical d'atenció a treballadors estrangers. Unpublished PhD thesis, Universitat de Barcelona, Barcelona.

Codó, E. (2008) *Immigration and Bureaucratic Control: Language Practices in Public Administration.* Berlin: Mouton de Gruyter.

Codó, E. and Garrido M.R. (2010) Ideologies and practices of multilingualism in bureaucratic and legal advice encounters. *Sociolinguistic Studies* 4 (2), 297–332.

Colectivo IOÉ (2010) *Discursos de la población migrante entorno a su instalación en España. Investigación cualitativa.* Colección Opiniones y Actitudes 64. Madrid: Centro de Investigaciones Sociológicas.

Ewing, K.D. (2005) The function of trade unions. *Industrial Law Journal* 34 (1), 1–22.

Gallin, D. (2000) Trade unions and NGOs: A necessary partnership for social development. *Paper 1.* Geneva: UNRISD Publications.

Garrido, M.R. (2010a) 'If you slept in Catalunya you know that here it's a paradise': Multilingual practices and ideologies in a residential project for migrants. Unpublished MA thesis. Universitat Autònoma de Barcelona, Barcelona.

Garrido, M.R. (2010b) Tensions ideològiques sobre la 'llengua d'acollida' en un projecte residencial per a migrants. *Llengua, Societat i Comunicació* 8, 19–26.

Gilbert, N. (2004) *Transformation of the Welfare State: The Silent Surrender of Public Responsibility.* Oxford: Oxford University Press.

Giménez Romero, C. (2003) *¿Qué es la inmigración?* Barcelona: RBA/Integral.

Gogia, N. (2006) Unpacking corporeal mobilities: The global voyages of labour and leisure. *Environment and Planning* 38, 359–375.

Gómez Gil, C. (2005) *Las ONG en España: De la apariencia a la realidad.* Madrid: Catarata.

González Enríquez, C. (ed.) (2008) *Los sindicatos ante la inmigración.* Documentos del Observatorio Permanente de la Inmigración 18. Madrid: Ministerio de Trabajo e Inmigración.

Herranz Bascones, R. (2005) *Las organizaciones no gubernamentales: un modelo integral de gestión y control*. Madrid: Asociación Española de Contabilidad y Administración de Empresas.

Inda, J.X. (2006) *Targeting Immigrants: Government, Technology, and Ethics*. Oxford: Wiley-Blackwell.

Joseph, M. (2002) *Against the Romance of Community*. Minneapolis, MN: University of Minnesota Press.

Kostova Karaboytcheva, M. (2006) Una evaluación del último proceso de regularización de trabajadores extranjeros en España (febrero–mayo de 2005). Un año después. Documento de Trabajo (DT) 5/2006. Madrid: Real Instituto Elcano.

LIPPS Group (2000) The LIDES Coding Manual: A document for preparing and analysing language interaction data. *International Journal of Bilingualism* 4 (2), 131–271.

McIlroy, J. (2008) Ten years of New Labour: Workplace learning, social partnership and union revitalization in Britain. *British Journal of International Relations* 46 (2), 283–313.

Moyer, M. and Martín Rojo, L. (2007) Language, migration and citizenship: New challenges for the regulation of bilingualism. In M. Heller (ed.) *Bilingualism: A Social Approach* (pp. 137–160). London: Palgrave.

Parella Rubio, S. (2003) *Mujer, inmigrante y trabajadora: la triple discriminación*. Rubí (Barcelona): Anthropos.

Penninx, R. and Roosblad, J. (2000) *Trade Unions, Immigration, and Immigrants in Europe, 1960–1993: A Comparative Study of the Attitudes and Actions of Trade Unions in Seven West European Countries*. Amsterdam: Berghahn Books.

Porta Perales, M. (2009) Se busca sindicato moderno con buena presencia. *ABC*, 1 June 2009, accessed 17 October 2011. http://www.almendron.com/tribuna/25300/se-precisa-sindicato-moderno-con-buena-presencia/.

Ryfman, P. (2009) *Les ONG*. Paris: La Découverte.

Sabaté, M. (2010) Voices from a locutorio: Telecommunications and migrant networking. Unpublished PhD dissertation, Universitat Autònoma de Barcelona, Barcelona.

Solé, C. and Parella, S. (2003) The labour market and racial discrimination in Spain. *Journal of Ethnic and Migration Studies* 29 (1), 121–140.

Song, J. (2009) *South Koreans in the Debt Crisis: The Creation of a Neoliberal Welfare Society*. Durham, NC and London: Duke University Press.

Subirós, P. (ed.) (2010) *Ser immigrant a Catalunya. El testimoni de vint-i-dos protagonistes*. Barcelona: Edicions 62.

Urry, J. (2000) *Sociology Beyond Societies: Mobilities for the Twenty-First Century*. London: Routledge.

Weber, M. (1948) *Essays in Sociology*. London: Routledge & Kegan Paul.

Woolard, K. and Frekko, S. (2013) Catalan in the 21st century. Special issue of the *International Journal of Bilingual Education and Bilingualism* 16 (2), 100.

3 Skilling the Self: The Communicability of Immigrants as Flexible Labour

Kori Allan

Introduction

'English is key', Naeem 'Nick' Noorani exhorts, making it number one of his '7 Secrets of Success for Canadian Immigrants', his keynote address for the 2008 Teachers of English as a Second Language (TESL) conference in Toronto, Canada. Later, he described how 'one lady, who did not speak English' asked him if he could make his book, *Arrival Survival*, and his *Canadian Immigrant Magazine* available in other languages. 'No', he said, for the 'language of success is English ... even if you have a PhD, if you have no English, how can you demonstrate your skills?'.

Noorani's speech focused on professional immigrants, whose integration is primarily measured in terms of their success in the Canadian labour market. However, professional immigrants are overwhelmingly underemployed in Canada; that is, they are not employed in jobs commensurate with their professional training. Although immigrants are twice as likely to have a university education than Canadian-born workers, the earnings gap continues to widen between them, with the former earning significantly less.[1] Like Noorani, Citizenship and Immigration Canada (CIC) cast this 'professional immigrant underemployment problem' as, in part, a language problem, arguing that some immigrants 'do not have the language skills in either English or French to be able to use their skills optimally. Increasing the current levels of language training would help realise the human capital gained through immigration'.[2] Consequently, the federal government introduced the Enhanced Language Training Initiative (ELT) in 2003–2004, which offers advanced and sector-specific language training for professional immigrants. Although language is often cited as a key barrier to immigrants' labour market integration, or rather as the key to success, what the buzz phrase 'language barrier' constitutes is fuzzy and contested in integration circles. In the ELT classes that I observed in Toronto in 2008, teachers did not focus primarily on advanced or sector-specific technical language (as advertised), but rather on 'good' communication skills, to prepare job-seeking immigrants for interviewing, networking and meeting with recruiters. This chapter argues that ELT problematically individualised the 'professional immigrant under-employment problem'; that is, it addressed individual skills deficits rather than the systemic and structural conditions that contribute to professional immigrants' 'de-skilling'. I demonstrate how this is accomplished in two ways. First, I show how language training, which primarily consisted of prescribing communicative norms, was a governmental 'technology of citizenship' (Cruikshank, 1999), or rather, a means through which ELT instructors attempted to produce 'good' future-citizen-workers, capable of self-governance and deemed appropriate for Canada's knowledge-based economy. These technologies individualised the 'professional immigrant underemployment problem' by encouraging newcomers to view the self as a project of improvement and to entrepreneurially sell themselves while accepting responsibility for their own un- and underemployment. Secondly, the focus on 'language as a barrier to labour market integration' is often a way of ascribing attitudinal deficiencies; that is, in practice, lack of language skills gets conflated with lack of appropriate cultural and behavioural attributes. Rather than challenging systemic and hegemonic workplace norms, language and communication skills training focused on changing individual immigrants' behaviour. Finally, I argue that by focusing on re-training the individual rather than on addressing structural barriers to employment, such as credential recognition problems and the nature of the labour market, ELT contributed to the (re)production and regulation of flexible labour. Before outlining the above arguments, I will discuss, in more detail, how 'the professional immigrant underemployment problem' arose in Canada as well as describe my theoretical framework and methodology.

Canada's 'Professional Immigrant Underemployment Problem'

In the 1990s the Government of Canada reconfigured its labour and immigration policies to address a perceived 'skills dilemma': Canada needed more highly skilled workers to develop innovative industries in the increasingly competitive 'new global economy'.[3] The government's perception of a skilled labour shortage continues, due to Canada's aging workforce and negative population growth. CIC thus admits immigrants who possess the skills deemed valuable in Canada's knowledge-based economy through the skilled worker class. Potential skilled immigrants are assessed by a points system that measures their value in terms of human capital theory, in which people's knowledge and skills – acquired through investments in education, training and work experience – are a factor in production (Abu-Laban & Gabriel, 2002: 65). These selection criteria award the most points for one's education and knowledge of Canada's official languages, privileging those with post-secondary education.[4] However, despite the tendency of policy documents to valorise their international capital in the global economy,[5] professional immigrants are subject to 'de-skilling' in Canada, as employers are reluctant to hire professionals without Canadian credentials or work experience. While in the 1980s immigrants earned $19,130.30 less on average than their Canadian-born counterparts, recent immigrants with university degrees who came to Canada between 2001 and 2006 earn $41,760.70 less than Canadian-born workers with the same education (Preston et al., 2010: 8). There is thus a disjuncture between the evaluation of professional immigrants' human capital at the border and its devaluation in Canadian labour markets. In the 2000s, the underemployment of professional immigrants was problematised and was seen as requiring governmental intervention.

ELT was introduced as part of the Internationally Trained Workers (ITW) Initiative,[6] which arose out of the concern that immigrants' skills were not being efficiently utilised, thereby costing Canada potential profit as well as posing 'risk', or rather 'social unrest', producible by frustrated underemployed immigrants. ELT, in particular, aimed to address a perceived gap in language services, which previously focused on basic language training. Existing language services, primarily Language Instruction for Newcomers to Canada (LINC), were problematised as focusing on 'survival English', which is too rudimentary for professional work and for immigrants who were largely admitted with (at least) basic language skills. ELT, in contrast, allocates funding for projects that deliver sector-specific and higher levels of language training, coupled with education on Canadian workplace culture. Although the programme is primarily concerned with language training, it also offers employment support. It provides employment counsellors whose mandate is to help clients obtain jobs, mentorships or volunteer placements once the language training has been completed. ELT is thus conceptualised as a bridging programme and was designed to solve the 'underemployment problem' by enabling professional immigrants to obtain jobs commensurate with their skills and qualifications, so that they could be 'productive and valued asset(s) in the Canadian workforce'.[7] However, in practice, I found that ELT largely failed to ameliorate the underemployment of their clients. It did, however, facilitate the (re)production of the active un(der)employed who aimed to increase their employability (i.e. human capital) through language training.

Language and Communication in the New Economy

Many scholars have examined the privileging of language and communication skills in the 'new economy' – 'when the exchange of information becomes a primary form of production' (Budach et al., 2003; see also Cameron, 2000; Duchêne, 2009; Gee et al., 1996; Heller, 2003; Urciuoli, 2008). When language and communication are conceptualised as a set of measurable skills (Budach et al., 2003: 606–607; Heller, 2003: 474), it 'becomes legitimate to regulate and assess the way employees talk' (Cameron, 2000: 18). The accompanying institutionalisation of 'some people's preferred practices as norms … define large numbers of other people as inadequate or "substandard communicators"' (Cameron, 2002: 80). Control over what constitutes legitimate linguistic and communicative practice thus 'regulate(s) access to other resources', such as jobs and economic capital (Heller & Martin-Jones, 2001: 2). ELT teachers thus attempted to teach such preferred norms to their students. The prescription of such norms, however, simultaneously involved the prescription of particular values and attributes (Cameron, 1996). Briggs (2005) and Inoue (2006) usefully combine studies of Foucauldian productive power with studies of language ideologies to demonstrate how the forms of communicative events or texts produce particular kinds of (neoliberal) subjectivities. Ideologies assign language value through processes in which different referents become associated with languages or styles of speaking (Briggs, 1998; Gal, 1998; Woolard, 1998). Drawing on these insights, I loosely adopt Briggs' (2005) term *communicability* to examine how ideologies of language and communication in ELT classrooms produce particular citizen-worker subjectivities.

By simultaneously prescribing particular subjectivities and values, language and communication skills training became a governmental[8] 'technology of citizenship' (Cruikshank, 1999; see also Ong, 2003). According to Cruikshank, 'individual subjects are transformed into citizens by … technologies of citizenship: discourses, programmes, and other tactics aimed at making individuals … capable of self-government' (Cruikshank, 1999: 1), by conducting people to conduct themselves (Dean, 1999; Foucault, 1991).[9] Although the prescription of communicative norms may be well intentioned, for mastering certain kinds of personhood is essential for obtaining professional employment (see Roberts, this volume), such practices are nevertheless simultaneous attempts to 'constitut[e] and regulat[e] citizens: that is, strategies for governing the very subjects whose problems they seek to redress' (Cruikshank, 1999: 2). However, such technologies do not necessarily produce docile subjects, for ELT students often challenged, even as they may have simultaneously reproduced, hegemonic norms and values. Nevertheless, these language training programmes were a means of regulating labour and of (re)producing citizen-workers (Bjornson, 2007), who manage their own employment risks.

Methodology

This chapter is part of a larger project that examines how governmental programmes construct the 'professional immigrant underemployment problem' as well as how they develop solutions and techniques to address it. Taking my cue from scholars of government (Dean, 1999; Rose, 1999), I am not concerned with assessing whether or not these programmes are 'right' or successful according to their own criteria. Rather, I examine what their actual effects are, that is, how 'the institutionalised production of certain kinds of ideas' results in 'the production of certain sorts of structural change' (Ferguson, 1994: xv). To do so, I rely on the tools of discourse analysis from linguistic anthropology and sociolinguistics, examining the ways in which discourses of integration are reproduced or contested through practice (Heller, 2001). Specifically, I conducted 16 months of ethnographic fieldwork in immigrant service agencies (ISAs) and in the immigrant settlement and integration sector more broadly in Toronto, Canada. Toronto is a key site for studying integration, as its immigrant population is larger than that of any other Canadian city. According to Statistics Canada (2001 Census), 43.7% of Toronto's population is foreign born (Stasiulis et al., 2011: 91). Since cities are neither bounded nor isolated, I consider how national policy impacts Toronto and how 'Canadian culture' is constructed from this particular locale. However, my data cannot be generalised to represent Canada, since Toronto has a unique history of immigration as well as context-specific political and economic conditions.

This fieldwork, which spanned from November 2007 to March 2009, consisted of participant-observation, document analysis and interviews. The primary methodology was participant-observation, which requires one to learn the tacit knowledge reproduced in everyday practice and which shows 'the production and reproduction of social forms is a result of what people do' rather than what they intend (Simon & Dippo, 1986: 157–158). I also conducted 43 interviews, 27 of which were in depth (recorded, often over multiple sessions) with settlement workers, policy makers and new immigrants. This research also included analysis of 10 individual immigrant employment trajectories over the span of at least a year following the fieldwork period (several are over the course of three years) as well as follow-up research and interviews from March 2009 to the present.

I conducted daily participant-observation at two different ISAs in 2008, focusing on ELT since it was the primary programme offered to professional immigrants seeking employment. I examined a total of five ELT programmes in detail, observing and participating in three programmes from start to finish. These classes offered training for people in the engineering, health, financial, information technology and customer service sectors. I chose to examine these programmes at two organisations for comparative purposes, to ensure that the patterns I observed were indicative of the immigrant settlement sector, rather than particular to specific agencies. My data from this participant-observation are comprised of conversations with staff and clients and observations of staff–client interactions, as well as participation in informal lunch and coffee breaks. At both organisations the clients accessing the services were from a variety of countries, including the Ukraine, China, Pakistan, Syria and Brazil, to mention a select few. The majority of my informants had come through the skilled worker immigration stream, which privileged professional immigrants, even though permanent residents from other immigration classes were eligible for these programmes (if they had been in Canada for less than three years). In addition to capturing the nature of interactions in these agencies, I immersed myself in the life of my informants as much as possible, participating in various kinds of social events beyond the agencies. I also attended job fairs and recruiting sessions recommended to skilled immigrants by ISAs. Additionally, I participated in a variety of events in the immigrant integration sector which enabled me to determine what data from my two key field sites were indicative of the sector as a whole. I also conducted analysis of policy documents (from all levels of government), programme evaluation contracts, guidelines, advertisements, curriculum, etc. The examples examined in this chapter are indicative of social processes prevalent in this larger corpus of data.

Prescribing and Selling the Ideal Worker-citizen

Before being placed in ELT, newcomers' language proficiency is assessed by the Canadian Language Benchmarks (CLB), which is a national framework for regulating government-funded ESL training in Canada. Established by

CIC in 1998, this framework does not measure '"absolute" language ability,' but rather it measures communicative proficiency, defined as 'the ability to use the English language to accomplish communication tasks' (Pawlikowska-Smith, 2002: 6). Learning communicative competence requires background knowledge about communicative appropriateness, which 'depends on a range of previous experiences, including cultural and educational experiences, and not necessarily on the learner's formal knowledge of the language' (Pawlikowska-Smith, 2002: 23). CLB therefore recommends that background knowledge be addressed in ESL training in 'a systematic manner' in order to help learners achieve Benchmark competencies (Pawlikowska-Smith, 2002: 23). CLB's evaluative system has 12 Benchmarks or reference points that 'describe a clear hierarchy, or a progressive continuum of knowledge and skills that underlie language proficiency' (Pawlikowska-Smith, 2000: viii). Competencies are tested according to 'performance outcomes' of language use in 'increasingly demanding communicative contexts' (Pawlikowska-Smith, 2002: 25–26). ELT offers training in Benchmarks (B) 7–10, which span from the intermediate to the advanced ranges.[10]

Drawing on the CLB model, ELT curriculum identifies communicative tasks needed in particular professional fields, such as customer service interactions, writing memos, telephone conversations, etc. However, this sector-specific curriculum was rarely followed in the ELT classrooms I observed. Rather, employment counsellors and ELT teachers drew on widely available human resource materials to promote standardised ways of communicating through frequent lessons and workshops that taught job search skills, or rather how to 'sell yourself' within a vague and monolithic 'Canadian workplace culture'. Role-playing activities, presentations, self-promotional infomercials and mock interviews were evaluated by the teachers based on how speakers presented their arguments, used body language and conveyed appropriate attitudes. To help ELT students answer interview questions, instructors tried to make explicit the implicit cultural background knowledge they needed to know in order to answer appropriately, for they recognised that language practice is cultural. For example, Sophia,[11] a workshop facilitator, handed out an 'interview practice worksheet' that listed questions that were accompanied by explanations of the intent behind each question. She further explained the philosophy underlying such 'behavioural based interviews': 'your resume is a marketing tool, but nowadays there are behavioural questions, which are based on the assumption that how you acted in the past predicts your future behaviour'. Sophia explained that 'employers want examples in your near past, this is why it is crucial to think about the skills you have, the average person has 500 skills by the way'. Sophia, like other instructors, encouraged individuals to reflect upon their talents and work-related competences, including communicative competence, by conceptualising them as skills, which workers can acquire to increase their value or human capital (Heller, 2003). One settlement worker noted that new immigrants were not seen as needing skills upgrading in the 'old sense' (as a specific manual or technical operation), because they were professionals. Rather, skill 'now denotes any practice, form or knowledge, or way of being constituting productive labor' (Urciuoli, 2008: 212), making it possible for one to have 500 skills! In a network society the operationalisation of persons' abilities and characters as 'skills' attribute persons with economic value or at least signal a conception of the self in terms of productivity (Boltanski & Chiapello, 2005; Urciuoli, 2008).

To help ELT students answer behavioural-based interview questions and to present one's skills effectively, Sophia explained that 'you're being asked to talk about a specific example from your professional history' and emphasised that 'it is vital you give them an organized, articulate story'. Sophia recommended giving short, sweet and to the point examples using the STAR technique, which entails stating a situation, a task, an action and a result.[12] She illustrated the STAR technique by drawing on her experience as a salsa teacher: 'I am a salsa teacher. This is the *situation*: I have a difficult client who has two left feet. My *task* is to deal with the client. My *action* is: I approached the client and said don't worry it is normal at the beginning, how about you stand in front of the mirror and practice this basic step. The *result* is the client is not intimidated.' Sophia demonstrates that useful examples draw on personal experience to highlight one's skills and to demonstrate in a linear manner that the speaker could self-reflexively evaluate past actions.

Students were further asked to reflexively think of themselves as projects of self-improvement and to identify with work, as part of a construction of personal growth and self-worth. For example, an ELT teacher, Miro, asked a student the following mock interview question: 'What is your philosophy towards work?' Lily, a chemical engineer from China, succinctly replied: 'I work, I get the money.' Miro responded: 'we wouldn't talk about money, you work for more than money. How do you like work to be done?' After further explanation, Lily answered the question again: 'If I work I create more value, then contribution for company, I increase my knowledge and experience, I feel I'm a useful person.' Like Lily, many quickly learned that selling yourself requires constructing a 'therapeutic [notion] of the self as a reflexive project requiring work to perfect' (Cameron, 2002: 76). Indeed, another workshop facilitator claimed that: 'in

Canada no one is perfect: recognize your problem and say I can fix it'. One ELT teacher, Carl, tells his students: 'They [interviewers] will ask: "Tell me about your strengths", "Tell me about your weaknesses". In advance of the interview choose your weakness. Use the word BUT' [he writes 'but' on the chalkboard]. He recommended that newcomers say their weakness is English, 'BUT you are taking courses and you believe in lifelong learning. Turn a negative into a positive with the use of but. We are doing things to improve the weaknesses. Choose a weakness that you can change'. The STAR technique and the use of the conjunction BUT to modify one's weaknesses constructed narratives around the reflexive recognition of a 'problem' or task, and then one's capacity and willingness to fix or address it.

These communicative techniques thus encouraged ELT students to adopt a reflexive notion of the self as well as to embody the ideal worker-citizen subjectivity that is dedicated to lifelong learning. The ideology of lifelong learning constitutes workers as infinitely knowledgeable subjects (Olssen, 2008: 39) who should continually acquire new (commodifiable) skills to improve themselves. The *communicability* (cf. Briggs, 2005) of immigrants' experience or knowledge in recruitment processes, then, depended upon whether or not it was framed by a capitalisation of knowledge and of the self or rather the *ability* to communicate an appropriate relation to the self. The experiential narrative is an authoritative communicative genre within the immigrant service sector and in behavioural-based interviews precisely because of its self-reflective function, for it encourages workers to accept responsibility for their personal and professional development. ELT instructors made these implicit values of self-discipline and of self-improvement explicit when students criticised the government. For example, ELT students often complained that while the points system admitted them based on their hard skills, ELT gave the impression that soft skills, such as communication skills, were the key to getting a job. One student wryly suggested that the government should admit them based on their soft skills, since their hard skills seemed to be irrelevant. When students complained about such contradictions, counsellors encouraged them to reform themselves, rather than focus on what they could not change. For instance, Sophia explained that 'this society welcomes you but because it is individualistic you need to create a change for yourself'. ELT counsellors thereby attempted to govern the very subjects whose problems they sought to redress (Cruikshank, 1999), by persuading them to accept responsibility for their underemployment, rather than locate responsibility in the state, the market or in other systemic barriers, such as professional accreditation bodies.[13]

Personality Profiling: Conflating Language, Communication and Attitude

While emulating appropriately logical and effective styles of communicating to sell themselves, students were paradoxically asked to present an authentic self who had to nevertheless be relatable according to norms often glossed as Canadian. The focus on Canadian soft skills, such as being a team player, etc., increases the potential for discrimination, as 'fit' with a company's values is a legitimate basis for evaluating potential employees and by extension ELT students in the knowledge-based economy. I refer to this process as attitudinal or *personality profiling*. ELT counsellors consequently tried to foster the right attitudes in their clients, as is evident in the following example. After each student presented using the STAR technique, Sophia gave 'constructive feedback'. In addition to urging them to provide specific examples of how they wanted to advance their careers and to improve and enhance their skills, she told them that: 'no one maintained eye contact, it is important in Canadian workplace culture. Also you made everything about you. Check in with the person who is asking the question, touch base. We also didn't see your character, you were all serious.' Here she urges ELT students to conform to Canadian workplace norms, while also showing one's character. At another point, Sophia also told the class that there are 'cultural differences that you need to know'. For example, she tells one student that 'maybe you are perceived as aggressive in this culture ... soften up'. Yet ultimately she insists that 'the bottom line is to be yourself, be aware of your skills, you need to remember you have skills otherwise your self-esteem will go down and you lose confidence'. There are thus tensions between standardisation and individualisation that underlie job-searching processes: candidates must show they are uniquely valuable and relatable as well as 'be themselves' (that is, authentic), but within a narrow set of culturally acceptable norms and fairly standardised communicative genres. The preoccupation with authenticity threatens to unmask newcomers' entrepreneurial performances of the self, as the following example illustrates.

A recruiter for a mining company, who visited an engineering ELT class, started his presentation by espousing the value of diversity and the value of international workers' foreign language skills. After his opening speech, everyone in the room introduced themselves, according to the scripts they had learned in class, straightforwardly stating their name and professional background. After a few exchanges, the recruiter made it clear that he was disappointed with their level of language proficiency, commenting: *'language is a barrier,* you need to be able to read and write or you are off the job because if there is a sign and they say read it and you can't you are off the job because of safety. It is not like in the old days.' This response is perplexing for several reasons. First, we had assumed that he was hiring engineers, but he seemed to downgrade the types of work ELT students could be hired for after he heard them introduce themselves. Also, foreign language skills were clearly only valuable once one had mastery of English. Finally, it seemed evident that his phrase 'language as a barrier' referred to more than just English competency, but rather an ability to communicate an appropriate self. After talking with the students, he seemed to feel that he had not connected with them, stating:

> You know I would like a 1/2 paragraph on who they are ... Just so I get to see them as a person. ... If I have a stack of resumes up to here (he places his hand above his head), and I get a resume with a name I can't pronounce, you know ... I would like to know about your character, social clubs etc. People from the Philippines often have a picture attached; its personalized. I think this person looks nice, or maybe they look like Jack the Ripper, but usually they don't. And you need to talk about continuous education. You have to be a good employee, a good Canadian. What church work do you do, scouts, I want to see your hobbies. If I have two people with equal skills, both top of their class ... I'll look at their sports, hobbies, if one plays tennis and the other football and hockey I'll choose the one who plays team sports because I know he can be a team player. Well I wish you well. You need to change your resume, spiff it up a bit or get Asma [employment counsellor] to spiff it up. You need to sell a product, smile, win them over with a smile.

Here, he highlights the applicants' foreignness as a barrier, for he implies that he does not know what to do with a resume with a name he cannot pronounce. He needs to see if such foreigners are okay and not like 'Jack the Ripper'. He thus demonstrates that it is particularly important for new immigrants to communicate a relatable and acceptable self. The recruiter requests entrepreneurial values such as selling a product and 'good' Canadian characteristics, like volunteerism and being a team player. Here Canadian and workplace values are conflated. While the recruiter may be seen as uncharacteristically unprofessional, as the employment counsellors viewed him, he made explicit what behavioural-based interviews are premised upon. It was clear that he wanted to understand people readily and to be able to get a sense of their 'authentic' personality and the kinds of workers they would be through their introductions. There is thus a contradictory relationship between language and identity in professional interviews. On the one hand, language is a skill that can be evaluated independent of the speaker and their identity. Yet talk is also evaluated in job interviews as inseparable from the candidate's personality and fit with corporate values. As Boltanski and Chiapello (2005) have outlined, the *ability to relate* and *a capacity to communicate* have played a role in job selection, for in a 'network society':

> transverse modes of co-ordination (teams, projects, etc.) place greater weight not only on specifically linguistic mastery, but also on qualities that might be called more 'personal', more clearly bound up with the 'character' of the person – for example, openness, self-control, availability, good humour, composure – which were by no means so highly prized in the old work culture. The techniques of enterprise psychology (interviews, graphology, etc.) are used to pinpoint these propensities in candidates for a job. (Boltanski & Chiapello, 2005: 241)

The desire to trust and relate to the candidate authentically, through common-sense cultural modes of relate-ability, reveals anxiety about the commodification of authenticity.[14] Here communication skills are meant to demonstrate that one genuinely has the right attitude and values needed (i.e. for teamwork). 'Being yourself', then, is a self-effacing discourse that encourages one to accept a conception of the self as both entrepreneurial and cooperative. Such 'fit' candidates are valued because they can monitor themselves in line with the organisation's interests and thus decrease training and management costs (Urciuoli, 2008).

The inability to convey the right personality to interviewers can therefore restrict one's access to employment. However, as I have shown, authenticity must be recognisable and communicable through standardised narrative forms. Campbell and Roberts (2007) have similarly demonstrated that interviews require interviewees to synthesise work and personal identities and 'resolve in their interview performance the unstated internal contradictions of a new work order that simultaneously calls up discourses of individual empowerment while circumscribing and standardising the attitudes and competences which (potential) employees should have' (Campbell & Roberts, 2007: 244). Such interview techniques that attempt to test personal capacities may marginalise technical skills and privilege soft skills (Grugulis & Vincent, 2009: 597). Whether or not soft skills are evaluated above technical skills, they nevertheless naturalise the commodification of one's self as well as 'structure the conditions under which workers are recruited into the labor market' (Urciuoli, 2008: 224), and can act as gatekeeping devices. This is particularly difficult for immigrant job-seekers, as Campbell and Roberts (2007) show. I would add that such post-Fordist modes of 'selection' open up a space for covert discrimination as, 'Personal attributes, attitudes to work and individual qualities are extremely difficult to evaluate and, in practice, proxies are used' (Grugulis & Vincent, 2009: 599), such as evaluations based on gender and race, even though such grounds for discrimination are illegal. The treating of personal attributes as skills that can be accumulated in the individual also downplays their reciprocal and relational elements (Grugulis & Vincent, 2009: 599), such as how one is perceived by an interviewer. For example, the recruiter in the above example wanted to gauge (from interviews and resumes) whether people looked like 'Jack the Ripper' and what kind of personal characteristics and attitudes they had, more than what their technical skills were. Within the regime of immigrant integration such personality profiling, which can amount to cultural-cum-racial profiling, largely gets sanitised by the discourse of communication and soft skills. When language is cited as a barrier to integration, as it was by the recruiter, it is often a gloss for many other things, as language, communication, culture and identity are conflated. One ELT language assessor notes that: 'when language as a barrier quote unquote is used I think it actually means a lot and sometimes people also lack the proper terminology to say I don't get that person and that person doesn't get me and by that we don't mean the words'.

Integration policy and well-meaning ELT instructors try to make the unknown expectations of job interviews known to newcomers. They attempt to codify immigrants' value into seemingly universal skills that merely need to be translated through a strong grasp of a national language, effective communicative genres, and the background knowledge needed to successfully deploy them. However, such language training and the 'language as a barrier to integration' discourse not only glossed over complex processes of personality profiling, but also a set of discriminatory systemic and structural constraints that new immigrants face, which I will outline in the following section.

The Lack of Canadian (Work) Experience

It has become a cliché in the regime of immigrant integration that employers are preoccupied with 'Canadian experience'. However, it is not an unfounded cliché, for many of my informants reported that employers explicitly asked them whether or not they had 'Canadian experience'. Risk-adverse employers frequently used 'lack of Canadian experience' as a reason for not hiring newcomers. This phrase could be a gloss for discriminatory evaluations, but also for systemic issues like lack of local industry knowledge or Canadian credentials. ELT teachers tried to teach their clients how to portray their value and knowledge of Canadian workplace culture through communicative practice and particular genres such as the STAR technique. As I have shown, it is imperative to demonstrate one's skills through narratives of personal experience that demonstrate self-reflexivity. However, newcomers' experience from 'Other' contexts was often a priori devalued, for their skills and use-value could not be readily assessed (i.e. university and company reputations). ELT students recognised that their interlocutors evaluated them based on 'Other' indexes, such as their perceived foreignness (as the recruiter did).[15] In doing so, they simultaneously questioned the ideology of communication and soft skills as the keys to integration and even that by having the right attitude and communication skills one is guaranteed to get a job. Indeed, students largely did not focus on language as their greatest barrier to integration, but rather on their lack of what employers called 'Canadian experience' and which they understood to mean working or earning a degree in Canada, as we can see in the following example.

In one ELT class, the teacher, Carl, continually told the students that they needed to work on their soft skills in order to get a job. In one lesson, he asked: 'if you don't have a certificate on your resume that they are looking for how can you explain that in an interview?'. Vik, a nuclear engineer who emigrated from the Ukraine, replied: 'if you don't have the certificate you won't get an interview.' Vik questioned the assumption that he would even get an opportunity to explain himself if he did not have Canadian certificates. In another class, a guest speaker asserted that 'it's easy to get a job in Canada. All you have to do is write a resume and they will believe you. You can say you worked on the moon and they will believe you.' The students responded as follows:

Vik:	but what if they ask for a reference from the moon?
Mikhail:	Canadian experience?
Guest Speaker:	how do you answer that question?
Besnik:	a lot
Guest Speaker:	I hate that question, true I don't have Canadian experience but I have international experience ... make it a positive thing never a negative.

In this response the students cleverly point out that the 'foreignness' of their references often hinders immigrant job applicants, as does their lack of Canadian work experience. Newcomers recognised that, regardless of how they sell themselves, their personal experience is fraught with problems in local labour markets that value 'Canadian experience' over 'international' or foreign experience, despite the valuing of the latter in policy and business rhetoric. Indeed, many scholars have shown that the lack of recognition of professional immigrants' credentials and foreign work experience are the main contributing factors to their downward mobility (Guo, 2007; Kustec *et al.*, 2007), which is particularly problematic given that the points system admits immigrants based on their education and work experience.

The ELT programmes I observed focused almost entirely on soft skills and were largely unsuccessful at helping ELT students obtain work placements or internships that students found valuable. Students thus often expressed their frustration after hearing the same tired advice on soft skills and improving the self, rather than receiving concrete employer connections through ELT. It was not that they felt learning language and communication skills was completely irrelevant, but that their importance was inflated at the expense of concrete employment support. Furthermore, several ELT students told me that they understood they had to sell themselves from the first lesson, but changing their behaviour or 'soft skills' through short-term prescriptive 'language training' seemed unachievable. One student told me, 'this is not something you can learn in a workshop'. However, counsellors evaluated criticisms of ELT not as indicative of the quality of their services or as an opportunity to challenge governmental policy or to practice more critical pedagogy, but rather as characteristic of attitudes in need of adjustment, and the line between skills training and attitude adjustment became blurred (Dunk, 1996).

Carl and Vik, for instance, frequently disagreed over the value of soft skills. Carl told Vik, who was from the Ukraine, that he would fail if he applied his 'European thinking' that 'focuses on hard skills' in Canada: 'I will be blunt if you are an asshole and inflexible and don't have soft skills you will not get a job'. What led up to this comment was a disagreement between Vik, Besnik and Carl over how long it takes to train new workers. Someone in class asked what 'phase out retirement' meant, which was referenced in an article the class was reading. Carl described phase out retirement by drawing diagrams on the chalkboard. He explained that someone gradually works less, while passing on their experience and knowledge to other employees. A student from Albania, Besnik, questioned Carl's assertion that it takes a long time for their experience to be passed on to other employees. He noted: 'I worked at an organization of 350 employees, the government. After about 5 years I could replace anyone there, not a big difference with technology and so on, these days.' While Carl disagreed, Vik supported Besnik, noting that Carl's model was flawed for an 'entry level person would not be taking over the retirees job'. He went up to the front of the room and started to change Carl's model on the chalkboard, outlining the chain of managers that people worked their way up through, explaining 'so you would not need so much transition time'. Although Vik and Besnik presented relevant and logical arguments, Carl reiterated that he was talking about highly complex, specialised jobs and that by following the simple model ('it doesn't work like that in Canada'), Vik had 'flawed thinking'. Carl then continued to discuss how Vik's inflexibility makes him unemployable.

Carl marked Vik as an outsider, who lacked knowledge of Canadian norms, while suggesting that without the right attitude – a compliant one – he would not have the soft skills to get a job. Instructors often asserted their legitimacy to prescribe particular norms by claiming superior knowledge of 'Canadian (workplace) culture', a claim that several students, like Vik and Besnik often refuted. Indeed, it is not obvious that Vik or Besnik's professional opinions do not apply to the Canadian context. This was not an isolated incident. In another class, when Vik disagreed with Carl, the latter noted that ' if Vik is an *evil* engineer he won't get a job, he will end up working at [a corner store]'. Carl also made a joke about employers wanting to make sure you're not a 'terrorist' through behavioural-based interview questions. Such comments play on culturalising and racialising stereotypes of the 'Other'. These stereotypes are also implicit in advice given to ELT students on Canadian workplace culture. For example, a pamphlet I received at a conference for 'internationally educated professionals' lists a series of tips on how to adapt to Canadian workplace culture, including the following: 'In Canada a person's authority is related to their position and responsibility. Women hold the same kinds of positions as men and have the same level of authority.' Here, the stereotypical and culturalised subject of the patriarchal male immigrant is reproduced. In these examples communication skills training becomes a way of addressing perceived cultural deficiencies and of prescribing certain kinds of 'good' Canadian workplace values while attempting to adjust the attitudes of new immigrants. The above example illustrates that, at times, teaching the sociocultural knowledge needed to understand hegemonic communicative practice can become a 'technology of citizenship' or rather a means of managing ELT students. I refer to this process of turning the 'professional immigrant underemployment problem' into a 'lack of soft and communication skills' problem as *skill-washing*. This phrase plays on the term white-washing in order to highlight how counsellors glossed over systemic discrimination in the classroom and instead encouraged professional immigrants to become more 'flexible'.

'De-skilling' Flexible Labour

Frustrated that ELT was not helping him get a job or improve his English, Vik astutely noted one day, 'I realized why they have all these (un) employment agencies, to create jobs'. Indeed, there is a large market that sells flexibility: recruiters and agencies make a living off the flexible labour that emerges in the regime of flexible accumulation. ELT clients' choices are often limited to accepting precarious work, or to continually upgrade themselves as flexible 'knowledge' workers, to fill a gap in the labour market by, for example, obtaining a Canadian post-secondary degree. Through processes of de-skilling and retraining, immigrants 'are coming to be used increasingly as a part of a "flexible" and disposable labour force suited to the demands of the globalized just-in-time economy' (Shields, 2003: 2). Overall, new immigrants are faring less well than earlier waves of immigrants because of the rise of the tertiary service sector, that includes not only high-paying jobs, but the 'proliferation of contingent forms of employment' (Shields, 2003: 1). Currently, although the immigration points system and skilled worker category favours professional immigrants, a third of all immigrant workers are absorbed in the sales and services occupations, which are 'characterized by both high turnover rates and low wages' (Shields, 2003: 29).

Although the ELT programmes I examined were largely unsuccessful in helping their clients find professional work at their desired skill level, they were successful in helping students who sought employment in social work, since the settlement sector could offer them Canadian job experience. Maria, who had a degree in economics and who had worked in the social welfare field in Albania, obtained employment as a refugee counsellor in Toronto. She got this placement only after volunteering in the settlement sector as a translator for free, and because she spoke Albanian (which many of her clients spoke). Here her multilingualism was 'added value'. Another ELT student, Anna, who was originally from Belarus, had obtained a PhD in education from a university in New York before immigrating to Canada. She received a receptionist position at an ISA because she spoke Russian and English, but only after working at a retail store for a year, and only after volunteering in the sector for several months. Both of these jobs, earned after months of free labour, were contract positions, typical in the precarious settlement sector. As of the summer of 2011, Maria was no longer working as a refugee counsellor, since her original contract was a temporary one, covering a worker's maternity leave. While she still volunteers with seniors twice a week, she has recently received a real estate license with hopes for yet another career. Anna, who has recently completed a college degree in HR, is currently establishing herself as a self-employed recruiter. She wonders whether she made the right educational investment.

Common in integration documents is the diversity discourse in which immigrants' ethnic backgrounds and multilingualism are converted into commodifiable knowledge and skills that can help Canada gain access to 'other' markets in the competitive global economy. Referring to the ITW Initiative, a government document claims: 'The strategy will also help ensure that we have a diverse work force of people who understand the language, culture and marketplace of the world's nations, giving Canada a distinct competitive advantage globally.'[16] This discourse of diversity, which was espoused by the recruiter above, characterises diversity as enriching.[17] However, my research shows that ELT often does not guarantee the valuing of one's multilingualism in high-paying professional work, but rather it is 'de-skilled' in low-paying, precarious settlement work. Duchêne's (2011) work at a Swiss international airport has similarly shown how, despite a discourse that values multilingualism, low-paying workers such as baggage carriers are not remunerated for their multilingual work. The governmental concern that the underutilisation of immigrants' skills costs the Canadian government millions of dollars in profit potential does not take into account the loss of the countries and immigrants who made the initial investment, nor does it recognise that labour markets profit in other ways, such as the settlement sectors' profiting from new immigrants' multilingualism.

Conclusions

Well-meaning ELT instructors understood the politics of indexicality, that linguistic forms signal particular attributes, but their attempts to fill in immigrants' cultural/experiential deficits by prescribing appropriate skills problematically assumed that individuals can own and 'accumulate forms of capital' (Adkins, 2005: 112) independent of how they are evaluated and by whom. The important recognition that language is cultural, here becomes a dangerous terrain of governmental intervention and of behavioural adjustment. By construing the 'underemployment problem' as 'a skills deficit problem', communication skills training became, in part, a technique of neoliberal governance (Inoue, 2006). Such governance encouraged future citizens to continuously increase their own human capital, accepting responsibility for their employability in discriminatory and insecure labour markets. By not adequately addressing the political and economic conditions of un(der)employment, ELT also contributed to the reproduction of flexible labour forces that shuffle through contingent employment in the 'just-in-time' economy.

Neoliberal government however, is a contested process and ELT programmes and government policy produce entrepreneurial worker-citizens and flexible labour with varying success. Furthermore, some policy makers and immigrant service sector workers have questioned the policy focus on language. For instance, one settlement worker noted that there was a 'language overload in Toronto' and that she wanted more funding for skills training. Policy discussions with CIC in 2010 considered developing policy that 'goes beyond official language ability' to focus on soft skills, which addresses the conflation of soft and communication skills I discuss in this chapter. However, the importance of one's language competency continues to be emphasised, as the government has introduced changes to the points system that make official language ability the most important selection factor. In both instances, the policy makers continue to skill-ify behavioural attributes and language in an attempt to universalise and standardise employability. However, such skill-washing is far from neutral; rather, it continues to problematically download the risks and costs of integration onto individual immigrants.

Acknowledgments

The author would like to thank Bonnie McElhinny, Monica Heller, the Dissertation Writing Workshop participants (Anthropology, University of Toronto) and the Linguistic Prescriptivism and Patriotism Working Group (especially Lyda Fens) for their comments on earlier drafts of this chapter. She would also like to thank her fellow panellists at the 2011 American Anthropological Association session *Language-ing Labour* (particularly Lindsay Bell and Alexandre Duchêne), and colleagues at the AILA 2010 Seminar, *Language, Migration and Labour*, where she presented shorter versions of this chapter. She also wants to thank the editors, Celia Roberts and Melissa Moyer, for their detailed feedback. Finally, the author is grateful to the Social Sciences and Humanities Research Council for funding this research. Any shortcomings are, of course, the author's own.

Notes

(1) See Statistics Canada (http://www.statcan.gc.ca/pub/75-001-x/2008112/article/10766-eng.htm).
(2) 'ELT communiqué', Citizenship and Immigration Canada, December 2003. This chapter focuses on English, although these programmes are also offered in French. For information on the commodification of French in Canada, see da Silva *et al.* (2007).
(3) See, for example, the government report, *People and Skills in the New Global Economy* (1990). This report signals a shift from a Keynesian rationality of government – where the state could intervene in economic processes to decrease social risk – to a

neoliberal rationality in which the autonomy of the free market is privileged. To address the perceived 'skills dilemma' and in line with a neoliberal view of the economy, the social role of government in the 1990s was reconceptualised as needing to provide adequate training to help citizens cope with the inevitable market changes. Rather than ensure social equity, the social role of governance was seen as needing to create equal opportunity by providing access to skills retraining in flexible, transferable skills (Dunk, 1996). In this neoliberal rationality, which informs ELT, freedom 'is redefined: it is no longer freedom from want, which might be provided by a cosseted life on benefits: it is the capacity for self-realization' (Rose, 1999: 145).

(4) The point system (in 2002) consisted of the following six selection criteria, followed by the maximum points awarded for each criterion: education (25); ability in English and/or French (24); experience (21); age (10); arranged employment in Canada (10); and adaptability (10). Maximum points for education were awarded for a Masters or PhD.

(5) See, for example, CIC (1997) *Not Just Numbers: A Canadian Framework for Future Immigration*, and CIC (1998) *Building on a Strong Foundation for the 21st Century: New Directions for Immigration and Refugee Policy and Legislation*.

(6) The ITW Initiative recognised that lack of language skills was not the sole reason for underemployment. For instance, it also provided funding to develop better foreign credential recognition procedures. However, such developments have been inadequate and they focus on making procedures transparent rather than on systemic change.

(7) Niagara College Canada advertisement for ELT (2006) 'Enhanced language training for employment'.

(8) I mean government in the broadest sense as per the governmentality approach that confounds binary oppositions between the state and civil society. In the governmentality frame the state 'is but one node (although at times a 'coordinating' node) in a horizontal network of institutions and individuals through which power is exercised' (Sharma & Gupta, 2006: 25). Furthermore, the government-funded ELT programmes I examined were delivered by non-profit organisations.

(9) Foucault's (1991) concept of governmentality includes simultaneously governing at the level of the population and at the level of the individual, through the 'conduct of conduct'. Government aims to optimise the health and wealth of a population by steering individuals to conduct or govern themselves (through their freedom) in ways deemed advantageous to each person and to the population as a whole.

(10) The CLB importantly understands the significance of sociocultural knowledge in language use (cf. Gumperz, 1982). However, the CLB model is problematically premised on the ideology of communication as 'aimed at cooperation and maintenance of social relations' (Pawlikowska-Smith, 2002: 25). This view of communication as a cooperative transaction from which both parties benefit is a sanitised one which underplays the significance of power relations within communicative contexts. Communication is not necessarily approached cooperatively – rather misunderstanding can be used as a strategy to maintain social inequality. Furthermore, in practice cultural background knowledge is over-essentialised (see critiques of Gumperz model by Sarangi, 1994; Singh *et al.*, 1988; Kandiah, 1991).

(11) All the names used in this chapter are pseudonyms.

(12) Roberts and Cooke (2009) found that the UK business sector also uses the STAR technique. This commonality raises questions about the (international) standardisation of human resource material that needs to be further explored.

(13) ELT instructors and settlement workers were often aware of the limitedness of their interventions, but in everyday practice these interventions nevertheless had material

effects, often at odds with their own intentions and beliefs (i.e. that underemployment is not merely a skills-deficit problem).

(14) Being authentic is valued in the post-Fordist era, as a critique of the standardisation of Fordism (Boltanski & Chiapello, 2005: 441). However, the commodification of the authentic 'creates new forms of anxiety about the authenticity of things or persons; one no longer knows if they are 'authentic' or 'inauthentic', spontaneous or re-engineered for commercial ends' (Boltanski & Chiapello, 2005: 447).

(15) For example, studies have shown that applicants with resumes that had foreign names were three times less likely to be interviewed than those with English names (Oreopoulos, 2009).

(16) 'Overview: The Internationally Trained Workers Initiative'. Human Resources and Skills Development Canada.

(17) This discourse is also exemplified in a government-sponsored commercial advertising language training programmes. This commercial, which aired in 2006, features a South Asian woman in a business suit, who walks briskly through a smart office space as she speaks on her cell phone in her mother tongue. She hangs up the phone as she enters a conference room and switches to English to tell her co-workers that her 'contacts in Mumbai' will have the shipment ready tomorrow. The commercial ends with a voiceover that claims the government is ensuring that immigrants are being integrated into Canada by offering language training. An immigrant woman is thereby represented as contributing to the Canadian economy by using her bilingualism as a resource. However, her 'mother tongue' is only of added value if she has knowledge of a national language (the commercial is in French as well).

References

Abu-Laban, Y. and Gabriel, C. (2002) *Selling Diversity: Immigration, Multiculturalism, Employment Equity, and Globalization.* Toronto: Broadview Press.

Adkins, L. (2005) The new economy, property and personhood. *Theory, Culture & Society* 22 (1), 111–130.

Bjornson, M. (2007) Speaking of citizenship: Language ideologies in Dutch citizenship regimes. *Focaal: European Journal of Anthropology* 49, 65–80.

Boltanski, L. and Chiapello, E. (2005) *The New Spirit of Capitalism.* London: Verso.

Briggs, C.L. (1998) 'You're a liar – you're just like a woman!': Constructing dominant ideologies of language in Warao men's gossip. In B.B. Schieffelin, K.A. Woolard and P.V. Kroskrity (eds) *Language Ideologies: Practice and Theory* (pp. 229–255). New York and Oxford: Oxford University Press.

Briggs, C.L. (2005) Communicability, racial discourse and disease. *Annual Review of Anthropology* 34, 269–291.

Budach, G., Roy, S. and Heller, M. (2003) Community and commodity in French Ontario. *Language in Society* 32, 603–627.

Cameron, D. (1996) *Verbal Hygiene.* London: Routledge.

Cameron, D. (2000) *Good to Talk?: Living and Working in a Communication Culture.* London: Sage.

Cameron, D. (2002) Globalization and the teaching of 'communication skills'. In D. Block and D. Cameron (eds) *Globalization and Language Teaching* (pp. 67–82). London: Routledge.

Campbell, S. and Roberts, C. (2007) Migration, ethnicity and competing discourses in the job interview: Synthesizing the institutional and personal. *Discourse and Society* 18 (3), 243–271.

CIC (1997) *Not Just Numbers: A Canadian Framework for Future Immigration.* Immigration Legislative Review Advisory Group. Ottawa: Citizenship and Immigration Canada.

CIC (1998) *Building on a Strong Foundation for the 21st Century: New Directions for Immigration and Refugee Policy and Legislation.* Ottawa: Citizenship and Immigration Canada.

Cruikshank, B. (1999) *The Will to Empower: Democratic Citizens and Other Subjects.* Ithaca, NY: Cornell University Press.

da Silva, E., McLaughlin, M. and Richards, M. (2007) Bilingualism and the globalized new economy: The commodification of language and identity. In M. Heller (ed.) *Bilingualism: A Social Approach* (pp. 183–206). Basingstoke: Palgrave Macmillan.

Dean, M. (1999) *Governmentality: Power and Rule in Modern Society.* London: Sage.

Duchêne, A. (2009) Marketing, management and performance: Multilingualism as commodity in a tourism call centre. *Language Policy* 8, 27–50.

Duchêne, A. (2011) Néolibéralisme, inégalités sociales et plurilinguisme: l'exploitation des ressources langagières et des locuteurs. *Langage et société* 136 (2), 81–108.

Dunk, T. (1996) Culture, skill, masculinity and whiteness: Training and the politics of identity. In T. Dunk, S. McBride and R.W. Nelson (eds) *The Training Trap: Ideology, Training, and the Labour Market* (pp. 101–123). Winnipeg: Fernwood Publishing.

Ferguson, J. (1994) *The Anti-Politics Machine: 'Development,' Depoliticization, and Bureaucratic Power in Lesotho.* Minneapolis: University of Minnesota Press.

Foucault, M. (1991) Governmentality. In G. Burchell, C. Gordon and P. Miller (eds) *The Foucault Effect: Studies in Governmentality* (pp. 87–104). Chicago: University of Chicago Press.

Gal, S. (1998) Multiplicity and contention among language ideologies: A commentary. In B.B. Schieffelin, K.A. Woolard and P.V. Kroskrity (eds) *Language Ideologies: Practice and Theory* (pp. 317–332). New York and Oxford: Oxford University Press.

Gee, J.P., Hull, G. and Lankshear, C. (1996) *The New Work Order: Behind the Language of the New Capitalism.* Boulder: Westview Press.

Grugulis, I. and Vincent, S. (2009) Whose skill is it anyway?: 'Soft' skills and polarization. *Work, Employment & Society* 23 (4), 597–615.

Gumperz, J. (1982) *Discourse Strategies.* Cambridge: Cambridge University Press.

Guo, S. (2007) Tracing the roots of non-recognition of foreign credentials. *Canadian Issues* Spring, 36–38.

Heller, M. (2001) Critique and sociolinguistic analysis of discourse. *Critique of Anthropology* 21 (2), 117–141.

Heller, M. (2003) Globalization, the new economy, and the commodification of language and identity. *Journal of Sociolinguistics* 7 (4), 473–492.

Heller, M. and Martin-Jones, M. (2001) Introduction: Symbolic domination, education, and linguistic difference. In M. Heller and M. Martin-Jones (eds) *Voices of Authority: Education and Linguistic Difference* (pp. 1–28). Westport: Ablex Publishing.

Inoue, M. (2006) Language and gender in an age of neoliberalism. *Gender and Language* 1 (1), 79–92.

Kandiah, T. (1991) Extenuatory sociolinguistics: Diversity attention from issues to symptoms in cross-cultural communication studies. *Multilingua* 10 (4), 345–379.

Kustec, S., Thompson, E. and Xue, L. (2007) Foreign credentials: The tools for research. *Canadian Issues* Spring, 26–30.

Noorani, N. and Noorani, S. (2008) *Arrival Survival Canada: A Handbook for New Immigrants*. Oxford: Oxford University Press.

Olssen, M. (2008) Understanding the mechanisms of neoliberal control: Lifelong learning, flexibility and knowledge capitalism. In A. Fejes and K. Nicoll (eds) *Foucault and Lifelong Learning: Governing the Subject* (pp. 34–47). London: Routledge.

Ong, A. (2003) *Buddha Is Hiding: Refugees, Citizenship, the New America*. Berkeley: University of California Press.

Ontario Premier's Council (1990) *People and Skills in the New Global Economy: Premier's Council Report*.

Oreopoulos, P. (2009) *Why Do Skilled Immigrants Struggle in the Labor Market?: A Field Experiment with Six Thousand Resumes*. National Bureau of Economic Research (NBER) Working Paper No. 15036, June 2009. http://www.nber.org/papers/w15036.

Pawlikowska-Smith, G. (2000) *Canadian Benchmarks 2000: English as a Second Language – For Adults*. Ottawa: Centre for Canadian Language Benchmarks.

Pawlikowska-Smith, G. (2002) *Centre for Canadian Language Benchmarks 2000: Theoretical Framework*, March. Ottawa: Centre for Canadian Language Benchmarks.

Preston, V., Damsbaek, N., Kelly, P., Lemoine, M., Lo, L. and Shields, J. (2010) What are the labour market outcomes for university-educated immigrants? Toronto Immigrant Employment Data Initiative Analytical Report No. 8. Toronto: TIEDI, York University.

Roberts, C. and Cooke, M. (2009) Authenticity in the adult ESOL classroom and beyond. *TESOL Quarterly* 43 (4), 620–642.

Rose, N. (1999) *Powers and Freedoms: Reframing Political Thought*. Cambridge: Cambridge University Press.

Sarangi, S. (1994) Intercultural or not?: Beyond celebration of cultural differences in miscommunication analysis. *Pragmatics* 4 (3), 409–427.

Sharma, A. and Gupta, A. (2006) Introduction: Rethinking theories of the state in an age of globalization. In A. Sharma and A. Gupta (eds) *The Anthropology of the State* (pp. 1–41). Malden: Blackwell Publishing.

Shields, J. (2003) No safe haven: Markets, welfare, and migrants. CERIS Working Paper No. 22 (pp. 1–39). Joint Centre of Excellence for Research on Immigration and Settlement, Toronto.

Simon, R. and Dippo, D. (1986) On critical ethnographic work. *Anthropology and Education Quarterly* 17, 195–202.

Singh, R., Lele, J. and Martohardjono, G. (1988) Communication in a multilingual society: Some missed opportunities. *Language in Society* 17, 43–59.

Stasiulis, D., Hughes, C. and Amery, Z. (2011) From government to multilevel governance of immigrant settlement in Ontario's city-regions. In E. Tolley and R. Young (eds) *Immigrant Settlement Policy in Canadian Municipalities* (pp. 73–147). Montreal and Kingston: McGill-Queens University Press.

Urciuoli, B. (2008) Skills and selves in the new workplace. *American Ethnologist* 35 (20), 211–228.

Woolard, K.A. (1998) Introduction: Language ideology as a field of inquiry. In B.B. Schieffelin, K.A. Woolard and P.V. Kroskrity (eds) *Language Ideologies: Practice and Theory* (pp. 3–50). New York and Oxford: Oxford University Press.

Part 2

Sites of Selection

4 The Gatekeeping of Babel: Job Interviews and the Linguistic Penalty

Celia Roberts

People are not becoming more free by becoming more mobile
Blommaert, 2005

Introduction

In many of the globalised countries of the western world, and the UK is a prime example, the face-to-face interview remains the ultimate method for selecting candidates for a job. It is the endgame of a long discursive process which includes hard copy and online application forms, a range of, usually, online aptitude, attitude and literacy and numeracy tests, and assessment centres where candidates are put through a range of exercises. These selection processes reflect and help to sustain a two-tier labour market. The lower tier consists of irregular, low-paid, insecure work with the poorest conditions, often done in unsocial hours, rendering the workers invisible. There are few if any formal selection processes for this work and many day labourers are recruited by a gang leader on the basis that they are available for work. Contemporary migrants are overrepresented in this tier, as I detail below. The higher tier consists of more secure work with better conditions and more opportunities for advancement and extends from low-paid work in, for example, supermarkets to high-level professional and managerial jobs. This chapter examines the selection interview as a barrier to those in the lower tier or who are unemployed, and explores the specific kinds of discursive skills that it requires. Outside the two-tier market are the increasing numbers of minority ethnic groups and migrants who are

Table 4.1 Contrasting sociolinguistics in migration studies

• Youth sub-culture	• Institutional encounters
• Celebratory	• Problem-oriented
• Communicative practice and changes	• Communicative norms and stabilities
• New forms that contrast and challenge the standard	• Dominant, standardised languages – 'linguistic capital'
(Günthner, 2011; Hewitt, 1986; Jacquemet, 2005; Rampton, 1995)	(Codó, 2008; Erickson & Shultz, 1982; Gumperz, 1982; Maryns, 2006)

self-employed, partly as a result of these exclusionary selection processes, and this phenomenon is the subject of other chapters in this book (e.g. Sabaté, this volume).

The institutionalised workplace is one of several key research sites within the sociolinguistics of globalisation and migration. These fall broadly into two contrasting categories as shown in Table 4.1. The studies in the right-hand column focus on the broad processes of categorisation, regulation and legitimation that form the institutional order and into which those who have moved countries are inserted. Within these studies, it is possible to make a further categorisation between those encounters which are constituted by the migrant experience and those which are not. It will come as no surprise that the former type of encounters, where migrants are the objects of specific policies, are almost exclusively concerned with assessments and judgements related to legitimacy, eligibility and appropriacy: in asylum seeker interviews (Belgium, Albania), immigration advice/information (Spain) or in special programmes for migrants to access the labour market, for example, internship interviews (Denmark). However, for the great majority of migrants, establishing their legitimacy is only the entry point in the more general societal competition for scarce resources such as healthcare, housing and secure employment. And in the case of the selection interview, migrant candidates' communicative performance must be at least as 'bureaucratically processible' (Iedema, 2003) and socially engaging as that of all other candidates.

The Selection Interview as a Language Game

Although communication skills are routinely mentioned in the design of interviews and in individual candidate assessment, the fact that interviews are made of talk and regulated by normative ways of speaking is not explicitly acknowledged. The value given to certain modes of language which are built into interview design and its realisation in face-to-face encounters is taken for granted by institutions and creates a demand for linguistic capital which outweighs all other selection criteria. For most routine and relatively low paid jobs, the linguistic demands of the job interview are greater than those of the job itself.

The capitalisation of language, in Bourdieu's terms, is based on a unified linguistic market in which all talk is measured against the 'legitimate or official language' of the dominant group. This institutional discourse is characterised by 'impartiality, symmetry, balance, propriety, decency and discretion' (Bourdieu, 1991: 130) and so by more abstract formulations, distant from concrete ways of doing and saying (Iedema, 2003). Bourdieu's formulation assumes there is only one form of linguistic capital: a formal register in a lexico-grammatical standard variety only associated with the dominant class. But the official language of the job interview, while highly conventionalised, is a mix or blending of 'legitimate language' and a more narrative, personal or dramatic mode. There is more variation in routine language practices than the over-arching genre of the job interview presupposes: more 'cockney' and less 'posh' (Rampton, 2006). So, the particular field of the job interview for routine/low-paid jobs values a blended or hybrid mode of talk as the acceptable linguistic capital. In this first example (from a real job interview, as are all the data on which this research are based), a local white candidate responds to a typical institutional question about his capacity to undertake routine, repetitive work:

Example 1

(1) **I:** so all we're looking for here is er:m
(2) an example where you have done similar type of routine repetitive work
(3) **C:** painting magnolia for three weeks ((laugh))
(4) that was the most (.) painting
(5) you couldn't get anything more er repetitive (2)
(6) walls with nothing just walls the size of hhh
(7) just giant walls in a warehouse say fifty feet high (.)
(8) painting one colour (.) day in and day out day in and day out ((laugh))
(9) there ain't nothing more repetitive than that (.)
(10) you'll be pleased to be paint (.)
(11) white ceilings was was a bit of a pleasure (2)
(12) and with printing as well (.) it's d- I'll let write (5)
(13) **I:** ((laugh)) (3) and this this what you're talking about
(14) except you (was) seven hours a day as well [(that long)
(15) **C:** yeah you we're] talking r- half hour half hour lunch and it's wouldn't even class it as lunch eating on the job (.)

This successful candidate responds to the question with a vivid personal narrative far removed from the impersonal and discreet institutional mode that Bourdieu describes and from the formality that a job interview implies, but entirely acceptable within the cultural context of this type of job interview in the UK today. Indeed, the 'experientially grounded', vivid detail of the account is not only acceptable but persuasive and credible (Edwards, 1991).

The hybrid discourses and interactional regimes that form the required linguistic capital for the selection interview are the product of both state regulation and the neoliberal economic order which has permeated both public and private sector organisations. One element of this regulation is the equal opportunities requirement or, in more recent discourses, diversity management (DM), or indeed some mix of the two (Scheepers, 2011). The interviews based on traditional equal opportunity (EO) lines lead to highly designed, scripted encounters with no opportunity to negotiate meaning. All interviews are expected to be entirely consistent on the principle that all interviews must offer the same opportunity to all candidates and on the false assumption that interaction can be strictly regulated. The DM approach stems from a neoliberal model of individual talents and close identification of the individual with the culture of the workplace. The argument here is that the organisation is open to selecting candidates from all and any ethnic cultural backgrounds provided that they align with its organisational culture, and so, by implication, with the culture of the interview. In other words, you can be as diverse as you like as long as you are like us.

The contemporary British job interview increasingly relies on a competency model which is largely derived from the neo-liberal new capitalism or 'new work order' (Gee et al., 1996), and so fits well with the DM approach but also persists with elements of the EO structure, most frequently in public sector jobs in, for example, health and education. The flattened hierarchies and constant requirements for flexibility at shop-floor level of this 'new work order' require a new focus on personality and buying into core organisational values in the 'enterprise' culture (du Gay, 1996). Even in low-paid jobs, individuals are expected to be autonomous and self-regulating and part of self-managing teams. This produces a new focus on the 'self' and individual agency which the competency model aims to assess. These new discourses claim to value and assess individualism and the interviews are designed to elicit vivid narratives and self-reflection which display the enterprising self. However, this new work order produces its own contradictions since the agentive and enterprising elements remain part of a regulatory framework of standardised attitudes and competences of the organisation's mission or vision. The job interview is therefore a potent mix of regulation and standardisation on the one hand and relative freedom and relaxation on the other. Elements of EO, DM and the competency framework itself create an interview design and interactional climate which is contradictory and hybrid and which requires artful synthesisation of the more personal and institutional discourses in order to be successful (Campbell & Roberts, 2007).

Competency Frameworks and 'Linguistic Penalties'

Competency frameworks are widely used to structure selection practices and assess performance at work (Wood & Payne, 1998). Typical competences are the ability to work as a team, self-organise, be flexible, cope with change and cope with repetitive work. Implied in these abstract formulations are a set of orientations to the self and to work which go beyond any narrow sense of skills for a particular job and require a blend of discursive capacities that align with the institutional and more abstract elements of the interview while also conveying an agentive and engaged personality. The interview, therefore, invokes particular forms of argumentation, reasoning, narrative and inferencing which are taken for granted by the interviewers and which mask the cultural specificity of the interview as a gatekeeping activity (Erickson, 2011; Erickson & Shultz, 1982).

This particular form of linguistic capital, like other forms, requires access to the means of its acquisition through intense participation in environments where it is produced. Transnationals who have not received their education in the UK and who are unemployed or working in ethnic work units in the lower tier labour market do not have such access. On the analogy of the ethnic penalty, the interview creates a 'linguistic penalty' for this group.

'Ethnic penalty' is a term used to describe the processes in the labour market which lead to black and minority ethnic (BME) jobseekers being less likely than their white counterparts to gain employment (Heath & Cheung, 2006). Drawing on Bourdieusian notions of linguistic capital, a 'linguistic penalty' is a combination of all the sources of disadvantage which might lead a linguistic minority group to fare less well in the selection/evaluation process generally and specifically in the labour market. While the notion of an ethnic penalty relates to explicit factors that account for BME disadvantage, the linguistic penalty of the job interview includes the idea that the very processes used to apparently offer an open and fair opportunity mask the social inequalities that these interviews produce. The competency-based interview is one of the technologies that helps to produce the linguistic market and whose very machinery obscures the powerful interests they serve (Foucault, 1983). Such interviews are widely assumed to be fair and the special reasoning and inferencing that their discursive regimes require are not critiqued or unmasked as valuing and serving the interests of the institution which produces them.

One of the typical competences mentioned above is that of coping with repetitive work. Despite the organisational discourses of the new capitalism which centre on flexibility and dynamism, much relatively low paid work is routine and repetitive. Within the competency framework, the expectation is that the candidate is not only willing to do this kind of work but is also sufficiently self-organised and self-aware to reflect on how they will manage the boredom of repetitive work in order to fulfil the required tasks. The design of competency questions usually takes two forms: the first is to elicit a narrative of experience, grounded in detail and personal engagement (such as example 1 above, 'Magnolia paint')' the second type of question is designed to funnel down to a more analytic and reflective stage, especially if the opening narrative has not included this element (Roberts & Campbell, 2005). The next two examples illustrate these two forms.

In Example 2, a local white candidate is asked to give an example where he has done repetitive work:

Example 2

(1) **C:** well one specific agency contract I got (.)
(2)   it was only four months
(3)   but it was the complete mind numbingly same repetitive stuff
(4) **I:** okay
(5) **C:** I was working for (name of company) in Harrow
(6)   and we were building headsets for helicopter pilots
(7)   and my specific task was to get this tiny little ear piece
(8)   and get a little drill and glue that
(9)   and that was all I had to do (.)
(10)   all day everyday (.)
(11)   I didn't have problem with that
(12)   because I was sat round a table with half a dozen other blokes
(13)   and you know (.) you don't really need to turn your brain on
(14)   to do something like that
(15)   you can just chat
(16)   and get the job done
(17)   and its (.) you got to keep yourself amused for boring jobs

The candidate's narrative follows the well-known Labovian structure (Labov & Waletzsky, 1967) for Anglo narratives. Not only does his narrative follow a conventional format, but the organisation to which he is applying has designed the form the interviewers will fill out around a widely used mnemonic, the STAR structure: situation, task, action, result, originally developed in the United States. The candidate's normative structure follows the STAR format with lines 1–3 (S) providing the Labovian abstract and lines 5–6 (T) the orientation, lines 7–10 (A) the crux of the story and in lines 11–17 (R) an extended evaluation which shows the interviewer the necessary display of competence. The final two stages of the conventional narrative structure, the result and coda, are usually collapsed into the evaluation phase, as in this case. As Labov and Waletzsky comment, evaluation is not a fixed stage and an evaluative component is already introduced in the opening abstract in this example. The normative Anglo narrative and the institution's bureaucratic assessment form map on to each other precisely.

The next example is taken from the second stage of the competency question about managing repetitive work. Here the candidate has given some examples of work where his work has been repetitive and how he coped. Now the interviewer funnels down to a more analytic, abstract and institutional form of question:

Example 3

(1) **I:** right what would you tell me is the advantage of a repetitive job (1)
(2) **C:** advantage of a
(3) **I:** repetitive job (1)
(4) **C:** er I mean the advantage of a repetitive job is that er:m
    it makes you it it keeps you going (.)
(5)   er it doesn't make you bored (.) you don't feel bored
(6)   you keep on going and (.)
(7)   I mean I me- a (.)
(8)   and also it it puts a smile on your
(9)   face you come in it puts a smile on your face
(10)   you feel happy to come to the job
(11)   the job will (trust) you
(12) **I:** you don't get to know it better
(13) **C:** sorry
(14) **I:** you don't get to know it better
(15) **C:** yeah we get to know the job better
(16)   we I mean we learn new ideas
(17)   lots of new ideas as well
(18) **I:** right what is the disadvantage of a repetitive job
(19) **C:** well (.) disadvantage er:m (.) er disadvantages (1)

(20)   you may you may f- offend customers
(21)   you may f- offend our customers
(22) **C:** in there that's a disadvantage of it
(23) **I:** you don't find it boring
(24) **C:** yeah it could also be boring (.)
(25)   to be boring and you and you (.)
(26)   yet by being bored you may offend the customers
(27) **I:** how how would you offend them by being bored
(28) **C:** by not putting a smile on your face
(29) **I:** right

This candidate was considered borderline and the interviewer expressed particular concerns about his answer to this question. He attempts to answer it by putting as positive a gloss as he can on how he could cope with such work. However, since the conventionalised expectations that the interviewer brings to the interview are hidden from him, he fails to give the preferred response and he is penalised for this. The same difficulty arises when he is asked about the disadvantages at line 18 and there is evidence in his pausing and repetition that he cannot easily find a suitable response. Although he does then offer a very plausible response, it is not readily accepted by the interviewer (lines 23 and 27). He fails to acknowledge that repetitive work is boring but that he has strategies for dealing with this, in other words, that he is a reflective, self-organised worker.

The Linguistic Penalty and the Production of Social Inequality

The examples in this chapter are taken from two studies of UK job interviews carried out between 2003 and 2007.[1] 70 interviews were video-recorded with candidates from 21 different linguistic backgrounds and ethnographic information was collected on candidates' and interviewers' responses to the interviews. The context within which this study was undertaken was one of increasing migration and 'superdiversity' (Vertovec, 2007), particularly in large urban centres and, very significantly, in London. For example, 25% of the London population are born abroad (BA) (Kyambi, 2005) and BME groups and migrants constitute 35% of the working-age population in London (GLA, 2005). Migrants are less able to access the labour market than the population as a whole (Kyambi, 2005) and are much more likely than the general population to be in the lowest paid jobs and those with the poorest conditions (Evans *et al.,*

2005). Furthermore, over 50% of migrants in these lower tier jobs have tertiary-level qualifications but are unable to break into the higher tier into jobs which are commensurable with their education and expertise (GLA, 2005).

Our studies show that despite the organisational discourses of equality and diversity, those born abroad suffer a linguistic penalty from the job interview. The Commission for Racial Equality's (2006) Code of Practice stated that: interviews should assess 'solely on ability to do the job satisfactorily' (para 4.28) and that 'A language requirement for a job may be indirectly discriminatory and unlawful unless it is necessary for the satisfactory performance of the job' (para 4.51). However, the discursive skills to produce a hybrid of institutional and personal discourse and structure narrative examples in Anglo ways are unnecessary for stacking shelves, packing factory products, undertaking simple reception work or delivering parcels, which were the typical low-paid jobs in both the private and public sectors that candidates were applying for. The difference in success rates for these types of jobs was stark (see Figure 4.1).

It is typical for this type of work for employers to hold assessment days and to interview large numbers of people with a view to taking on the majority who apply. In the case of white British and ethnic minority British this was the case. However, those born abroad were markedly less successful and were more likely to fail than pass, despite being more qualified. The discursive skills required at the competency-based job interview bundle up specific kinds of workplace sociocultural knowledge with normative styles of self-presentation (Gumperz, 1992). These skills have to be displayed within the synthetic environment of the selection process where both formality and informality have to be artfully blended.

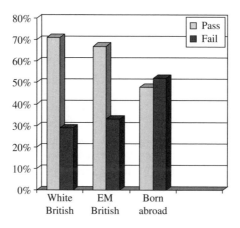

Figure 4.1 Success levels of BME candidates

The competency design requires the special inferencing to bridge the gap between the abstract formulations of the competence under scrutiny, for example, the ability to manage change or take ownership, and the initial narratavised expected answer. It also requires the candidate to produce responses couched in analytic terms such as the arguments for and against repetitive work, as in Example 2. As well as these discursive skills, there is an assumed perspective about how to present oneself in relation to work, for example, how to cope with repetitive work and a presumption that stories can be structured in Anglo ways and performed with the vivid vocabulary and prosody of a lively yarn.

All this is taken for granted by the designers of such interviews and by most, albeit not all, interviewers and those who train them. In this regard the institutionalised workplace is no different from other institutions bound together by common classifications and categories which become taken for granted and are presented as natural and reasonable (Douglas, 1986): 'This is how ... we build institutions, squeezing each other's ideas into a common shape' (Douglas, 1986: 91). So the production and maintenance of the contemporary job interview is as much about defending the institution as it is about selecting fairly. Janus-like, it looks out to the candidates but also in on itself and the business of 'harnessing all information processes to the task of establishing' itself (Douglas, 1986: 102).

Where interviews were not going well, the interactional regime became markedly more institutional and less informal. This occurred much more frequently when the candidates were migrants than otherwise and this increased institutionalisation itself created more interactional problems and fewer affordances for candidates to present themselves in acceptable ways. This occurred in three main ways: more control over candidate talk, more negativity and less helpfulness and stricter alignment to formal participation roles (Campbell & Roberts, 2007). Control was exercised through longer reformulations of questions, through 'talking down' (Erickson & Shultz, 1982), and through more interruptions and sudden topic shifts which fragmented the candidates' narratives and so constructed them as less coherent. More negativity was apparent in the foregrounding of questions with built-in negative assumptions and implied or explicit critical assessment of responses, as in Example 3, and in fewer helpful or embedded questions and responses. For example, successful candidates were often rewarded with responses such as: 'I imagine that was difficult/interesting/hard work, etc.', where the interviewers put themselves on an empathetic footing with the candidate. Thirdly, in less successful encounters, interviewers would align more rigidly to their role as interviewers by orientating more to the documents of the interview and animating talk that they had not authored (Goffman, 1981). For example, they would read questions verbatim from the question sheet and so foreground their work as institutional representatives rather than conversational partners. Such conduct was a response to candidate performance but also, crucially, served to construct what was perceived as less than adequate performance which, in turn, could be used defensively to justify rejection.

Although candidate success or failure was jointly and interactionally produced, there was no recognition of this since the institutional position was that all candidates were given an equal opportunity at the interview. The specific linguistic capital was invisible to the institutions which had delineated it. However, its role in the hierarchy of language power is clear. In this particular field, it was less about standardised language and more about managing hybrid discourses. These discursive skills are valued more highly than an undifferentiated institutional voice and storytelling is more persuasive for some responses than more formal, analytic stances. However, the latter is also expected at other points in the interview. The linguistic resources that all migrant candidates brought to the interview as multilingual speakers were never acknowledged at any time either in the interviews or, subsequently, in the decision-making process. These resources were not capitalised despite their potential value in the workplace.

Conclusions

In access to the labour market, language is, simultaneously, over-used as an explanatory phenomenon and yet under-recognised and under-specified. It is an easy notion to call up in order to rationalise gatekeeping decisions or as a clarion call around which doubts and negativity may coalesce. The discourses on integration or on job-seeking are obvious examples where '(not) speaking English' is used as the lead explanation for what is seen as a 'migrant problem'. However, its powerful role in decision making goes unnoticed. The linguistic capital of the interview is not recognised since its complex cultural and language requirements are not valued as such but treated as transparent means to arrive at personal skills. Migrant candidates are much more likely than others to have the gatekeeper close the gate on them because they are seen as, individually, lacking the competences. Judgements by gatekeepers of an applicant's competency or personality ('I didn't really trust him') are based on assessments of the adequacy of how he or she talks, but there is no institutionalised space for this to be acknowledged.

The selection interview requires both bureaucratically processable talk and a vivid social performance, subtly blended together to produce a credible and persuasive self which aligns with the ideal worker in the new capitalist workplace. Small interactional differences and difficulties feed into larger scale judgements and institutional orders which, in turn, press down on individual decision making.

The bureaucratic interview assumes a certain type of linguistic capital which is not readily available to those who are unemployed or working in ethnic work units in lower tier work where migrant workers are over-represented. So it produces a linguistic penalty for these groups and as such contributes to the production and re-production of social inequality. As in many bureaucratic settings, the discourses of the gatekeeping encounter require a level of linguistic capital incommensurate with its outcome. Candidates may well be competent for the job but they are excluded from it because they are not competent for the interview.

The linguistic and cultural processes of the job interview are rendered invisible by the current ideologies of competency frameworks and reliance on common sense which institutions use to defend their decision-making processes. While the formal selection interview remains the ultimate method for choosing candidates, it will continue to perform a linguistic gatekeeping role that sustains the gap between the majority group and ethnic/linguistic minorities in the low-paid job market.

However, there are some reasons to be hopeful that the interview's role in producing inequality will gradually diminish. While the competency framework used for interviews is imperfect, it represents a distinct improvement on the old-style biographical interview with questions such as 'Where do you see yourself in five years' time?'. There is also increasing reliance in the selection process on tasks that simulate the actual duties of the job. And finally, DVDs based on this research have been shown to contribute to job-seekers' success in interviews, suggesting that many of the rules of the job interview game can be learnt. The larger task, and one that could lead to more fundamental changes, is to work on the public understanding of language so that organisations recognise the linguistic penalty and act to eliminate it.

Note

(1) The two studies were funded by the UK Government's Department for Work and Pensions and are available on their website, *Talk on Trial* (Research Report No. 344) and *Talking Like a Manager* (Research Report No. 501), at http://research.dwp.gov.uk/asd/asd5/rrs-index.asp.

References

Blommaert, J. (2005) *Discourse*. Cambridge: Cambridge University Press.
Bourdieu, P. (1991) *Language and Symbolic Power*. Cambridge: Polity.

Campbell, S. and Roberts, C. (2007) Migration, ethnicity and competing discourses in the job interview: Synthesising the institutional and personal. *Discourse and Society* 18 (3), 243–271.

Codó, E. (2008) *Immigration and Bureaucratic Control.* Berlin: Mouton de Gruyter.

Commission for Racial Equality (2006) *Statutory Code of Practices on Race Equality in Employment.* London: CRE.

Douglas, M. (1986) *How Institutions Think.* Syracuse: Syracuse University Press.

du Gay, P. (1996) *Consumption and Identity at Work.* London: Sage.

Edwards, D. (1991) Categories are for talking: On the cognitive and discursive bases of categorisation. *Theory and Psychology* 1 (4), 515–542.

Erickson, F. and Shultz, J. (1982) *The Counselor as Gatekeeper: Social Interaction in Interviews.* New York: Academic Press.

Erickson, F. (2011) From speech as 'situated' to speech as 'situating': insights from John Gumperz on the practical conduct of talk as social action. *Text and Talk* 31 (4), 395–406.

Evans, Y., Herbert, J., Datta, K., May, J., McIlwaine, C. and Wills, J. (2005) *Making the City Work: Low Paid Employment in London.* London: Queen Mary College, University of London.

Foucault, M. (1983) The subject and power. In H. Dreyfus and P. Rabinow (eds) *Michel Foucault: Beyond Structuralism and Hermeneutics* (2nd edn) (pp. 208–228). Chicago: University of Chicago Press.

Gee, J., Hull, G. and Lankshear, C. (1996) *The New Work Order: Behind the Language of the New Capitalism.* St Leonards: Allen & Unwin.

GLA (2005) Country of birth and labour market outcomes in London. An analysis of Labour Force Survey and Census data. DMAG Briefing 2005-1. Greater London Assembly, London.

Goffman, E. (1981) *Forms of Talk.* Oxford: Blackwell.

Gumperz, J. (1982) *Discourse Strategies.* Cambridge: Cambridge University Press.

Gumperz, J. (1992) Interviewing in intercultural situations. In P. Drew and J. Heritage (eds) *Talk at Work* (pp. 302–327). Cambridge: Cambridge University Press.

Günthner, S. (2011) The dynamics of communicative practice in transmigrational contexts: 'Insulting remarks', and 'stylised category animations' in everyday interactions among male youth in Germany. *Text and Talk* 31 (4), 447–474.

Heath, A. and Cheung S.Y. (2006) Ethnic penalties in the labour market: Employers and discrimination. DWP Research Report No. 341. Department for Work & Pensions, Sheffield.

Hewitt, R. (1986) *White Talk. Black Talk: Inter-racial Friendship and Communication Among Adolescents.* Cambridge: Cambridge University Press.

Iedema, R. (2003) *Discourses of Post-Bureaucratic Organisation.* Amsterdam: John Benjamins.

Jacquemet, M. (2005) Transidiomatic practices: Language and power in the age of globalisation. *Language and Communication* 25, 257–277.

Kyambi, S. (2005) *Beyond Black and White: Mapping New Immigrant Communities.* London: IPPR.

Labov, W. and Waletzsky, J. (1967) Narrative analysis. In J. Helm (ed.) *Essays on the Verbal and Visual Arts* (pp. 12–44). Seattle: University of Washington Press.

Maryns, K. (2006) *The Asylum Speaker.* Manchester: St Jerome.

Rampton, B. (1995) *Crossing: Language and Ethnicity Among Adolescents.* London: Longman.

Rampton, B. (2006) *Language in Late Modernity: Interaction in an Urban School.* Cambridge: Cambridge University Press.

Roberts, C. and Campbell, S. (2005) Fitting stories into boxes: Rhetorical and textual constraints on candidates' performances in British job interviews. *Journal of Applied Linguistics* 2 (1), 45–73.

Scheepers, S. (2011) Equality for those who are competent. Discourses on competencies, diversity and equality in the public sector. In K. Pelsmaekers, C. Rollo, T. van Hout and P . Heynderickx (eds) *Displaying Competence in Organisations* (pp. 27–44). Basingstoke: Palgrave.

Vertovec, S. (2007) Superdiversity and its implications. *Ethnic and Racial Studies* 29 (6), 1024–1054.

Wood, R. and Payne, T. (1998) *Competency Based Recruitment and Selection.* Chichester: Wiley.

5 Language Work Aboard the Low-cost Airline

Ingrid Piller and Kimie Takahashi

Introduction

Flight attendants can be considered as transnational workers par excellence: transnational mobility is what they 'do' on a daily basis. In addition to doing transnational mobility for a living, they could also be considered prototypical service workers: despite the heavy physical demands of flight attendance work, it is considered low-skilled work and flight attendants are mostly judged for the emotional, aesthetic and linguistic work they perform. Finally, they are also typical of the neoliberal global economic order in that theirs is a low-wage sector where, since the deregulation of the aviation industry from the 1980s onwards, competition has largely been fought on the terrain of labour costs. In contrast to most other low-wage sectors, however, flight attendant work is widely seen as desirable and even glamorous. Consequently, flight attendant work can be considered an ideal site to explore the intersections between mobility, institutions and language. In this chapter we do so by focusing on the selection practices of a transnational airline operating in the Asia-Pacific and how these are experienced by a group of Japan-born and Australia-based flight attendants working for that airline.

Employment as a flight attendant holds a very special place in the dreams and aspirations of many young women in Japan. Being a flight attendant is seen as an opportunity to move overseas and to develop a glamorous identity as a multilingual cosmopolitan. These aspirations coincide with the recruitment strategies of Australian airlines, which increasingly hire Asian flight attendants as a way of extending their operations into Asia. We thus find that their mobility is embedded in a global system of ideologies and practices that pit English against other languages, native speakers of English against non-native speakers of English, women seen as naturally demure and caring against men, Asians seen as naturally graceful and docile against Westerns, and nationals of developed countries who are seen as spoilt and demanding against nationals from the global South, who are seen as 'hungry' enough to make submissive workers. Japanese flight attendants occupy conflicting positions in these global hierarchies: their work entails doing 'being Japanese' but also doing 'being not Australian' and 'being not Thai'.

The remainder of this chapter is structured as follows. In the next section, we will introduce the context of our study, namely the changing role of flight attendant work, Asia-Pacific aviation as an employment sector, and the low-cost carrier for which our participants worked at the time of data collection in 2008. We will call that airline *Flying High*. In this background section we draw on previous research, career guides and media reports. We then introduce our participants, four female and one male Japan-born and Australia-based flight attendants working for *Flying High*. Their narratives demonstrate that ideology and practice intersect in complex ways on the terrains of work, gender, culture, nationality, location and language. We structure our exploration of these intersections around the two languages central to our participants' experiences of selection: Japanese, as the language that got them their dream job, and English, as the language through which daily exclusions, from being under heightened surveillance to not being rostered for desirable routes, are played out.

Flying High with *Flying High*?

Since the beginning of commercial aviation in Japan in the 1950s, employment as a flight attendant has held a special place in the dreams of many young women, as is true internationally (Baum, 2010). In the early days, the actual opportunity to become a flight attendant was exclusive to the daughters of the upper-middle class (Chizuko Kawamura, personal communication). In this, too, Japan was no exception (Baum, 2010). With flying being the prerogative of a relatively small elite, airlines sought to employ women of a certain upper-class sociability and sophistication to match their passengers' sensibilities. As far as female occupations go, a career as a flight attendant provided a relatively high status, salary and job security. This started to change with the deregulation of the aviation industry from the 1980s onwards, first in the USA and a few years later in Asia and Europe. Neoliberals like to cite the fact that airfares have fallen around 25% since 1990 as evidence of the unequivocal success of removing government controls and turning aviation over to the free market (Smith & Cox, 2008). By contrast, labour analysts point to the fact that the drop in airfares (and the concomitant rise in profits) has mostly been achieved through the reduction of labour costs. In Australia, for instance, pilots' wages have dropped by as much as 50% since the 1990s while job security has disappeared and workloads have increased (Schulte & Zhu, 2005). For flight attendants, these indicators are even more dramatic, with the low-cost carrier Virgin Australia (formerly Virgin Blue), for instance, paying wages of only 34% of those that used to be paid by the national carriers Ansett Australia and Qantas (Weller, 2008). Furthermore, low-cost carriers operating in and into Australia are 'Australian' only in name and branding but, in actual fact, are multinational corporations employing staff in different locations according to local labour markets and subject to local industrial relations policies.

In mid-2011, for instance, exploitative employment conditions at low-cost carrier Jetstar, a fully owned Qantas subsidiary, became a national concern when it emerged that Thailand-based flight attendants were paid less than a tenth that of Australia-based crew (Cannane, 2011). Additionally, the Thai flight attendants' employment contracts stipulate 20-hour shifts and these can even be extended at the employer's discretion, raising serious fatigue concerns. Furthermore, they are virtually indentured because they have to pay back 4.5 months' worth of salary when they leave their contract prematurely (Cannane, 2011). Jetstar responded to these revelations by claiming that they had no control over local market conditions, particularly as they did not actually employ Thailand-based flight attendants themselves but had outsourced flight attendant contracting in Thailand to tourism employment agency Tour East Thailand. In a further twist, Tour East Thailand is partly owned by the Qantas Group, Jetstar's parent company. Qantas has similar partly owned employment agencies to source crew operating, inter alia, out of Indonesia, the Philippines, Singapore and Vietnam (Sandilands, 2011).

The dire reality of flight attendant work that has emerged in recent years has done little to dent its glamorous image, as Baum (2010) observes in his analysis of the fictional representations of UK and US flight attendants in the period from 1930 to 2010. In Japan, the image of flight attendants has been strongly shaped by the 1980s megahit TV melodrama スチュワーデス物語 [*Stewardess Story*]. *Stewardess Story* was about a group of young women training to be flight attendants for Japan Airlines (JAL), which, at that time, was one of Japan's flagship carriers and the largest Asian airline (客室乗務員 [Flight attendant], 2011). In contrast to the upper-class image that flight attendant work still held at the time, the main character, Chiaki, was an ordinary woman, with limited English, whose eventual success in passing the training was presented as due to her determination, her hard work, and the help she received from her fellow trainees and a passionate male instructor. *Stewardess Story* inspired desire and raised the hopes of many 'ordinary' young girls of that generation that a glamorous career as a flight attendant was an attainable career goal for them, too.

The glamorous fictional representations of flight attendants in Japan and internationally are echoed in – and further cemented through – career guides and training institutes. 'Cool career' guides such as Thomas and Nations (2009), a US publication, abound. In Japan, the glamour of flight attendants is inextricably linked to the glamour of English as an indispensable career tool for women, which we have analysed elsewhere (Piller & Takahashi, 2006, 2010). To demonstrate that point further we will here examine two such career guides in some more detail, namely 語学を生かして、世界で働く [Career overseas by using language skills] (Itakura, 2006) and 英語でリッチ！ [Get rich with English!] (Sasaki, 2006).

Itakura (2006) lists 19 desirable English-related careers in four job categories, namely international relations, tourism, language study and business. Each job entry consists of a short narrative of a woman holding that particular job, followed by the author's advice on how to obtain the job. One of the jobs listed in the tourism section is flight attendant, featuring the story of Miwako Leitmüller, who works for Lufthansa. Describing flight attending as her 'childhood dream', Miwako traces that dream back to *Stewardess Story*, which she says she watched enthusiastically. In a typical narrative complication, she initially has to give up her dream because her applications to Japan's two domestic airlines are unsuccessful. Instead, she settles for work with a travel agency, where she often gets to watch 'flight attendants wearing their cool uniforms walking by briskly with their carry-on luggage' (Itakura, 2006: 85). Motivated by envy, she resurrects her dream, attends a flight attendant school, polishes her English, and finds a job with the German flagship carrier Lufthansa. Sticking to her dream turns out to be beneficial all round because in addition to a job she also finds love in Germany. Her story's happy ending relates to both work and family: Lufthansa's flexible employment programme allows her to combine work and motherhood, something she thinks would have been impossible if she had worked for a Japanese company.

Sasaki's (2006) format is similar. Chapter Three, 'Using English in the Work of Your Dreams', starts with the story of 29-year-old Emi Kawamura, who flies for an unidentified Asian airline. Under the headline 'Never give up and be persistent when confronted with challenges! Achieving the dream of becoming a flight attendant after six years', Emi's story begins with her girlhood dream of becoming a flight attendant. In order to realise her dream, she goes to the UK to study as an overseas student, attends a flight attendant school and, additionally, a private English language school specializing in preparation for the Test of English for International Communication (TOEIC). In her case, the complication also results from the fact that her job applications for flight attendant work keep being rejected over a period of six years. The happy ending occurs when her persistence is finally rewarded and she is hired by a foreign airline based in Asia. The reader is left with Emi sharing her plans to move to the UK. While this is a non sequitur, its position in the story seems to suggest that flight attendant work in Asia is not an end in itself but a step to bigger and better things.

Neither story is a complete fairy tale. Itakura (2006) points out that flight attendant work is physically taxing, and involves irregular shifts and limited opportunities for career development. And, the promise of Sasaki's (2006) title, *Get Rich with English!*, notwithstanding, Emi's flight attendant dream job pays JPY30,000 less than her previous work. Reality also intrudes on websites where jobseekers discuss their experiences. In an exchange on *Yahoo Chiebukuro*, for example, someone wants to know whether being a flight attendant is the most popular occupation among women and the 'best' answer (as selected by the inquirer) says, 'The salary and benefits (because of the introduction of temping and hourly rates) are on the decline, and the nature of the work is simply hostessing and waitressing. Who wants to look after drunk customers or clean up their vomit and the toilets?'[1]

While the popularity of flight attending is evidently on the decline and the gap between dreams and reality is slowly starting to emerge, a 2005 survey found that flight attendants continue to be among the top 10 most popular careers for women in Japan.[2] In addition to fictional accounts and career guides, it is also flight attendant schools and English schools with their vested interest, which keep the dream alive. The websites of flight attendant schools[3] feature images of stunningly beautiful, confident-looking professional women, who look like feminine masters of the universe. In addition to flight attendant schools in Japan, there are now also schools in Australia targeting the Japanese market with the offer of a combination of flight attendant courses, English study and overseas experience, such as the Aviation Study Centre in Brisbane, where the low-cost carrier Virgin Australia happens to have its headquarters. The 'cabin crew course' on offer there provides evidence of the ways in which flight attendant work has been deskilled. In an eight-week course, and for a fee of AUD5950, students can gain four 'Australian government recognised certificates', namely a Certificate II in Transport & Distribution, a Security Services Certificate, a Senior First Aid Certificate and a Responsible Service of Alcohol Certificate.[4]

The ways to market the glamour of flight attendants and to turn the desire these discourses engender into a profit are seemingly endless. A major tourism provider, for instance, markets '7-day flight attendance experience tours' with Malaysia Airlines and Virgin Atlantic. For JPY194,000 (Malaysia) or JPY398,000 (Virgin), this package tour allows participants to spend a few days at a Malaysia site in Kuala Lumpur or a Virgin site in London and to experience training in flight attendant work, to attend English classes and to have a make-up and hairstyle makeover. On their last day, tour members get to wear authentic Malaysia or Virgin flight attendant uniforms and to have their picture taken in front of a branded airplane as if they were a real crew.[5]

The desire of many Japanese women for flight attendant work, for English and for an international career, coincides with Western stereotypes of Asian women as ideally and naturally suited for service work. Epitomised in the *Singapore Girl*, a trademark of Singapore Airlines, Asian flight attendants are often marketed as the serenely beautiful, warmly caring and demurely elegant embodiment of 'Asian values and hospitality' (Singapore Girl, 2011). Airlines with predominantly Asian crews have long used discourses of the essential Asian-ness of their flight attendants in their marketing. *Flying High*, too, promotes itself as 'the best of Australian and Asian hospitality' through the embodied identities of their 'warm, friendly and extremely attentive' flight attendants. For originally non-Asian airlines such as *Flying High*, the employment of Asian flight attendants has thus also been central to their attempts to break into the Asian market and to visibly 'demonstrate' their Asian-ness.

While Asian flight attendants have long been stereotyped as 'ideal' flight attendants and have come to serve as an embodiment of many airlines' brand identities, their image as docile, their relative lack of unionisation and, increasingly, the reality of their underpayment have made Asian flight attendants often unpopular with their Western colleagues. As early as 1983, Hochschild (2003: 130), for instance, was quoting a unionised flight attendant at PanAm as saying that management 'would love nothing better than to get rid of us [=US flight attendants] and fill the plane with loving, submissive Japanese women'.

In sum, in the course of the deregulation of aviation, flight attendant work has undergone dramatic changes from high-skilled, secure, well-paid and respected women's work to low-skilled, casual, poorly paid and devalued work. However, the perceived glamour of flight attendants has been much slower to die. As a matter of fact, fictional representations, women's magazines, career guides and training institutes continue to keep the dream alive and have found additional means to turn those desires into a profit. As a matter of fact, in some of these practices, such as study-abroad flight attendant schools or flight attendant experience package holidays, the boundary between work and leisure consumption has become blurred. The commodification of the dream of flight attending, both as a means to obscure the reality of exploitative labour practices and to promote consumption, is also apparent in the images particularly associated with Asian flight attendants. In the next section, we will now explore how these tensions play out in the narratives of five Japan-born and Australia-based flight attendants working for *Flying High*.

Participants

In 2008 we conducted fieldwork for a research project investigating the political economy of languages in tourism between Australia and Japan.[6] We interviewed two groups of participants in the Gold Coast and Sydney in Australia, and in Tokyo and Yokohama in Japan. The first group consisted of tourism service providers catering for Japanese tourists to Australia. The second group consisted of Japanese individuals who had travelled to or lived in Australia on a short-term basis. As part of the former group, KT interviewed five Japan-born and Australia-based flight attendants working for *Flying High* at the time. Each individual interview was conducted in Japanese and, with one exception, lasted for more than three hours. Interview questions were broad but centred on their language learning and career trajectories, their current work and their future plans. Table 5.1 provides an overview of the participants and we will now briefly introduce each participant.

At the time of the interview, Eri was 33 years old and had been based in Sydney for a little over a year. She had moved to Sydney for her job after having been hired by *Flying High* in Japan. Prior to her employment with *Flying High*, she had worked as a flight attendant based in Hong Kong and as grand hostess at Narita Airport after her graduation from a flight attendant school in Tokyo. Eri was the only participant who had previously worked for another airline; she chose to leave her better paid position with an Asian flagship carrier to work for *Flying High* because she was fed up with Hong Kong and had a positive image of Sydney from a previous visit. Despite her extensive experience in the sector, it was her dream to leave the tourism industry for a more rewarding sector and/or to start a family.

Fumie was 36 years old in 2008 and had lived in Australia since the age of 25, when she had arrived on a working holiday visa. At that time it had been her aim to improve her English and to live in a freer society away from Japan. Before joining *Flying High* in 2007, she had held a number of customer service positions in the tourism industry in several cities in Australia. She

Table 5.1 Overview of participants

Pseudonym	Year of birth	First visit to Australia	Visa status	Languages	Education	Previous work experience	Hiring location
Eri	1975	2001	Temporary work visa	Japanese, English, Spanish	Flight attendant school	Grand hostess and flight attendant in Hong Kong and Japan	Japan
Fumie	1972	1997	Permanent residency	Japanese, English, Korean	Hotel school	Various tourism-related customer service jobs in Australia and New Zealand	Australia
Juri	1974	1995	Temporary work visa	Japanese, English, French	Graduated from a women's university	Various tour guide roles in France, Japan and New Zealand	Japan
Ryoko	1982	2001	Temporary work visa	Japanese, English	Vocational hospitality degree	Various waitressing and receptionist roles in Australia	Japan
Takashi	1972	1997	Permanent residency	Japanese, English	Tourism degree	Various tourism-related service jobs in Australia and Japan	Australia

had obtained permanent residency (PR) through a previous Australian partner and she is proud of the fact that she is often taken for an Australian native on the basis of her accent. She was happy with the non-demanding nature of her job and had no further career goals. Her dream was to find a partner and start a family and she spoke at length about the difficulties of entering a stable relationship as a flight attendant, particularly for a budget airline.

Like Eri, Juri moved to Sydney because she had gained employment with *Flying High* in 2007 when she was 33 years old. However, this was not the first extended period she spent in Australia as she had spent most of her twenties travelling widely, including extended periods of working holidays in Australia, France and New Zealand. During these travels she gained extensive work experience in the tourism industry, particularly as a tour guide, tour conductor and tour coordinator. In her early thirties she had returned to Japan with the intention of settling down. However, her lack of networks and her age made it impossible for her to find a job in Tokyo and so she applied for a flight attendant job with *Flying High* when they advertised in Tokyo in 2007. Juri enjoyed the stress-free nature of her work and the fact that she got to see her family in Japan regularly. However, she feared that the physically demanding nature of the flight attendant job would mean that she would have to change careers again in the not-too-distant future.

At age 26, Ryoko was the youngest of our participants. Having failed to gain admission to a university in Japan, she came to Australia on a working holiday visa in 2001 at the age of 18. She travelled widely throughout Australia, mostly pursuing romantic interests, before she studied hospitality at college. After graduation, she worked in a Japanese restaurant and a five-star hotel before joining *Flying High* in 2007. Like the other participants, she described her work as easy and stress free but she suffered from a sense of loneliness and the limited opportunities to form solid relationships afforded by the nature of shift work. She talked extensively about her dilemma of having achieved her life dreams of high fluency in English and a career as a flight attendant while, at the same time, feeling empty, lonely and dissatisfied. She had no sense of direction as to how that dilemma could be resolved.

Takashi is the only male among our participants. In 2008, he was 36 years old and had lived in Australia since 1997. At that time, he had quit his secure job at a major Japanese tourism service provider because he wanted to improve his English and enjoy a freer lifestyle than was available to gay men in Japan. After studying English at a language school for six months, he went on to obtain a diploma of tourism, held several tourism-related jobs, both in outback Australia and in Sydney and, like Fumie, obtained PR through an Australian partner, prior to joining *Flying High* in 2007. He was the only participant who actually spoke about being inspired by *Stewardess Story* (see above). As male flight attendants are virtually non-existent in the Japanese airline industry, he never acted on his dream until he came to Australia. Like the gay US flight attendants interviewed by Hochschild (2003) in the 1980s, Takashi believes that gay men make ideal flight attendants because they are sensitive and caring, have good listening and conversational skills, a good sense of humour and physical strength. Takashi was the only participant who was unambiguously committed to his work. He was extremely ambitious and, in the 14 months he had been working for *Flying High* at the time of the interview, had managed to achieve promotion to in-flight trainer. He told us that he was one of the first-ever Asian flight attendants to achieve that level at *Flying High*.

There are a number of commonalities in our participants' profiles. They all came of age and entered the job market after the Japanese bubble economy burst in 1989; the 1990s, Japan's so-called 'lost decade', must be considered their formative period. In Japan, their generation forms a distinct demographic variously described as パラサイトシングル ('parasite singles') or フリーター ('freeters'). 'Parasite singles' is a generally negative term introduced by Yamada (1999) to refer to unmarried children who continue to live with and be dependent upon their parents well into their twenties or even thirties. The term 'freeter', which is coined on the basis of English *free* and German *Arbeiter* ('worker'), by contrast, is a positive term referring to the same demographic of young adults who are not regularly employed but 'pursue their dreams' by moving from one job to another. Both terms highlight the voluntary nature of being a 'parasite single' or a 'freeter'. However, as Genda (2005) explains, even if this aimlessness may appear as free choice to individuals, the reality is that they have little other choice as jobs with a structured career progression that could lead to lifetime employment have all but disappeared for this generation of Japanese. All our participants had worked in a variety of jobs and, with the exception of Takashi, none was expecting to work for *Flying High* for an extended period – a 'choice' that was inscribed in their three-year employment contracts (2007–2009). Indeed, at Australian low-cost carriers, the average age of their crews increases more slowly than the real age of the crew members, or even goes down over time, evidencing high levels of turnover and the replacement of crews with ever-younger entrants (Weller, 2008).

Our participants also have in common that, irrespective of whether they were hired in Japan (Eri, Juri, Ryoko) or in Australia (Fumie, Takashi), they had spent extended periods outside Japan, including Australia, prior to their employment with *Flying High*. They all described the initial purpose of their peregrinations as improving their English and experiencing a more liberal society than Japan. None had left Japan with the intention of migrating permanently and, despite that fact that, at the time of our interview, Australia and Japan were the two most 'fixed' locations in their lives, they all felt ready to move somewhere else if anything came up. Although they lacked deep local attachments, all of them considered a PR visa in Australia a good thing to have. However, the short-term nature of their employment contracts meant that the only realistic way to obtain PR was through family connections. Thus, again their 'choice' to be spatially relatively free-floating was inscribed in institutional practices, where the Australian state and their employers 'conspired' to make them permanently temporary.

In sum, the subjectivities of our participants 'happily' coincide with the neoliberal corporate workplace where industrial relations seem to have disappeared as an issue. Their personal flexibility, which they largely experienced as pleasurable and liberating, coincided with the labour flexibility demanded of them and which they increasingly experienced as an obstacle to leading fulfilling lives as they grew older. As such, their pursuit of flexible lifestyles simply helps to consolidate the global capitalist system, which in turn serves to trap them in a progressively more precarious situation, as Song (2009) has observed for demographically similar Korean women.

In the following we will now focus on the actual interview data to further explore the intersections between language, mobility and institutions with reference to Japanese and English.

The Value of Japanese

As part of its expansion strategy into the Asia-Pacific, *Flying High* advertised for Japanese-speaking flight attendants in 2007, both in Australia and Japan. The year 2007 was the first (and, at the time of writing in September 2011, the only) time *Flying High* recruited in Japan. For all our participants, those recruitment ads for Japanese-speaking flight attendants based in Australia appeared like a once-in-a-lifetime opportunity. Eri decided to apply because she was bored with life in Hong Kong and had a positive image of Australia, and particularly Sydney, from previous visits. Fumie applied because working as a flight attendant was a long-cherished dream of hers, which had been beyond her reach until this opening. She figured (correctly) that her Japanese language skills would outweigh her small height. Most airlines used to have minimum height requirements but with the emergence of low-cost carriers (and US anti-discrimination lawsuits) these have largely disappeared. Even so, for the job interview, Fumie wore padding inside her shoes to make her look a bit taller. Juri, who had wished to settle down in

Japan after her many years of travel and work overseas, applied because she could not find a job in Tokyo, and regular flight assignments to Japan would at least enable her to see her family periodically. Ryoko, too, was attracted by the prospect of being able to travel back and forth between Japan and Australia, as she feels attached to both locations. Additionally, being a flight attendant was the most prestigious customer service job she could imagine. Takashi, too, had held a lifelong dream of becoming a flight attendant and feels grateful to *Flying High* that they made it possible and, specifically, that they do not discriminate against (gay) men.

Fumie and Takashi, who by that time both held PR visas, applied in Sydney. Eri, Juri and Ryoko applied in Japan although only Juri resided in Japan at the time. When Eri and Ryoko were invited for an interview, they flew to Tokyo at their own expense from Hong Kong and Sydney, respectively. Job interviews were conducted in English in both these locations and none of the participants expressed any sense of anxiety about taking the interview in English. After all, they all had significant experience in English-speaking workplaces on top of many years of travel, English study and life in English-speaking environments. What worried them during the job interview then was the depth of their knowledge about *Flying High*'s destinations, the quality of their customer service skills, and whether they had the personality and looks that they thought *Flying High* was looking for. The urgency they all felt to get the job and the sense of destiny was best expressed by Takashi, who told the interviewer: 'My heart is already flying with *Flying High*!'

The fact that the participants were hired in different locations meant they received different employment contracts, based on different local-national employment legislation. We have already discussed above how such location-based contracts have come in for criticism with regard to Thai crews flying for Jetstar. While Thai labour laws are significantly weaker than Australian ones, the opposite is the case for Japan, and we suspect that that is the main reason why 2007 was *Flying High*'s only hiring season in Japan. At AUD4100 the monthly base salary of the participants hired in Japan was thus greater than that of those hired in Australia (AUD3200). However, flight attendants hired in Japan were not eligible for an AUD800 Japanese language allowance while those hired in Australia were. In our participants' understanding, the language allowance at *Flying High* was exclusive to the Japanese group, and flight attendants with other languages or who spoke Japanese as an additional language were not eligible to receive a language allowance.[7] In order to receive the language allowance, Fumie and Takashi had to sit a Japanese language test and thus formally prove their proficiency by achieving a certificate of *Nihongo Kentei* Level 6. Those hired in Japan, by contrast, did not need to have their Japanese certified. However, they had to have their English tested and a minimum score of 680 on the TOEIC was a requirement for being hired in Japan but not in Australia.

Ultimately, the salary and conditions of those of our participants hired in Australia and those hired in Japan were quite similar. When we asked them how they felt about their salaries (which were further increased by an overnight allowance of AUD150), all participants indicated that they were happy. Given the high cost of living and particularly accommodation in Sydney, they could not save but, as they were all single and without financial commitments such as a mortgage, they felt their wages enabled them to live a relatively carefree life. They had taken out insurance against various emergencies and misfortunes, and did not dwell on the fact that they were not able to save or build any equity for their old age. What discomforted them was the fact that they were aware of the low wages that their co-workers hired in other Asian countries received. They spoke about trying to hide their salary levels from those co-workers, who they thought had to work much harder to pull in less than half of what they earned. So, their satisfaction with their remuneration and conditions was not only an expression of the kind of life that their work allowed them to live but also an expression of the pressure and naked fear that the presence of underpaid colleagues doing exactly the same work created. The presence of 'cheap labour' made them feel sorry, worried and slightly guilty, as is evident in this quote from Eri:

Eri: 結構タイ人の子達やっぱ出来る子多いから。日本語。元日本の航空会社で働いていたとか多いんですよね。だから結構日本の日本語でサービスする事たたきこまれてる人達が多くって。関わらず、もう過酷な労働条件の下、ほんとにだからチープレイバーって言ったらチープレイバーなんですよねぇ。

Eri: Many Thai crew members are capable of speaking Japanese. Many used to work for a Japanese airline where they were strictly trained in customer service in Japanese. Still, they have to put up with such hard working conditions. Really, they are cheap labour.

They found it particularly unsettling that those underpaid Asians also spoke Japanese (but did not get a language allowance) and were also familiar with the Japanese style of customer service, which they uniformly considered superior to the Australian or Western style. The Japanese language and Japanese style of customer service were the two key areas where they unambiguously added value to *Flying High*. And yet, there too, they were replaceable because, the advertising rhetoric notwithstanding, quality did not really matter at *Flying High*, as Juri explained.

Juri: いっぱいいる。レジメに。日本の航空会社で働いていた人たちとかいるから。でも、もうほんっとたかが知れてるから。日本の会社とコードシェアとかに乗せたら、だから多分それは、後々問題に。
KT: あ、ほ〜んとに。喋れないの？
Juri: お飲み物は何に致しましょう？オレンジジュース。アップルジュース。みたいな。なんか問題があったら解決できるっていう事では。

Juri: In their resume, many Thai crew members include their work experience with a Japanese airline. But, it's not that good at all. If they fly on a code-share flight with a Japanese airline, problems arise.
KT: Oh really? They can't speak Japanese well?
Juri: 'What would you like to drink?' Like, 'Orange juice or apple juice?' Not at the level of proficiency where they could solve problems.

However, the threat of being undercut was not only coming from the natives of poorer Asian countries. As we said above, *Flying High* hired in Japan only once. However, from 2008 onwards *Flying High* began to hire Japanese nationals through another southeast Asian country, at conditions local to that country. While a more prosperous nation than Thailand, the base salary there is still significantly lower than the minimum wage in either Australia or Japan. To be undercut by about 60% by younger Japanese with a similar profile made them feel disposable and was only possible because of the widely circulating discourses about the desirability of flight attendant work, as Takashi explained.

Takashi: 結局、どんなに給料低くっても「あたしフライトアテンダントになりたい！」っていう若い日本人の女の子は数知れないでしょ？だから、いかにこれから会社に自分が貴重な存在になれるかだね。

Takashi: After all, no matter how low the salary is, there are endless numbers of young Japanese women who would say 'I want to be a flight attendant!' So, it's important to be seen as an asset to the company from now on.

Thus, despite the fact that they had been hired for their Japanese language skills and their experience in Japanese-style customer service, they felt that they would never be able to add enough value to *Flying High* to consider themselves worthy. Rather, they felt expendable.

Eri: でも私じゃなくてもいい訳じゃないですか？要は仕事に関して言うなら
ば、エアラインってどこもそうでしょうけど、誰か個人を必要として回って
る会社ってどこもないんですよね。きっと… 特にフライトアテンダントな
んて、若くてなりたい人もいっぱいいるし。だから、ね、それこそ誰でもで
きる仕事だと思うし、そういうのでね、私ってほんとに必要とされてるんだ
ろうか？とかふと思ったり。

Eri: But it doesn't have to be me, does it? In terms of my job, there is no
airline or company that needs one particular person. For sure, flight
attendant jobs are in demand as there are many young women who
want to be a flight attendant. I think anyone can do this job, and that's
why I sometimes wonder if I'm ever needed.

We now turn from Japanese as a selection criterion in the hiring process
to the ways in which the participants' identities as Japanese placed them
regularly in difficult positions as the expectations of Japanese customers
clashed with the services provided by *Flying High*. As 'designated' Japanese
flight attendants, our participants were most frequently rostered on flights
to and from Japanese destinations. Also, if there were problems with Japanese
customers, our participants were usually assigned to deal with them. This
placed them regularly in a difficult position as there was a clear mismatch
between Japanese customer expectations and *Flying High* service provisions,
and our participants were acutely aware that *Flying High* was falling short by
Japanese standards. As a result, they often had to bear the brunt of Japanese
customers' anger, as in this example offered by Ryoko.

Ryoko: お前日本人でねぇだろう。俺も会社立ち上げてやってきてるけど、お
前らみたいにどうたらこうたら、日本人として恥ずかしくねぇのか。み
たいな感じで。私は日本人代表じゃないけど@@@8 会社代表じゃ
ないけど@@@勝手に代表にされて日本人である事で。

Ryoko: He went like 'You are not Japanese! I run a business, but you all
are blah, blah, blah. Aren't you ashamed of yourself? Aren't you
ashamed to call yourself Japanese?' I was like, 'I don't represent
Japan.' @@@. I don't represent my company either @@@. He
made me a representative just because I'm Japanese.

Their most common response to such incidents was 'to let them wash over
me' and ignore them. Ryoko said it was her 'personal policy' to do only as
much as she was paid for, as does Juri.

Juri: もうあえてその努力をしてサービスやってます、っていうのは全く。私だ
から、とにかくうちの会社っていい加減だからその…毛布、オーバーナ

イトフライトなのに毛布がないとか。それを謝る時にやっぱりすごいね、
せっかくお金出してくれてるのにやっぱりお客さんにも文句があるか
ら、そん時あれだけど。でもまぁ私のせいじゃないし@@@

Juri:　I don't make an extra effort in customer service because our
company is so slack. Sometimes, we don't even have enough
blankets on overnight flights. I know customers are upset because
they paid for it, and we have to apologise. But it's not really my
fault@@@.

Although they understood that they were specifically in charge of
Japanese customers, another strategy to deal with the mismatch between the
high expectations of Japanese customers and their institutionalised inability
to meet those expectations was to refer any complaints to Australian colleagues, as Juri explained.

Juri:　また言葉が通じるから日本人変な所でごねると思うし。だからいつも何
か問題があったらオージーを連れて来て。外人に弱い日本人じゃないけ
ど、… 外人をガンっと連れてきて、その人がペラペラ話してそれを訳し
て、「こういっておりますが」っていうと収まるの… なのでもう日本、日
本にしない方がいい。このもうオージー！オーストラリア！ みたいな。こ
れの雰囲気。雰囲気を味わって@@@帰れるから。

Juri:　Japanese customers get more difficult with us because we have the
common language. That's why I bring in an Aussie when a problem
happens. Japanese are scared of foreigners. I bring in a foreigner, and
she will speak English and I translate it. Things get settled when I
translate and say 'This is what she's telling you'. So, we shouldn't
do it the Japanese way. Like, 'These are Aussies! This is Australia!
That's the experience.' They can go home with the experience of
Australia.

In sum, Japanese language skills had a distinct value when it came to
getting the job. At the same time, having been hired primarily on the basis
of their Japanese proficiency resulted in a strong sense of job insecurity as
other Japanese speakers were seen as being able to do the same job at ever
cheaper rates, depending on where they were based. The uncoupling of language and nationality/territory must thus be considered as a way to devalue
the commodity value of Japanese. Additionally, the value of Japanese proficiency and Japanese-style customer service was of limited value beyond job
entry because the conditions at *Flying High* were such that it was simply
impossible to meet the high expectations of Japanese customers. While our
participants dealt with this potentially stressful situation by 'letting it wash

over them' and by only doing as much as they were paid to do, they experienced considerable anxiety when it came to English, as we will explain in the next section.

The Burden of English

All our participants stressed repeatedly that the linguistic demands of their work – both in Japanese and English – were well below their proficiency levels. Prior to joining *Flying High*, they had all been led to believe that English proficiency levels for flight attendant work would have to be high but to their dismay, tinged with relief, they found that all that was needed was to be able to ask 'Chicken or beef?' and 'Apple or orange?'. That is how all of them caricatured the linguistic demands of their work to us. Nonetheless, English proved to be stressful for them – not because of the proficiency levels needed to do the job but because of *Flying High*'s English-only policy.

Passengers on *Flying High*'s international flights are served by multinational teams consisting of Australians, Japanese and other Asian nationals. With the exception of the provision of service to customers from the same national/linguistic background (e.g. Japanese flight attendant attending to Japanese customer), it is *Flying High* policy that all communication on board must be in English. Our participants found this policy particularly burdensome when it came to communicating with other Japanese crew members: while they were encouraged to speak Japanese to Japanese customers, they were prohibited from speaking Japanese to Japanese co-workers. In fact, the English-only policy extended to their time off-board, too, as it applies whenever and wherever they are in uniform.

Ryoko: そういうもうあからさまにするマネージャーとかもいますし […] ユニフォームだって覚えてる？みたいな感じで、ユニフォームだし英語で喋ってね。他のお客さんとかもいるから。とか。ユニフォーム着てる間はお客さんからみたら Flying High だって思われてるから、Flying High のクルーとしてちゃんとやっぱり、そういう風にして。

Ryoko: Some managers make it clear […] like, 'Remember you are wearing the uniform.' 'Speak English all the time when in uniform.' And like, 'Customers are always around.' 'When in uniform, customers identify you as representing *Flying High*.' 'Remember you represent *Flying High* as its crew member.'

All our participants found it inconvenient and bothersome to speak to Japanese colleagues in English and confessed to breaking the English-only policy when no Australians were around. They would switch to English as soon as an Australian came into sight (or earshot). They observed the same behaviour with other Asian crew-members, i.e. Japanese speakers broke the rule in the presence of Thai speakers, for instance, who also felt free to speak Thai to other Thai crew members in the presence of the Japanese but not in the presence of Australians. All participants confessed to this kind of illicit code-switching and, as a result, found – or felt – themselves under heightened linguistic surveillance. Ryoko, for instance, spoke about the feeling of being watched, particularly as she thought it was rude to respond in English if someone addressed her in Japanese.

Ryoko: あ、そういう時は日本語で喋ってますけど。でも感じる、オージーとか
が、ああ見てるなぁみたいな。で、そうするとやっぱちょっとして注意
されたりとか。

Ryoko: Well, I speak back to them in Japanese. But I feel it. The Aussies are watching us. Then we get warned later.

All our participants claimed that being reported to management by Australian co-workers for violating the English only rule was common. Any reported violation affected not only their reputation but also their performance review, including their promotion prospects. According to our participants, there are two levels of promotional opportunities for flight attendants at *Flying High*: flight attendants can become in-flight trainers (a status only Takashi had achieved) and beyond that, crew supervisor. While Takashi aspired to become a crew supervisor, Eri, Fumie, Juri and Ryoko were convinced that any promotion was out of their reach. An in-flight trainer is someone to whom new flight attendants are assigned for the first few weeks of their work for on-the-job training. A crew supervisor's duties include overseeing the crew of flight attendants on any given flight, making in-flight announcements, troubleshooting, dealing with customer complaints, communicating with pilots and writing flight reports. Our participants said that almost all in-flight trainers and crew supervisors were Australian. Indeed, Takashi prided himself on being only one of a handful of Asian in-flight trainers at *Flying High*. The reason the women initially gave for their lack of aspiration was that they felt that their English would not be enough to handle communication in an emergency situation. Given their obvious high proficiency levels this seemed surprising and when we probed further, they also confided that English was a terrain where race was played out. Juri, for instance, felt alienated because there were no Asians in managerial positions.

Juri: 上がね　オーストラリア人。ま、だからまぁそういう所でなんかこう、差別的なものじゃないけど、あ、やっぱり私達って第2外国人だなぁみたいな。まぁそれは感じますよね。

Juri: People in management are all Australian. That makes us feel discriminated, feeling like we are second class foreigners. That's what I feel.

When they said they did not have the English for managerial positions, they really seemed to say that they did not have authority in situations of inter-racial conflict, as Fumie explains.

Fumie: で、あのう、私、正直マネージングスキルあると思うんですよ。あのうマネージングもやってたし、日本でも。管理能力は全然できると思うんですけど、でも、やりたくないんですね。なぜそう思うかっていうと、管理できないから。っていうよりも、やっぱりそのネイティブイングリッシュスピーカーじゃないので、[...] で、しかもオーストラリアの会社で一番最初全部アナウンスとかは、全部マネージャーがやるんですよ。' Good morning, ladies and gentlemen. Welcome to ブラーブラー'、とかっつって。

KT: うん。全然できるじゃない!

Fumie: 違う、違う。でも出来るんですけど、でもやっぱりネイティブじゃない。オーストラリアのネイティブじゃない。やっぱりアクセントは絶対にあるし、で、やっぱりその緊急のエマージェンシーになった時のやっぱりそこまで　あれだけれども、でも、やっぱり緊急時のそうやっぱ人の命とか... うちらはやっぱりサービス要員の前に保安要員なんですよね。complaint のハンドルはできない事もないかもしれない。多分できると思う。普通の complaint も対応してるから。だけれども、多分 big complaint か何かなった時にじゃ、オージーのね下のクルーの子が complaint になって、じゃあマネージャー出せって私がぽ〜んって行った所で、はぁ?ってやっぱり。無きにしも非ずなんですよ。

Fumie: I think I have good management skills. I used to be a manager, too, in Japan. I am capable of managing, but I don't want to do it. Because I won't be able to manage. Or more like because I'm not a native English speaker. [...] also, managers have to do the announcements, like 'Good morning, ladies and gentlemen. Welcome to blah, blah, blah.'

KT: You can do that!

Fumie: No, no. Well, I could. But I'm not a native speaker. Not an Australian native speaker. I definitely have an accent, and in case of an emergency. We are safety providers first before we are

customer service staff. Maybe I can handle *complaints*, too.
Probably, I can. I have been able to manage *complaints* so far. But
in case of *big complaints*, and an Australian subordinate receives a
complaint, a manager gets called in, and I show up, it would be
like 'What?!' That's not an unlikely scenario.]

That Fumie is right and the scenario is not unlikely at all is confirmed by
Takashi, who describes how Australian trainees sometimes refuse to accept
Asian in-flight trainers. He himself had at that point only ever trained one
trainee, an Asian, and so wasn't speaking about his personal experience.

Takashi: だから多分、アジア人の人から習いたくない人も多いんだと思う。オ
              ージークルーの人はね。でもやっぱりアジア人クルーに習うと、結
              構あのう後でコンプレインしている新人の子もいる。…日本人とか
              言わないけどね。オージーの人は言う。はっきり言う。
KT: はぁ～。未だにあるのか。
Takashi: あるある。[…]
              うん。なんで英語もろくに喋れんのに習うのか?っていうのもある
              のね。

Takashi: Many don't want to be trained by Asians. Particularly
              Australian crew members. New recruits complain if they are
              trained by an Asian crew member. Japanese don't. Australians
              don't hesitate to complain.
KT: Something like that still happens, huh?
Takashi: Yeah, yeah, […] Like, 'How come I have to be trained by some-
              one who can't speak English properly?' It's like that.

White Australian co-workers are not the only ones reportedly having
difficulties dealing with Asian managers. Our participants repeatedly told us
stories of white Australian customers refusing to accept the authority of
Asian flight attendants, complaining about their English or pointing out
their visibility. Consequently, only relatively small contingents of Asian
flight attendants were rostered on routes that mostly carried Australian holi-
daymakers. Our participants were regretful that this practice limited their
opportunity to fly to 'fun' destinations such as Bali or Hawaii.

In sum, 'English' is a key site of contestation over the identity of what it
means to work for an 'Australian' airline. As we said earlier, the Australian-
ness – just as the Asian-ness – of *Flying High* is mostly a discursive construction and only to a lesser degree a material reality. 'English' is a terrain where
that discursive construction is achieved. *Flying High*'s English-only policy
makes the airline look (or sound) Australian. However, no matter how good

their English, speaking English cannot erase the embodied identities of our participants as Asians and, implicitly, as 'non-Australian'. This finding is in line with our observation elsewhere that, in multicultural Australia where race has become unmentionable, 'English proficiency' has come to serve as code for race (Piller & Takahashi, 2011a, 2011b).

Conclusions

In this chapter we have explored the selection processes played out on the terrain of Japanese and English in a prototypically mobile, neoliberal workplace, namely a low-cost airline operating in the Asia-Pacific. Flight attendant work for low-cost carriers such as the airline we have named *Flying High* is low-skilled, physically demanding, increasingly poorly paid and offering hardly any structured further training or career progression. Nonetheless, many discourses – both fictional and non-fictional – conspire to maintain the flight attendant glamour of a bygone era. Consequently, aspiring candidates have to invest heavily to gain entry into this job. Our participants had all invested many years of their lives in perfecting their English and their customer service skills to the levels that made them eligible to be considered for work with *Flying High*. Despite their substantial investment, the rewards were meagre and, in terms of career progression, the job seemed, for all except one, the end of the road. The best hope our female participants had was to find a partner and start a family so as to escape their dead-end job. The fact that the men they met in the course of their work were undesirable and that shift work limited their opportunities to meet potential partners outside work was a source of considerable anxiety for the women.

In addition to their desire for English and the West that shaped their careers prior to gaining entry to work at *Flying High*, it was their proficiency in Japanese that was most immediately relevant during the selection process. They were employed by *Flying High* because their linguistic, cultural, national and racial identities offered a fit with *Flying High*'s expansion strategy into Asian markets, particularly the Japanese market. At the same time, the recognition that they had been hired for their generic identity attributes rather than their personal achievements served to instil a sense of precariousness and insecurity. It was a constant reminder that there were many younger competitors with exactly the same attributes who could be hired in locations with lower wages and less stringent labour laws than Japan and Australia.

Finally, while their identities as Asians and as speakers of Japanese were an asset for *Flying High* internationally, they were a liability within Australia. The company's English-only policy can be understood as a way of holding on to an 'Australian' identity while being a multinational corporation that conducts different parts of its operations in whichever location generates the most profit for that particular aspect of the operation. As such, it seems to us that language and identity work in the context we have explored here is best understood as entirely subject to the profit motive (see also Duchêne, 2011, for a similar conclusion about language work at a Swiss airport).

We close by noting a large black spot in our data and our analysis: our participants saw themselves through the lenses of language, culture, nation, location and race and it was these aspects of their identities that enabled them to gain work as flight attendants and to perform that work well; it was also these identities that were remunerated and where they experienced inclusion and exclusion. What is strikingly absent from our data are our participants' class identities and their identities as workers. We contend that the success of the neoliberal multinational corporation is to a large degree built on identity politics and their moral relativism, while rendering class struggles and labour activism built on worker solidarity not only invisible but unimaginable.

Notes

(1) http://detail.chiebukuro.yahoo.co.jp/qa/question_detail/q1111062826, accessed 15 September 2011.
(2) http://allabout.co.jp/gm/gc/294698/, accessed 15 September 2011.
(3) E.g. http://www.ca-style.jp/ or http://www.airline.ecc.jp/, accessed 15 September 2011.
(4) http://www.aviationstudycentre.com/cabincrew.htm, accessed 15 September 2011.
(5) See http://www.travelvision.jp/news/detail.php?id = 48962 and http://www.his-j.com/tyo/group/2011mh_cabinattendant/ for details, accessed 15 September 2011.
(6) Funded by a Macquarie University Research Development Grant. We also gratefully acknowledge the research assistance provided by Kyoko Kanda.
(7) Formally, the requirement for the language allowance was to be able to pass the Japanese language test *Nihongo Kentei* at Level 6. Practically, this meant that only native speakers of Japanese were eligible because *Nihongo Kentei* is a Japanese language test aimed at native speakers. It is primarily formal levels of Japanese, including the number of *kanji,* that are being tested. See http://www.nihongokentei.jp/ for details, accessed 15 September 2011.
(8) @ indicates laughter.

References

Baum, T.G. (2010) From upper-class to underclass. Working the skies: Representations and reality, 1930–2010. CAUTHE Annual Conference, 1 February 2010, Hobart, Tasmania. http://strathprints.strath.ac.uk/15571/, accessed 15 September 2011.
Cannane, S. (2011) Jetstar crew members claim exploitation. *ABC Lateline*. http://www.abc.net.au/lateline/content/2011/s3279602.htm, accessed 15 September 2011.

Duchêne, A. (2011) Néolibéralisme, inégalités sociales et plurilinguisme: l'exploitation des ressources langagières et des locuteurs [Neoliberalism, social inequalities and multilingualism: The exploitation of linguistic resources and speakers]. *Langage et société* 136, 81–106.

客室乗務員 [Flight attendant] (2011) Wikipedia article. http://ja.wikipedia.org/wiki/%E 5%AE%A2%E5%AE%A4%E4%B9%97%E5%8B%99%E5%93%A1, accessed 25 June 2012.

Genda, Y. (2005) *A Nagging Sense of Job Insecurity: The New Reality Facing Japanese Youth.* Tokyo: International House of Japan.

Hochschild, A.R. (2003) *The Managed Heart: Commercialization of Human Feeling.* Berkeley: University of California Press.

Itakura, H. (2006) 語学を生かして、世界で働く:国際関係、旅行、語学、ビジネス *[Career Overseas by Using Language Skills: International Relations, Travel, Language Teaching, Business].* Tokyo: Rironsha.

Piller, I. and Takahashi, K. (2006) A passion for English: Desire and the language market. In A. Pavlenko (ed.) *Bilingual Minds: Emotional Experience, Expression, and Representation* (pp. 59–83). Clevedon: Multilingual Matters.

Piller, I. and Takahashi, K. (2010) At the intersection of gender, language and transnationalism. In N. Coupland (ed.) *Handbook of Language and Globalization* (pp. 540–554). Oxford: Blackwell.

Piller, I. and Takahashi, K. (2011a) Language, migration and human rights. In R. Wodak, B. Johnstone and P. Kerswill (eds) *Handbook of Sociolinguistics* (pp. 573–587). London: Sage.

Piller, I. and Takahashi, K. (2011b) Linguistic diversity and social inclusion. *International Journal of Bilingual Education and Bilingualism* 14 (4), 371–381.

Sandilands, B. (2011) Xenophon bill would outlaw foreign cabin crews on domestic Australian flights. *Crikey.* http://blogs.crikey.com.au/planetalking/2011/07/29/xenophon-bill-would-outlaw-foreign-cabin-crews-on-domestic-australian-flights/, accessed 15 September 2011.

Sasaki, M. (2006) 英語でリッチ! *[Get rich with English!].* Tokyo: Ark Shuppan.

Schulte, P. and Zhu, Y. (2005) Globalisation and labour relations in Australian airlines industry: A case study of pilot experience. *Proceedings of the 19th Conference of the Association of Industrial Relations Academics of Australia and New Zealand* (pp. 181–188). http://airaanz.econ.usyd.edu.au/papers/schulte_Zhu.pdf, accessed 15 September 2011.

Singapore Girl (2011) Wikipedia article. http://en.wikipedia.org/wiki/Singapore_Girl, accessed 25 June 2012.

Smith, F.L. Jr., and Cox, B. (2008) Airline deregulation. *The Concise Encyclopedia of Economics.* http://www.econlib.org/library/Enc/AirlineDeregulation.html, accessed 15 September 2011.

Song, J. (2009) Between flexible life and flexible labour: The inadvertent convergence of socialism and neoliberalism in South Korea. *Critique of Anthropology* 29 (2), 139–159.

Thomas, W.D. and Nations, S. (2009) *Flight Attendant.* New York: Gareth Stevens Publishing.

Weller, S.A. (2008) Are labour markets necessarily 'local'? Spatiality, segmentation and scale. *Urban Studies* 45 (11), 2203–2223.

Yamada, M. (1999) パラサイトシングルの時代 *[The Age of Parasite Singles].* Tokyo: Chikuma Shinsho.

6 (De)capitalising Students Through Linguistic Practices. A Comparative Analysis of New Educational Programmes in a Global Era

Luisa Martín Rojo

Reconfiguring the Linguistic Map in a New Sociopolitical and Economic Context

This chapter is part of a long-term study carried out over the last decade by a group of researchers in Madrid (Spain), seeking to better understand the role played by linguistic practices in the implementation of educational programmes and, particularly, new educational linguistic programmes (such as the Spanish as a second language programme for descendants of non-Spanish-speaking migrants) in maintaining, justifying and legitimating social selection processes in contemporary Spain (see Alcalá Recuerda, 2011; Mijares & Relaño Pastor, 2011; Patiños Santos, 2011). Within this frame, my personal research has taken into account the rising dropout rate of the immigrant population at the conclusion of obligatory education and their premature entry into the job market as unskilled workers, focusing on the role of the schools, and particularly on the role of linguistics practices in the classrooms, in the construction of social inequality (Martín Rojo, 2010, 2011). This chapter is a further contribution to that research. New linguistic programmes, aimed at the whole school population and particularly at students who are considered above average, are also included in the analysis (in this respect, see also Mijares & Relaño Pastor, 2011). Thus, a comparative analysis of the different programmes has been made to examine whether a hierarchisation process of the different linguistic programmes (and hence of the students) is taking place.

This analysis is focused on the educational programmes implemented in the Madrid region, one of the richest in Spain (at least before the current financial crisis), in which new economic forces and changing migration flows seem to have the most impact. In this region a neoliberal policy has been implemented for over 10 years, and particularly so since 2004, with the election of regional president, Esperanza Aguirre, representing the (conservative) Popular Party. Madrid has traditionally been a destination for migration from other parts of Spain, and was during the last two decades one of the preferred goals of workers from other countries, mainly from (and in this order) Ecuador, Colombia, Romania, Peru, Morocco, Bolivia, China and the Dominican Republic. The proportion of immigrants to local inhabitants in the city of Madrid is approaching that of other European cities like Barcelona, London, Paris and Amsterdam. According to the data published by Madrid City Hall, students of foreign origin now represent around 15.5% of the total school population in the Madrid region, while in the city centre this figure rises to 34% (see Madrid City Council, 2005). As a result, the cultural and sociolinguistic environment has also evolved and school populations are less homogeneous than they used to be. Indeed, over 50 languages can now be heard within the primary schools in the region (Broeder & Mijares, 2004).[1] However, this tendency seems to have changed recently with the current crisis. For the first time in recent years, immigration is decreasing.

This brief introduction highlights the extent to which Spain in general, and Madrid in particular, reflects the impact of the current social transformation and changes in the economy, and specifically the diasporic and migration-related mobility of individuals around the globe, together with the demands of professionals trained to work in a global market for a general picture of the socio-political transformation of Spain, see Piedrafita, Steinberg, and Torreblanca, 2006). Thus, the schools in Madrid, as in other parts of the world, are being transformed.

It is in the context of these trends – increases in population flows, and a progressive incorporation into a global economy – that the two new educational linguistic programmes, described above, have been implemented. These programmes are in fact shaped by the regional linguistic policy. The regional government has not publicly declared its linguistic policy, although it has made significant interventions in the language field, focusing on Spanish as the transaction language in social services and in the administration, and promoting the incorporation of other languages related to tourism and other economic interests.

Within this framework of a rapidly evolving society and economy, the aim of this article is to explore the role played by languages in these changes, and their consequences for language policies and educational programmes. The implementation of these new linguistic programmes in education has influenced the definition of the 'language of instruction', but, as I explore in this chapter, this implementation has also had a broader impact on how language and cultural capital are valued, on students' trajectories, and on how schools organise their activities. In order to understand how these social processes take place, we carried out a comparative analysis of the educational linguistics programmes implemented in a Madrid secondary school, in which both linguistic programmes were provided simultaneously until last year, when the Spanish as a second language programme was withdrawn.

Analysis of the interactional dynamics within the classrooms, and of in-depth interviews with teachers and students, shows how symbolic capital is managed in both programmes, and enables us to consider whether this management could give rise to the processes of capitalisation and decapitalisation that I propose (Martín Rojo, 2010).

In the next section, 'New Educational Programmes for a Global Era', I present the socio-educational context of this reconfiguration of the linguistic map. The analytical approach and the ethnographic site are presented in the section following, entitled 'A Sociolinguistic Ethnographic Approach to Explore a Social Process of Selection through Linguistic Practices in Villababel Secondary School'. In order to understand how these social processes take place, I then present a comparative analysis of the educational linguistics programmes implemented in a Madrid secondary school, in which both linguistic programmes were provided simultaneously until 2010, when the Spanish as a second language programme was almost withdrawn. That section, 'The Management of Linguistic Resources: A Comparative Analysis', analyses the interactional dynamics within the classrooms (participants' linguistic choices and practices, linguistic norms, interpretation of the linguistic choices by participants, etc.), showing how symbolic capital is managed in both programmes, and enabling us to consider whether this management could give rise to processes of capitalisation and decapitalisation among the students studied (see also, for these processes, Martín Rojo, 2010). The implementation of these new linguistic programmes in education has influenced the definition of 'language of instruction', but could also have a broader impact on how language and cultural capitals are valued on students' trajectories. In the section on 'Social Mobility, Linguistic Ideologies and Education Programmes', some conclusions are drawn on the social implications and the linguistic ideologies which shape linguistic practices and the contradictions and inconsistencies which emerge. The final section concludes.

New Educational Programmes for a Global Era

To shed some light on the interest raised by the social, economic and educational changes that have taken place in Spain in recent decades and, in particular, their impact on language management in schools and its social implications, this chapter begins by opening the doors to a classroom in the Madrid region to see just what is happening in relation to the distribution and management of linguistic and cultural capital by participants, and the potential consequences of this. The following excerpts illustrate some of the developments in schools over the last few years that have arisen from the attempts to adapt education to new communicative and neoliberal demands (following related work by Duchêne & Heller, 2011). This adaptation is governed by certain principles, of course, and follows specific national and economic guidelines that will be analysed in this chapter.

Excerpt 1[2] introduces us to a common classroom situation, illustrating the kind of programmes which have been designed to deal with social transformations and with increasing social and linguistic diversity. This excerpt comes from a history and geography class in the second year of compulsory secondary education (Educación Secundaria Obligatoria (ESO)) in a school in a working-class neighbourhood south of Madrid.

In this history class, the language of instruction is no longer Spanish, but English. Moreover, the teaching focus has changed: the teacher does not consider the class content as the sole aim of his educational task, but also the linguistic form, specifically the students' English pronunciation, as shown in line 2 and lines 11–13, where the teacher explicitly points out the problem to the student and what he might need to do to prevent potential confusion.

Excerpt 1[3]   Mario (teacher); David A (student)

1	**David A**	he find an unknown
2	**Mario**	he what?
3	**Student**	he found
4	**David A**	he found
5	**Mario**	thank you
6	**David A**	[he found] =
7		[he found

8	**David A**	= an unknown new continent between
9	**Mario**	Mm
10	**Alex**	he found
11	**Mario**	ok I think I need I need your
12		pronunciation / here a better
13		pronunciation here I understood

This English–Spanish bilingual programme began to be implemented in Madrid in 2004/2005 in primary education, and in 2008/2009 in secondary education. During 2008/2009, there were about 180 such bilingual schools at primary level, distributed throughout the region.[4] In primary schools, bilingual education is based on a whole-school approach; that is, all the children at the school have the same educational opportunities, regardless of socio-economic or other circumstances. In secondary education, however, bilingual education is not offered to the whole school, but is only available for those students considered competent in the two languages of instruction, Spanish and English. Thus, in this secondary school there is only one group taking the bilingual programme in each grade. The students in this group have either successfully completed a bilingual programme in primary education or have demonstrated sufficient competence in both languages to enter the secondary education programme. This condition represents a de facto selection of students regarded as above average. The facts and figures show that in secondary schools those enrolled are mainly Spaniards and, occasionally, Spanish-speaking newcomers from Latin America. Other newcomers arriving from non-Spanish-speaking countries such as India or Pakistan could be denied access, despite their knowledge of English, if their written and spoken skills in Spanish are not considered sufficient for them to attend classes given in this language (such as Spanish language or mathematics).

Over the past five years, the Madrid regional government has made great efforts to promote the knowledge of other European national languages (mainly English), and to overcome the former monolingualism in the education sector. This greater openness to other languages is rooted in the public belief that the monolingual tradition inherited from the Franco era created a burden on the educational, cultural and scientific development of the country, and an obstacle to the personal and occupational advancement of its people. The bilingual evolution, however, has not benefited the languages of immigrants, or the other languages used in Spain, but rather has strengthened the position of English, a language from another EU nation-state, and one that is already highly valued.

As we see in Excerpt 1, this new programme for bilingual instruction has been developed using a content-based approach,[5] known in Europe as content and language integrated learning (CLIL; see EURYDICE, 2006, for an over-view of the implementation of this programme in the EU). This model con-trasts with the content-based programmes implemented in Canada and the USA, giving that in this place the target language is an international lan-guage of prestige that is not the language of origin of any of the country's minorities. This fact underlies some of the fundamental characteristics of this programme, such as its undeniable prestige and elitism. For example, on comparing what happens in the dual language programmes in Spanish and English, implemented in cities like New York, the commodification of Spanish as a language to open up career opportunities and enable a certain degree of upward mobility is still in its infancy, while in the case of English-language instruction in Madrid, this is an established phenomenon. In New York, on the other hand, Spanish is the language of the Hispanic minority, and has a corresponding association with certain social and ethnic groups and with the lower standing in which they are generally regarded.

Excerpt 2 presents another kind of linguistic education programme, one that coexists with the first in Madrid schools. The aim of the programme is to teach Spanish, as the language of instruction in Madrid schools, to incom-ing students from non-Spanish speaking countries. In this particular class, the students are mainly from Morocco.

In this programme, the language of instruction is 'Spanish only' (see Martín Rojo & Mijares, 2007). In fact, this class is Spanish as a second lan-guage for newcomers, who need to learn the language in order to integrate fully into the school. Nevertheless, as we see in the excerpt, the class cannot be seen as monolingual; rather, the students contribute their linguistic capi-tal, or at least try to do so, as part of the learning process (see Fatima's con-tribution at lines 8–11 and the teacher's immediate and deliberate inattention to this form of capital as a means of truncating it in favour of her educational agenda, lines 12–15: Spanish only).

Excerpt 2⁶: Alicia (teacher); Fatima (student)

1	**Alicia**	¿dudas¿	*any questions¿*
2	**Todos**	Muchísimas	*lots*
3	**Alicia**	pero si no has empezado a	*but you haven't even started*
4		leer	*reading*
5		{risas, que se mantienen	*{laughter, continues*
6		durante las siguientes	*during the following*
7		intervenciones}	*items}*
8	**Fatima**	¿sabes qué es dudas en	*do you know what questions*

9		árabe / profe¿	*means in Arabic / miss¿*
10	**Alicia**	qué	*what*
11	**Fatima**	**&gusanos**	*&worms*
12	**Alicia**	&gusanos es / bueno pues /	*worms is / well then /*
13		mira / gu- / no gusanos no	*look / wo- / worms you*
14		tenéis / no estaba entre	*don't have to / that*
15		los animales que he copiao	*wasn't among the animals I*
16		/ pero la MARIPOSA / tiene	*copied out / but the*
17		una etapa de su vida que	*BUTTERFLY / has a stage in*
18		es **gusano** // pues fíjate /	*its life when it's a worm*
19		tiene una etapa de su vida	*// so think about it / it*
20		que es dudas / la mariposa	*has a stage in its life*
			*that is **questions**/ the*
			butterfly

This second excerpt is taken from a class set up as part of an educational programme which began to operate in Madrid in 2002.[7] In fact, it wasn't until this year that the first specific programme for the children of immigrant workers was set up, namely the 'Welcome Programme', in which a fundamental role is played by the Spanish as a second language programme, called 'Bridging classes' (for an in-depth study of this programme, see Martin Rojo, 2010; Martín Rojo & Mijares, 2007; Pérez Milans, 2007a, 2007b). The focus of this programme is to develop skills in the language of instruction, so that students with limited proficiency in this language may make the transition to mainstream instruction as rapidly as possible. In order to do so, the students attend mainstream classes and receive additional periods of instruction aimed at developing language skills in the language of instruction. In this respect, the Madrid region parallels the general trend observed in many European countries. In terms of general approaches to supporting students with limited proficiency in the language of instruction, a surprisingly homogeneous picture emerges (see PISA Report, 2003: Tables 5.4a and 5.4b).[8] On many occasions, the aim that this programme should facilitate the transition to mainstream schooling is not achieved, and students are transferred from this programme to others that lead to early entry into the labour market. As I have observed previously, the orientation applied to language teaching in these classes, and the fact that emphasis is not placed on preparing the content and language skills required in the subjects studied in the mainstream groups, is one of the main reasons why full integration does not take place (Martín Rojo, 2010).

Thus, in both cases – the English/Spanish bilingual programme and the Spanish as a second language programme – a linguistic goal is established, which for the students means that they must master a new language of instruction. Both programmes feature the underlying assumption that the provision of a second language increases the students' chances of academic success and social integration. Furthermore, in spite of the common goal proclaimed for the two programmes, they differ: (i) in the financial support received from the regional government (one in three of all primary schools in the area are now 'bilingual'); (ii) in the teaching procedures, methods and goals (content-based language teaching versus Spanish as a second language) practised by the teachers; and (iii) in the students targeted (the Spanish as a second language programme provides the instructional language to newcomers to the educational system, while the bilingual programme provides an additional language of instruction to students who are already within the educational system). In view of this, the following questions arise:

(1)   To what extent do everyday linguistic practices increase the differences between the two programmes? In particular, how does this occur through the way in which capitals are distributed and managed, and, more specifically, through processes of capitalisation and decapitalisation?

(2)   To what extent is the introduction of these two programmes changing Spanish schools? Could the prestigious Bilingual Education Programme (BEP) be contributing not only to devaluing the Spanish as a second language programme but also the Spanish monolingual mainstream programme. In particular, is the commodification of languages creating new programme hierarchies? And how is this hierarchisation of programmes being acknowledged (and voiced) by the participants (teachers/students)?

(3)   Is it possible that both the way in which the administration is managing these programmes and the way in which they are being implemented, i.e. the distribution of linguistic resources in the classrooms, are reinforcing social stratification and producing a social selection process? If so, how is social stratification taking place? And what are the consequences of these practices and ideologies for students coming from different backgrounds?

The main focus of the following sections is to address the above questions.

A Sociolinguistic Ethnographic Approach to Explore a Social Process of Selection Through Linguistic Practices in Villababel Secondary School

In order to study the linguistic and educational transformation of schools in the Madrid region, the team involved in this R&D project on educational linguistic programmes implemented in Madrid carried out ethnographic field-work in a secondary school in southeast Madrid, in a traditionally working-class area. This area has experienced the arrival of diverse groups of migrants over the years, both national, i.e. people who originally lived in Spanish regions other than Madrid, such as Andalusia, Castilla-La Mancha and Extremadura, and who settled here in large numbers in the 1960s, and foreign immigrants, who have been coming in different waves since the early 1990s, and who now form an important proportion of the population in this neigh-bourhood. Migrant students, mainly from Ecuador, Morocco and Romania, represent 25% of the student population. The school has a pyramidal struc-ture, with seven groups in the first grade of compulsory secondary education (ESO) and only one group in the top grade (*Bachillerato*), reflecting the high dropout rate between ESO and the advanced levels. Students in the English bilingual programme constitute only 180 of the 780 students in the school, and only seven of them are from a migrant background. Some 20 students, in two classes, were enrolled in the Spanish as a second language programme when this study was carried out. In addition, a considerable number of stu-dents (around 30%) were taking special programmes, with curricular adapta-tions to the regular syllabus. Following a critical approach, in analysing the data compiled I will explore the links between local discourse practices (such as interactional routines in classrooms) and wider, complex social processes, such as social selection processes. Thus, I develop a broad, encompassing approach, seeking to integrate sociolinguistics, critical discourse studies and ethnography, relating the analysis of classroom interactions to the discursive representations which emerge in agents' discourses, both of these factors being addressed through ethnography.

This perspective not only shapes the aim of the research, but also impacts on both the definition of what is actually under study and on how it is to be studied. The corpus of this research responds, therefore, to this critical approach, seeking to examine how teaching and learning are partly discur-sive. Thus, the analysis focuses on the educational practices in classroom interactions, in particular, on how they are organised and regulated, on the participation framework and on the placement of students' resources in the backstage or in the frontstage of the class setting.

As Cicourel notices, 'ecological validity' cannot be achieved solely by close analysis of recordings of interactions; it also requires broader ethnographic research that enables researchers to place a particular encounter in the context of texts, interactions and institutional practices. Thus, considering that 'bureaucratic settings trigger, guide and constrain communicative exchanges' (Cicourel, 2002: 4) and that 'speech events frame and are framed by informal (often implicit or tacit) organisational policies and routine work practices' (Cicourel, 2002: 3), as the principal researcher I designed a 'task-oriented ethnography' (Cicourel, 2000: 115), which was conducted by a team of four researchers.[9]

The corpus gathered comprised a total of 92 audio-recorded interactions and three filmed videos at the two educational programmes under study (the 'Bridging classes' and the bilingual programme (72 days going to the field-work site).[10] In line with a multimodal understanding of the interaction, we sought to address the different aspects constituting the unit of analysis (i.e. interactions in the classroom), which led us to note, as well as the oral exchanges, the teaching materials employed (books, maps, photocopies, etc.) and the writing activities (blackboard exercises, use of notebooks), as these comprise an inseparable part of the teaching and learning process. Together with these sets of data, institutional documentation (syllabus, classroom programmes, information on the composition of the student body, tests and scores, etc.) were compiled and analysed. In addition, in-depth interviews with teachers and students were carried out. Thus, the research team built up a net of discursive data and observations which contributes to the corpus' 'ecological validity'.

The analysis of linguistic practices enables us not only to capture the results of a social process of selection – for example, if students of a certain origin suffer exclusion – but also to reveal how, in social agents' everyday practices, such a selection takes place. My proposal, therefore, is that the analysis should focus on how symbolic capital is managed in the classroom.[11] From this analysis, we can both witness these practices and also achieve a better understanding of the social process of social selection itself. In this particular case, what the analysis shows is that selection occurs not only when access to a certain social field, such as education and specialised programmes in the field, is hampered, being reserved for those who meet the capital requirements established (in the academic world, the mastery of two languages), but also in day-to-day interaction, whereby speakers try to gain capital, to position themselves, to improve their situation and to learn. However, these capitalisation moves may be constrained or even impeded by other participants. In fact, in social selection processes, the impact appears to be particularly strong when the capital required in an educational

programme (for example, the academic variety of the language of instruction) is not presented, or when social agents are prevented from gaining
capital (see the section on 'Social Mobility, Linguistic Ideologies and
Education Programmes'). It is precisely this phenomenon, that of not providing and of preventing the capitalisation of social agents, which I term
'decapitalisation'.

Thus, my analysis will be focused on the distribution of symbolic capital
in the class. In order to do that, I shall apply Goffman's (1959) distinction
between backstage and frontstage (also used in classroom research by Heller
& Martin-Jones, 2001). Furthermore, this spatial metaphor allows us to see
the class from a perspective which is not teacher centred and also to take into
account tensions and conflicts among participants (see also Duff, 2002: 220).
Frontstage is where the performance takes place and where the performers
and the audience are present. When teachers decide who is a ratified participant and what is a relevant activity, a legitimate topic and a legitimate language to be used, they are also deciding what can be placed at the front. In
the backstage, on the other hand, there may appear facts, contributions,
topics and languages which are not considered a legitimate part of the class.
Given that students in the backstage manifest their loyalty as team members, resistance usually emerges here. However, in the course of resistance
sequences, students might conquer the frontstage and impose new topics,
languages and activities, as we will see in the following examples (see
Excerpts 3 and 5).

With this encompassing approach I address the question of how the distribution of symbolic capital through linguistic practices takes place:

> What languages, knowledge and participants can enter the scenario?
> That is, which elements are allowed frontstage and which are forced
> backstage.
>   This placement encompasses: (i) the languages and topics allowed at
> the front versus at the back; (ii) the knowledge presupposed and the
> inferences required; (iii) the patterns of participation allowed in relation
> to the frontstage versus backstage positions.

The data analyses made are interaction based (focused on some excerpts
from the 65 classroom interactions recorded in both programmes), but going
beyond the fine-grained scrutiny of language practices in education. The
corpus compiled for this research also includes the institutional documentation of the school and the educational programmes (school projects, subject
syllabuses, information on the composition of the student body, etc.), focus
groups with the students and two in-depth interviews with the teachers,
and data on students' marks and trajectories (triangulation).

The Management of Linguistic Resources: A Comparative Analysis

In order to study the management of symbolic capital, in this section my analysis focuses on which resources can enter the frontstage in both programmes. Excerpt (3) comes from the History and Geography class in the second year of compulsory secondary education in the English/Spanish bilingual programme cited above (as Excerpt 1). The teacher and the students are reading a text about Christopher Columbus, in which it is stated that America was an 'unknown new continent'. In line 2, Mario interrupts the reading. As the IRE (Initiation/Response/Evaluation) pattern shows, the teacher's focus is on the production of a 'correct' linguistic form (line 4), which is validated by the teacher in line 5 (thank you). This interactional pattern characterises the language-centred interactions, rather than content-centred ones (in Kasper's [1986] terms), because, as the previous IRE pattern shows, the teacher's focus is on the production of a standard or 'correct' linguistic form. Seedhouse (2004) has studied this type of exclusively form-focused or accuracy-focused classroom activity, in which the organisation of interaction, and the students' contributions, although perfectly acceptable in 'natural' conversations, are strongly constrained.

Alex intervenes, and again the teachers open a new accuracy-focus sequence in lines 2–3. David tries to continue, in line 7, and then the teacher interrupts again, this time focusing on the words 'an / unknown'. This sequence is interrupted by another student in line 13 with a statement in which we can see how Spanish erupts in the class and that this expression in colloquial Spanish, together with items in English, greatly amuses the class (line 15).

Excerpt 3[12]   Mario (teacher); David A and Mario (students)

	1	**Alex**	he found
→	2	**Mario**	ok I think I need I need your pronunciation / here a
	3		better pronunciation here I understood
	4	**David A**	he faund
	5	**Mario**	he faund
	6	**David A**	an / unknown
→	7	**Mario**	an unknown ok make it clear an unknown
	8	**David A**	an unknown a new continent between
	9	**Mario**	ok too many ans in here

10	**Student**	an unknown continent
11	**Mario**	an unknown new continent / a new unknown
12		continent
→ 13	**Student**	**pero** unknown **del todo no era**
14	*Translation*	***but it wasn't totally*** *unknown*
15		Everybody laughs
16	**David A**	Yes
17	**Mario**	yes it was [well u-unless you think that the
18		Vikings reached there which is really possible]

Furthermore, and what seems to be more significant, taking into account the other examples analysed in each of the linguistic programmes, is the fact that the teacher and the students share their interpretation of the communicative intent, with both languages emerging and co-existing in the class. The language shift is a contextualisation cue (Gumperz, 1982), which marks a feature of particular interest to the students, and an attempt to change the activity, from reading to a more interesting debate. Mario's answer in 17, and the acceptance of the student's remark as a new topic for the class, shows that for the teacher and in fact, for all the participants, this contextualisation cue does not index a change in the communication frame, from a class activity to a side-play event, or from involvement in the class to a show of resistance.

Naturally, this management of linguistic resources could be explained, at least in part, by the fact that all the participants share a knowledge of Spanish, and by the fact that Spanish is the traditional language of instruction in monolingual areas in Spain, and in Madrid in particular it is seen as the language of the nation, as well.

However, it is important to note that the appearance of Spanish is not exceptional in these lessons; on the contrary, it undertakes an important role as a working language and for learning.

In this regard, it is interesting to compare what happens in the above class with others where activities are not so teacher focused. Thus, I have analysed how Spanish is integrated into the development of more complex activities, which the teacher uses to activate and assess different language skills. Of particular interest is one that continued over several sessions, involving cooperative work in which students had to first gather and classify information on the different professions in the services sector. They were then asked to write an essay on one of these professions, and finally to present it to the rest of the class.

The analysis shows how the management of linguistic capital was not the same in the different stages of the activity. Thus, in the first session, in which the teacher explained the task to the students and how it would be evaluated, it was the teacher himself who encouraged the students to state – in Spanish – the service-sector professions they were aware of, and in which they were interested: *'you will give me / all the Spanish words you don't know / we will put them on the blackboard / and you will have an opportunity to say / how they are / said in English.'*

In this class, Spanish is often used as a learning tool for the students, but also for the teacher; moreover, when it is used, it is under the assumption that the students already possess some knowledge about the professions in the third sector economy, and they need to learn vocabulary.

At other moments in the development of the activity, the presence of Spanish acquires a different value. When the lesson material is being compiled by the student teams, the working language is Spanish and only isolated terms in English are employed. Nevertheless, the teacher does not insist on the use of English as the working language. Finally, when the class presentations are made, Spanish appears, framing the activity, although only among the students, for comments, jokes or to reduce nervousness, while the actual presentations are given in English.

Thus, the type of activity and the degree to which its development is teacher centred, or whether it requires more or less cooperative work influences how the two languages are used, and the roles they play. However, in all these cases, the teacher and the students take the same approach and believe that translinguistic practices (such as translation, language change, code-switching or code-mixing) do not impair the students' involvement in the activity (García, 2006: xiii; forthcoming).

In the Spanish as a second language class mentioned above, in Excerpt 2, we have seen how the students – in this case students from Morocco, who have lived in Madrid for some time – are still in the Bridging programme and are working and having recourse to other languages. Nadya, Fatima and Zaynab have been given a reading exercise but do not understand what they have to do. Alicia, the teacher, has instructed them to read about certain animals (dragonfly, chameleon, starfish, koala and butterfly). After reading the texts, the students are supposed to explain to each other in their own words what they have understood. In this excerpt, they are sharing an anecdote about animals in Arabic and are laughing among themselves.

In line 1 of Excerpt 2, Alicia, the teacher, asks *¿duda?* (any questions?). The pronunciation of 'duda' in Spanish corresponds to the word 'worm' in Arabic. In lines 8–11, we see that the student informs the teacher of the meaning in Arabic of the Spanish word and of the misunderstandings that could thus arise.

The teacher seems to respond to this attempt by the student to bring her closer to the learning process; indeed, the teacher plays with the double meaning of the word in line 20. In a subsequent interactional segment that has been omitted due to space constraints, Nadya initiates a narrative sequence, but the teacher ignores this attempt, refocusing on the activity in the next turn, and failing to take advantage of the linguistic resource offered by the student, to develop a possible activity based on animal names in the two languages, or perhaps on a related grammar subject that might be of interest, such as false friends, homonyms or polysemy. Thus, Arabic does not enter the frontstage, although the girls do play a part in this management of the languages, as shown in the continuation of the interaction in Excerpt 4[13].

Excerpt 4   Alicia (teacher); Fatima and Nadyar (students); Laura (researcher)

		(...)	(...)	(...)
	32		{5 minutos despuès}	{5 minutes later}
	33	**Zaynab**	({riéndose}: (() maɛeftš	({laughing}) ( )) I
	34		ɛela men kanfetšu (())	don't know what we're
	35		(3")	looking for here
				(3")
	36	**Nadya**	((estás muerta de	((literally, you're
	37		verdad))	really dead; I haven't
				a clue))
	38	**Alicia**	{hablando consigo	talking to herself}:
	39		misma}: a ver / eeh	let's see / eeh
→	40	**Fatima**	kantfeker e-nnhār	I remember that day
	41		(2") {los estudiantes	(2") {the students
	42		se ríen y hay mucho	laugh and there is a
	43		ruido en la clase.	lot of noise in the
	44		//llegan varios alumnos	class // several students come in
→	45	**Nadya**	menin kuntiI meña	when you were with you
	46		yemak	mother
	47	**Fatima**	((menin gālt lek))	((when she told
→	48		detha el essbitār dial	you...)) I took her to
	49		e-ssbeniol	hospital (.) Spanish Spanish

50		{cuando menciona la	{when she
51		palabra "español" o	mentions the word
52		"España", se oye una	"Spanish" or "Spain",
53		gran carcajada}	there is loud laughter}
→ 54	**Nadya**	e-ttbiba katqul liha	the doctor asked her if
55		wašandek ši duda u	she had any questions
56		hiya katqul liha duda	(duda) / and she
57		ej	answered QUESTIONS¿
			(¿DUDA¿) how
			disgusting!!
58		{Laura se ríe}	{Laura laughs}
59	**Alicia**	{hablando consigo	{talking to herself}:
60		misma}: vale	ok
61	**Nadya**	pero ¡tiene que decirla	but you have to say it
62		en español qué ((tu	in Spanish! what ((you
63		hablas))	speak))!
64		{se ríen de fondo las	{students laugh in the
65		estudiantes}	background}
66	**Fatima**	ġultlek sāfi	I've told you this is
			enough
67	**Nadya**	ella no sabía como dice	she didn't know how to
68		en español / y le dice	say it in Spanish /and
69		aal médico / ¡es duda!	she tells the doctor /
			it's doubt (duda)!
70		(4") {varias	(4") {some students and
71		estudiantes y Laura se	Laura laugh}
72		ríen}	
73	**Nadya**	((nunca lo voy a	((I'll never forget
74		olvidar))	it))
→ 75	**Fatima**	sāfi sāfi	(ok stop enough
76	**Alicia**	{ahora dirigiéndose a	{now addressing the
77		las estudiantes}: vale	students}: ok /from
78		/ de aquí para abajo	here on you don't have
79		no↓ / ¿vale¿ porque	to read /ok¿ Because
80		estos son todos nombres	these are all
81		científicos- >	scientific names- >
→ 82	**Nadya**	¿esto no voy a leerlo¿	so I don't have to read
83			this¿
84	**Alicia**	no =	no =

85	**Nadya**	Waja	*((ok))*
→ 86	**Alicia**	[=porque estoo	*[=because this*
87		noo =]	*isn'ttt =]*
88	**Nadya**	[(no hace falta) °]	*[(there's no need) °]*
89	**Alicia**	= de momento no vas a	*= right now you're not*
90		ser bióloga	*going to be a biologist*
91		{se ríe alguna	*{a student laughs*
92		estudiante en bajito}	*softly}*

In line 40, Fatima reinitiates the narrative introduced at the beginning of the class (Excerpt 2), which was not followed up by the teacher at the frontstage, and this time Nadya joins her to co-construct the narrative, by adopting the role of story recipient and animator (in line 45). This time she starts to construct the narrative in Arabic, and the teacher becomes an unaddressed participant. These two students play the most active role in the group co-construction of the narrative in the following turns. They are supposed to complete the activity designed by the teacher, while the teacher seems to be absorbed in preparing more materials for the class. In lines 48–49, Fatima presents the main character and the scene of the narrative (She took her mother to the hospital), and we see how the whole group can anticipate what is about to happen during the doctor's examination when she said the hospital was a Spanish one. The whole group has some knowledge of both languages and of the misunderstandings that may occur. They also seem to know about Fatima's mother's lack of competence in Spanish. In this line it is significant how, at the same time, she is dispossessed of agency ('I took her to the hospital'). Her role in the narrative is to represent a lack of knowledge 'as I didn't know …'). The whole anecdote is constructed out loud, without pretence, and during it the students switch between Arabic (40–57, 66, 75) and Spanish (61–63, 67–74) at different moments. In fact the narrative ends in Arabic, with Fatima attempting to return to the set task. The researcher, Laura (who understands Arabic), participates in the co-construction of the story, laughing at the climax, when the mother tells the doctor 'ʕDUDAʕ/ how disgusting!'. As a whole, this narrative reflects not only bilingual language competence, but also that a knowledge of both languages is positively valued by the students.

In this second attempt to build this narrative, the teacher seems to have changed her position of ratified participant to unaddressed participant, and her lack of visible orientation to the students shows how she has chosen not to attend to the discourse but to position herself as a bystander. One might think that this is because she is unfamiliar with one of the languages involved. However, as we saw in the example above, both Fatima and Nadya previously tried to include her in this exchange, and to advance the narrative to the frontstage and to incorporate it in the main activity. In this second attempt, the teacher remains untouched by the exchange, concentrating on her class papers, while the girls work, and talk about what has happened and laugh out loud.

Taking participation into account enables us to understand the internal organisation of the story, but also to see how these local practices reflect larger social and political processes connected to globalisation. This story is linked to a course of action and is part of the educational process. Thus, it sheds new light on the erasure of other languages (Irvine & Gal, 2000: 38), non-Spanish ones, which are relegated to the backstage. In the meantime, the students' insistence shows how they manage the linguistic resources of their growing repertoires. This ideological erasure is in part derived from the fact that a monolingual norm is often enacted in these classes, as shown by a sign on the wall stating the rule: 'Spanish only'. Students have contested this sign stating this norm, writing the same message in standard Arabic beside the Spanish, and this contestation has been in some way allowed. Thus, at least, the fact that these students are not monolingual is a statement visible at all times in the class.

Although the monolingual norm is imposed in the classroom through interaction, in this class the students do not renounce the use of these language varieties. Thus, the instances of code-switching that take place – i.e. the 'juxtaposition of grammatically distinct subsystems to generate conversational inferences' (Gumperz, 1982: 97) – constitute a discursive practice which is not identically valued and interpreted by the different participants. In the frame of Gumperz' conversational inference theory, code-switching comprises a contextualisation cue that 'index[es]' or 'invoke[s]' a frame of interpretation for the rest of the linguistic content of the utterance' (Gumperz, 1996: 379), and through which communicative intentions can be negotiated.

In this case, the students' use of Arabic as a learning tool and as part of the activity, and the lack of response by the teacher, shows, in the first place, a different valuation of languages. Let us recall, these students, like those in the English/Spanish class, are bilinguals in progress, and they also need to recall their home language as a learning strategy that allows them to collaborate and increase their involvement in the lesson. Translation, word games, highlighting 'false friends', comparing the linguistic features of the different languages ... these are all means of helping resolve doubts or of enabling the students to catch up with the class when they get lost, or of improving their performance (see Martín Rojo, 2010: 245–250). It is interesting to note that, while these linguistic resources are typically used in the so-called bilingual programme to facilitate acquisition, to raise students' awareness of linguistic and cultural differences and to enhance their cognitive and transferable skills, among other aspects, in this learning environment these resources are often ignored despite the students' efforts to the contrary. Might they be ignored as a result of the teacher's lack of bilingual competence and lack of training for this specific programme? Or might it be the result of the underlying ideology of the programmes? For the teacher, Arabic is not a language of instruction in Spanish schools, especially when a student 'has to learn Spanish', and when it is considered that maximum exposure to Spanish is required. Nevertheless, these students live in Spain and they are exposed to Spanish in many different places.

Depriving students of these learning tools has in fact a decapitalising effect. Ofelia García has shown similar effects drawn from the lack of adaptation of pedagogical practices to students' translingual practices (García, 2013). Data from a study of a secondary school for emergent bilingual students show how a pedagogy that builds on the fluid languaging of bilingual children holds much promise to meaningfully educate bilingual students, especially those from minority communities. In the same direction, Elana Shohamy analyses how students' multilingual functioning receives no attention in language testing practices, and this has a clear negative impact on their marks (see, among other publications, Shohamy, 2011).

With the concept of decapitalisation, I refer to the acts of discouraging capital formation, such as in the previous examples. If students do not learn Spanish, their access to higher education will be impeded, and they will be oriented to vocational educational programmes and to unskilled jobs in the labour market.

In this particular class, we see that, on the contrary to what happened in the bilingual class, the teacher and the students differ in their interpretation of code-switching. For the students, it clearly indexes a pedagogical frame, by means of which they try to follow the activity and to learn more. For the teacher, however, language switching does not seem to index a learning activity, but rather an in-group conversation, as evidenced by the teacher's lack of attention and response from the beginning of the narrative until line 86. This different interpretation can easily lead to misunderstanding, by means of which teachers' lack of attention can be seen as a lack of interest in the students' learning process, and the co-construction of the narrative can be seen as a lack of involvement in classroom activities.

Divergence in the interpretation of the students' multilingual practices activates an asymmetrical frame. In the cases examined, asymmetry is not due so much to the degree of linguistic knowledge as to diverse valuations of the different languages involved. The monolingual norm discourages students from assuming greater control over their own learning goals (Cummins, 1984: 28), limits their access to linguistic resources, and shows how control is exercised with respect to what learners can speak, in which spaces (frontstage versus backstage), how much they speak and what resources they can use (see Norton Pierce, 1995: 12).

Social Mobility, Linguistic Ideologies and Education Programmes

Although many such examples have been analysed previously in this and in other similar research, the focus of attention in this chapter concerns the consequences of the learning process itself, the management of students' linguistic capital and their social implications.

Bourdieu explained how schools perform this role in social stratification, through processes that 'convert' economic relations into symbolic capital (Bourdieu, 1977: 195). By means of this 'conversion', relations of dependence are presented as the consequence of inequalities of talent or educational ability. The concepts of 'conversion' and 'capital' immediately bring to mind others proposed by Bourdieu, namely those of 'value', 'measure' and 'market'. This value-giving process is inextricably bound to the representation of students as legitimate or non-legitimate participants in the education system. Furthermore, social and cultural conditions are changing and there is currently a great deal of tension and contradiction in the evaluation and legitimisation of knowledge capital, including languages.

As an effect of these changes, English language is a new required capital for success in Spanish schools. As Heller (1992, 1995, 2006) has shown, dominant groups rely on norms of linguistic resources and practices to maintain symbolic domination, while subordinate groups may use linguistic resources and practices, such as code-switching in everyday interactions within multilingual communities, to accommodate to a heterogeneous world, but also to resist or redefine the value of languages as symbolic resources in the linguistic marketplace. In fact, a pattern of imposition of new demands and standards and how they could be challenged and resisted by students' attempts to gain capital is what we observe in the examples analysed and seems to be the key to understanding the social implications of educational programmes, in particular in explaining educational failure in programmes based on a deficit approach (see Martín Rojo, 2010 for a detailed analysis of imposition and resistance in these educational programmes). The bilingual programme not only introduces new demands for success in education, but also provides some students with this capital. In this sense, a process of capitalisation can be detected in everyday practices in this programme.

Through the proposed concepts of capitalisation and decapitalisation (i.e. acts of subtracting capital and of discouraging capital formation), it can be understood how processes such as the dissimilar evaluations of linguistic resources and requirements, the deprivation of capital and the enforcement of new and more demanding norms, take place within everyday exchanges. And, what is more significant, through this kind of analysis, unified and static interpretations of the linguistic market concept are avoided.

The analysis of the distribution of symbolic capital between the frontstage and the backstage is related to capital evaluation and legitimacy. Bourdieu draws a parallel between the concept of symbolic capital and legitimate capital, because it is symbolic capital that defines what forms and uses of capital are recognised as legitimate bases of social positions in a given society. The effectiveness of symbolic capital depends on real practices of communication. Thus, the analysis of communicative practices reveals the participants' agency not only in reproducing, but also in challenging and resisting the value of symbolic resources and their social distribution in the linguistic marketplace.

Decapitalisation is seen to be a complex phenomenon which encompasses various aspects: firstly, the process by which value is assigned to linguistic varieties and communicative practices (for an in-depth analysis of the decapitalising effects of this educational focus and the selection of topics and methodologies, see Martín Rojo, 2010: 172–180). In relation to this, an analysis of processes of inference can also contribute to a better understanding of the different values assigned to the same linguistic practices by participants, and their differing interpretations of the activities in which they are engaged, and the different positions taken in relation to these activities and the distribution of capital.

The concept of decapitalisation refers to acts of subtracting capital, such as the lack of valuation of students' previous schooling, languages and knowledge, but also to acts of discouraging capital formation, as illustrated in the previous examples, with the tendency for educational programmes to orient students toward unskilled jobs and toward lower positions in the labour market (for the definition and functioning of this concept, see Martín Rojo, 2010).

If students from a migrant background achieve no more than an ESO diploma that gives no access to university education, but merely to unspecialised vocational programmes, they will reproduce a social class position in the wider social system, one of foreign workers with little access to skilled jobs. This social logic in the educational field may contribute to reproducing a social order that assigns foreign workers and their descendants to a weak social position. Similarly, although the process of decapitalisation does not necessarily lead to school failure, it may contribute to the rising dropout rate of the immigrant population at the conclusion of obligatory education and to their premature entry into the job market as unskilled labour.

The role of the school is analysed in a sociodemographic context that threatens the cultural homogeneity formerly observed in southern European schools. In this context, moreover, there seems to be occurring a progressive ethnic stratification[14] of the job market and of society as a whole (Cachón Rodríguez, 2002; García Borrego, 2007, 2011; López Sala & Cachón Rodríguez, 2007). If the educational programmes oriented to the integration of the students with a migrant background fail, schools would have a role in this stratification (Carrasco Pons, 2004; Franzé, 2002; Serra, 2004; Serra & Serra Palaudàrias, 2007).

The figures provided by the Ministry of Education[15] for this year (see Table 6.1) support this affirmation. That is, in everyday practice, older immigrant children are indeed propelled toward vocational and occupational studies related to an early entry into an increasingly ethno-stratified labour market.

The total figures for secondary studies after ESO by foreign students (FP: 7.39% and *Bachillerato*: 5.83%), are five percentage points below those for all students enrolled in PCPI (18.52%) – the vocational training programme below the secondary education level. López Blasco (2007: 37) stated that the educational level achieved by non-EU immigrants in their own countries was

Table 6.1 Foreign students in the general non-university education system as a proportion of all such school students, for the school year 2009–2010

Average proportion of foreign students in all non-university education	9.65%
Nursery education	6.94%
Primary education	10.97%
Obligatory secondary education (ESO)	12.09%
Initial professional qualification programme (PCPI)	18.52%
Occupational training (FP)	7.39%
Bachillerato (pre-university entrance)	5.83%

Source: VVAA (2011)

not being maintained by their children in Spain. This had also been observed some years previously, when Angulo Martín (2006: 50) commented that only one in 10 children of immigrant parents was enrolled in high school, while three times as many native Spanish students were so enrolled. This is evidence of a clear and disproportionate symbolic gap between the two student communities.

Conclusions

In relation to the research questions posed at the beginning of this chapter, we can conclude that, regarding the distribution of linguistic resources in the classrooms, the way in which the administration is managing these programmes and the way in which they are being implemented are reinforcing social stratification and producing a social selection process. The sons and daughters of immigrants not only inherit the 'immigrant status' of their parents, defined as a subordinate social status, but also, ultimately, the unskilled jobs reserved for them (López Blasco, 2007: 36).

The ethnographic data collected about students' educational trajectories confirm, at least in part, the potential effects of this decapitalisation process. In fact, our investigation clearly reveals society's lack of expectations, as a whole, regarding the schooling of students with a migrant background. Examination of the academic results obtained by such students at the schools visited shows there is a strong trend for them to leave school immediately following the obligatory stage, and a tendency towards early incorporation into the labour market (this has been corroborated by other studies: Cachón Rodríguez, 2002; Carrasco Pons, 2004; Franzé, 2002; García Borrego, 2007, 2011; López Sala & Cachón Rodríguez, 2007; Serra, 2004; Serra & Palaudàrias, 2007).

In relation to the second research question addressed by this chapter, we see that this new requirement, to master English and Spanish in an academic domain, could be contributing to devaluing the monolingual track and the Spanish as a second language programme by creating new programme hierarchies.

In interviews, teachers highlighted the social implications of this new requirement to be English and Spanish bilingual in school, and remarked on the extent to which this contributes to a lower valuation of students and programmes in Spanish, and to the construction of inequality in Madrid society. Some of these remarks are summarised by teachers: 'until you (the author) mentioned it we didn't realise we can have the same targets as the bilingual programme'; 'BEP is a separate elite section within the same school'; 'BEP is creating asymmetries among teachers and students' (research interviews).

It is precisely through new linguistic demands and requirements that a new process of hierarchisation of educational programmes and educational tracking is taking place. However, it is in everyday practices that social agents enforce or resist these demands, in their management of linguistic and learning resources. The academic credentials, to be in a bilingual programme (cultural and symbolic capital), is 'convertible' into economic capital on the job market.

Transcription conventions

Miguel:	participant
right (italics)	translation into English
{ }	comments made by the researcher
&	turn latched to previous turn
=	maintaining of a participant's turn in an overlap
[ ]	turn overlapping with similarly marked turn
-	re-starts and self-interruptions without any pause
	silence (lapse or interval) of 5 seconds
(5')	(when it is particularly meaningful, the number of seconds is indicated in pauses longer than one second)
/	short pause (0'5" seconds)
//	long pause (0'5–1'5" seconds)
↑	rising intonation
↓	falling intonation
→	intonation of suspension
RIGHT (all capital letters)	loud talking
(( ))	incomprehensible speech
pa´l	syntactical phonetic phenomena between words
( )°	low talking
aa (doubled vowels)	vowel lengthening
ss (doubled consonants)	consonant lengthening
¿	questions (also used for tag questions such as 'right¿', 'eh¿', 'you know¿')
!	exclamations
→	preceding elements of the excerpt that will be referred to in the running text

Acknowledgements

This chapter was written in the frame of the R&D Project, *Multilingualism in Schools: A Critical Sociolinguistic Analysis of Educational Linguistics Programs in the Madrid Region* (HUM2007-64694), financed by the National Plan of R&D&I of the Ministry of Science and Technology of Spain. The author also wishes to acknowledge the fruitful discussions with all the participants at the *17th International Workshop on Discourse Studies: Critique and Decolonization* (FFI2010-09407-E, Ministry of Science and Technology of Spain). The final draft of this chapter was made possible thanks to the Salvador de Madariaga Mobility Grant awarded by the Ministry of Science and Education (PR2011-0250). It also benefitted from the inspiring academic environment at the Department of Social and Cultural Analysis at NYU and the Centre for Language, Discourse and Communication at Kings College, London, and the fruitful discussions with Mary Louise Pratt, Constant Leung, Roxy Harris and Ben Rampton, who welcomed the author to their centres.

Notes

(1) Spain's migration flows changed radically in the last third of the 20th century, as the country evolved from its traditional role of sender to that of being a destination country for foreign workers, mostly from North Africa and Latin America, and for well-to-do immigrants from other EU countries. Now this tendency has been reversed by the high rate of unemployment.

(2) Recorder reference in MIRCO-ELMA Corpus: T081016SL.

(3) Recorder reference in MIRCO-ELMA Corpus: T081016SL_M: 1.

(4) A pilot programme with different characteristics run by the Spanish Ministry of Education and the British Council has been operating in state schools since 1996.

(5) In many of these schools, English is offered as a core subject and as the main language of instruction for other subjects, like history or biology, to be studied, together with Spanish language and mathematics.

(6) Recorder reference in MIRCO-ELMA Corpus: M90427AE.

(7) *Instructions from the Madrid Region Deputy Secretary of the Department of Education,* which regulates the Welcome Classes under the Welcome Programme, so that foreign students can join the educational system.

(8) Diverse programmes are offered, including immersion (students with limited proficiency in the language of instruction are taught in a mainstream classroom), immersion with systematic language support in L2 (students receive additional classes in specified periods of instruction aimed at the development of language skills in L2), immersion with an L2 monolingual preparatory phase, transitional bilingual education and maintenance bilingual education.

(9) The research team includes Esther Alcalá, Diana Labajos, Luisa Martín Rojo, Laura Mijares and Ana María Relaño.

(10) All participants received a detailed information sheet about the project and signed a written consent form. This documentation was translated into the languages of

the household. Parents or guardians provided the written consent for minors (aged under 18).
(11) Bourdieu identifies three dimensions of capital, each with its own relationship to class: economic, cultural and social capital. These three resources become socially effective, and their ownership is legitimised through the mediation of symbolic capital. Economic and cultural capital have their own modes of existence (money, shares; examinations and diplomas), whereas symbolic capital exist only in the 'eyes of the others'. It inevitably assumes an ideological function: it gives the legitimised forms of distinction and classification a taken-for-granted character, and thus conceals the arbitrary way in which the forms of capital are distributed among individuals in society (see Bourdieu, 1986).
(12) Recorder reference in MIRCO-ELMA Corpus: T081016SL_H: 31.
(13) Recorder reference in MIRCO-ELMA Corpus: M090427AE.
(14) Some authors call this phenomenon 'ethnic segmentation of the job market' (Bassarsky, 2009), or even 'ethno-fragmentation' (García Borrego, 2007; Pedreño Cánovas, 2007).
(15) Data from the research: Evolución y situación actual de la presencia del alumnado extranjero en el sistema educativo español (1999–2010). CREADE – Instituto de Formación del Profesorado, Investigación e Innovación Educativa (IFPIIE): https://www.educacion.gob.es/creade/IrASubSeccionFront.do?id=1201.

References

Alcalá Recuerda, E. (2011) Norm-transgression sequences in the classroom interaction at a Madrid high school. *Linguistics and Education* 21 (3), 195–212.
Angulo Martín, C. (2006) Evolución de las condiciones de vida de la población extranjera en España. *Temas para el debate* 136, 27–29.
Bassarsky, L. (2009) La segmentación 'étnica' del mercado de trabajo español ¿qué lugar ocupan los hijos de inmigrantes? *Actas VI Congreso sobre las migraciones en España* (pp. 1467–1482). Coruña University.
Broeder, P. and Mijares, L. (2004) *Multilingual Madrid. Languages at Home and at School.* Amsterdam: European Cultural Foundation.
Bourdieu, P. (1977) *Outline of a Theory of Practice.* Cambridge: Cambridge University Press.
Bourdieu, P. (1986) The forms of capital. In J.G. Richardson (ed.) *Handbook of Theory and Research for the Sociology of Education* (pp. 241–258). New York: Greenwood.
Cachón Rodríguez, L. (2002) La formación de la 'España inmigrante': Mercado y ciudadanía. *REIS (Revista Española de Investigaciones Sociológicas)* 97, 95–126.
Carrasco Pons, S. (2004) Inmigración, minorías y educación: Ensayar algunas respuestas y mejorar algunas preguntas a partir del modelo de Ogbu y su desarrollo. *Suplementos Ofrim* 11, 39–68.
Cicourel, A. (2000) What counts as data for modelling medical diagnostic reasoning and bureaucratic information processing in the workplace. *Intellectica* 30, 115–149.
Cicourel, A. (2002) La gestion des rendez-vous dans un service médical specialisé: Organisation et communication en régime de 'surcharge cognitive'. *Actes de la Recherche en Sciences Sociales* 143, 3–17.
Cummins, J. (1984) *Bilingualism and Special Education: Issues in Assessment and Pedagogy.* Clevedon: Multilingual Matters.
Duchêne, A. and Heller, M. (2011) *Language in Late Capitalism: Pride and Profit.* London: Routledge.

Duff, P. (2002) The discursive co-construction of knowledge, identity and difference: An ethnography of communication in the high school mainstream. *Applied Linguistics* 23 (3), 289–322.

EURYDICE (2006) *Content and Language Integrated Learning (CLIL) at School in Europe*. Brussels: European Commission, accessed 7 January 2007. http://www.eurydice.org/ressources/eurydice/pdf/0_integral/071EN.pdf

Franzé, A. (2002) *Lo que sabía no valía. Escuela, diversidad e inmigración*. Madrid: Consejo Económico y Social, Comunidad de Madrid.

García, O. (2006) Foreword. In S. Makoni and A. Pennycook (eds) *Disinventing and Reconstituting Languages* (pp. xi–xv). Clevedon: Multilingual Matters.

García, O. (2013) Dual or dynamic bilingual education? Empowering bilingual communities. In R. Rubdy and L. Alsagoff (eds) *The Global–Local Interface and Hybridity: Exploring Language and Identity* (pp. 100–118). Bristol: Multilingual Matters.

García Borrego, I. (2007) Jóvenes migrantes y sociedades en tránsito. In A.M. López Sala and L. Cachón Rodríguez (eds) *Juventud e Inmigración. Desafíos para la Participación y para la Integración* (pp. 158–171). Las Palmas: Gobierno de Canarias, Dirección General de Juventud.

García Borrego, I. (2011) La difícil reproducción de las familias inmigrantes. ¿Hacia la formación de un proletariado étnico español? *Papers* 96 (1), 55–76.

Goffman, E. (1959) *The Presentation of Self in Everyday Life*. New York: Doubleday.

Gumperz, J. (1982) *Discourse Strategies*. Cambridge: Cambridge University Press.

Gumperz, J. (1996) The linguistic and cultural relativity of conversational inference. In J. Gumperz and S. Levinson (eds) *Rethinking Linguistic Relativity* (pp. 374–406). Cambridge: Cambridge University Press.

Heller, M. (1992) The politics of codeswitching and language choice. In C. Eastman (ed.) *Codeswitching* (pp. 123–142). Clevedon: Multilingual Matters.

Heller, M. (1995) Language choice, social institutions and symbolic domination. *Language and Society* 24 (3), 373–405.

Heller, M. (2006) *Linguistic Minorities and Modernity: A Sociolinguistic Ethnography*. London: Continuum.

Heller, M. and Martin-Jones, M. (2001) Introduction: Symbolic domination, education and linguistic difference. In M. Heller and M. Martin-Jones (eds) *Voices of Authority. Education and Linguistic Differences* (pp. 1–29). Westport, CT and London: Ablex.

Irvine, J.T. and Gal, S. (2000) Language ideology and linguistic differentiation. In P.V. Kroskrity (ed.) *Regimes of Language* (pp. 35–83). Santa Fe: School of American Research Press.

Kasper, G. (1986) Repair in foreign language teaching. In G. Kasper (ed.) *Learning, Teaching and Communication in the Foreign Language Classroom* (pp. 23–42). Aarhus: Aarhus University Press.

López Blasco, A. (2007) ¿Qué necesitamos saber de la 'juventud inmigrante'? Apuntes para la investigación y la política. In A.M. López Sala and L. Cachón Rodríguez (eds) *Juventud e Inmigración. Desafíos para la Participación y para la Integración* (pp. 27–44). Las Palmas: Gobierno de Canarias, Dirección General de Juventud.

López Sala, A.M. and Cachón Rodríguez, L. (eds) (2007) *Juventud e Inmigración. Desafíos para la Participación y para la Integración*. Las Palmas: Gobierno de Canarias, Dirección General de Juventud.

Madrid City Council (2005) *Madrid Plan on Social and Intercultural Coexistence*. Madrid: Ayuntamiento de Madrid, Dirección General de Inmigración y Cooperación al Desarrollo.

Martín Rojo, L. (2010) *Constructing Inequality in Multilingual Classrooms*. Berlin: Mouton de Gruyter.
Martín Rojo, L. (2011) Discourse and school. In R. Wodak, B. Johnstone, and P.E. Kerswill (eds) *Sage Handbook of Sociolinguistics* (pp. 345–360). London: Sage.
Martín Rojo, L. and Mijares, L. (2007) 'Sólo en español': una reflexión sobre la norma monolingüe y la realidad multilingüe en los centros escolares. *Revista de Educación Revista* 343, 93–112.
Mijares, L. and Relaño Pastor, A.M. (2011) Language programs at Villababel High: Rethinking ideologies of social inclusión. *International Journal of Bilingual Education and Bilingualism* 14 (4), 427–442.
Norton Pierce, B. (1995) Social identity, investment and language learning. *TESOL Quarterly* 29 (1), 9–32.
Patiño Santos, A. (2011) Negotiating power relations and ethnicity in a sociolinguistic ethnography in Madrid. *Journal of Language, Identity & Education* 10 (3), 145–163.
Pedreño Cánovas, A. (2007) Jóvenes españoles e inmigrantes en el espacio público: Una investigación sobre la realidad murciana. In A.M. López Sala and L. Cachón Rodríguez (eds) *Juventud e Inmigración. Desafíos para la Participación y para la Integración* (pp. 137–157). Las Palmas: Gobierno de Canarias, Dirección General de Juventud.
Pérez Milans, M. (2007a) Las aulas de enlace: Un islote de bienvenida. In L. Martín Rojo and L. Mijares (eds) *Voces del aula. Etnografías de la escuela multilingüe* (pp. 111–146). Madrid: Centro de Recursos para la Atención a la Diversidad Cultural en la Educación (CREADE), Centro de Investigación y Documentación Educativa (CIDE).
Pérez Milans, M. (2007b) Lectura y escritura en la enseñanza de español a escolares inmigrantes: El caso de los estudiantes chinos. In T. Álvarez Angulo (ed.) *La magia de las letras. El desarrollo de la lectura y la escritura en educación infantil y primaria* (pp. 273–319). Madrid: Instituto Superior de Formación del Profesorado, Ministerio de Educación y Ciencia (MEC).
Piedrafita, S., Steinberg, F. and Ignacio Torreblanca, J. (2006) *Twenty Years of Spain in the European Union (1986–2006)*. Madrid: Elcano Royal Institute, and European Parliament.
PISA (Programme for International Students Assessment) (2003) *Where Immigrant Students Succeed – A Comparative Review of Performance and Engagement in PISA 2003*. Paris: OECD, accessed 15 May 2006. http://www.oecd.org/dataoecd/2/38/36664934.pdf.
Regional Education Department (2003) *Instrucciones del 16 de julio de 2003 por las que se regulan, con carácter experimental, las Aulas de Enlace del programa 'Escuelas de Bienvenida' para la incorporación del alumnado extranjero al sistema educativo. Curso 2003–2004*. Madrid: Regional Education Department.
Regional Education Department (2005) Orden 2819/2005, de 26 de mayo, del Consejero de Educación, por la que se crean Secciones Lingüísticas de Lengua Inglesa en determinados Institutos de Educación Secundaria, en desarrollo del Convenio entre el Ministerio de Educación y the British Council. *Official Regional Government of Madrid Gazette (BOCM)* 135, 21.
Seedhouse, P. (2004) *The Interactional Architecture of the Language Classroom: A Conversation Analysis Perspective*. Oxford: Blackwell.
Serra, C. (2004) Rhetoric of exclusion and racist violence in a Catalan secondary school. *Anthropology & Education Quarterly* 35 (4), 433–450.

Serra, C. and Serra Palaudàrias, J.M. (2007) L'alumnat de nacionalitat estrangera en els estudis postobligtoris. In J. Larios and M. Nadal (eds) *L'estat de la immigració a Catalunya. Anuari 2006* (pp. 301–334). Barcelona: Mediterrània.

Shohamy, E. (2011) Assessing multilingual competencies: Adopting construct valid assessment policies. *Modern Language Journal* 95, 418–429.

VVAA (2011) *Evolución y situación actual de la presencia del alumnado extranjero en el sistema educativo español (1999–2010).* Madrid: CREADE – Instituto de Formación del Profesorado, Investigación e Innovación Educativa (IFPIIE).

7 From *kebapçı* to Professional: The Commodification of Language and Social Mobility in Turkish Complementary Schools in the UK

Vally Lytra

Introduction

This chapter explores the commodification of standard Turkish and the new vision of social mobility it introduces for the younger generation of mainly British-born Turkish-speaking young people attending two London Turkish complementary schools. Complementary schools, often referred to as 'community', 'supplementary' or 'Saturday' schools, are community-based voluntary organisations. They are set up by specific linguistic, cultural or religious communities for a range of functions, particularly the maintenance and development of the community language, culture and history. In his historical account of the emergence of complementary schooling in the UK, Li Wei (2006: 78) asserts that complementary schools were a 'response to the failure of the mainstream education system to meet the needs of ethnic minority children and their communities'. He maintains that 'despite the public debates over pluralistic, multicultural education over the decades, the UK governments have made no real attempt to address the criticisms that the mainstream education system was disabling and disempowering ethnic minority children and their communities' (Li Wei, 2006: 78).

As a result, the teaching and learning of community languages and cultures and the financial burden of running community schools has been largely left to the communities to deal with themselves.

Most Turkish complementary schools were set up from the late 1970s to early 1980s onwards in the context of the above-mentioned historical processes and attitudes to serve the social, linguistic and cultural needs of a heterogeneous community broadly consisting of families of Turkish-Cypriot, Turkish and Kurdish origins from mainland Turkey as well as Turkish-speaking families who had experienced secondary migration via other European Union countries and mixed heritage families. They emerged amid concern for the loss of the community language and culture and low academic achievement in mainstream education (Issa, 2005; Issa *et al.*, 2008; Mehmet Ali, 2001; Turkish Cypriot Forum, 1999). From their inception, their focus has been on the teaching and collective learning of standard Turkish and, largely, mainland Turkish history, cultural values and traditions (Blackledge & Creese, 2010; Lytra, 2011; Lytra & Baraç, 2008). Moreover, they have opened up spaces for the development of children's identities of choice in order to compensate for the lack of recognition of their multilingual realities in the broader British society (Issa, 2008; Lytra & Baraç, 2009). Last but not least, Turkish schools have focused on linking educational contexts, by providing support in mainstream education subjects, such as maths, English and science, and preparing children for Turkish language qualifications, notably GCSE (General Certificate of Secondary Education) and A-level (Advanced Level General Certificate of Education) examinations, which are recognised as the standard entry qualifications for studying at university in England. The emphasis on supporting mainstream education and attaining language qualifications has led to the development of an institutional discourse in Turkish complementary schools where Turkish language learning is seen as 'a resource with exchange value' (Heller, 2010: 101) and bilingual proficiency in standard Turkish and standard English as an indispensable skill to increase children's access to university and the professions (Creese *et al.*, 2008; Lytra, 2010; see also Francis *et al.*, 2009, 2010 for the development of similar discourses in Chinese complementary schools).

In this chapter, I examine the commodifying effect on language that the institutional discourse of the added value of standard Turkish has for the younger generation of mainly British-born Turkish-speaking youth in two London Turkish complementary schools. First, I situate the study in the research and policy context of community languages in the UK. Using field notes and interview data, I sketch out the profiles and investments of members of the Turkish-speaking élites in the management and teaching of Turkish complementary schools who articulated this institutional discourse and I address the following questions. (1) What are the key aspects and underlying assumptions of this institutional discourse? (2) In what ways does it consolidate dominant linguistic hierarchies? (3) What new vision of social mobility coming from within the Turkish-speaking communities does this institutional discourse put forth for the younger mainly British-born generation?

I illustrate how members of the Turkish-speaking élites discuss the economic value of standard Turkish as supplementing that of standard English. They link proficiency in standard Turkish to academic success in mainstream education, the attainment of Turkish language qualifications and access to tertiary education and professional opportunities for the future. I argue that this discourse reinforces linguistic hierarchies in the Turkish-speaking communities in London between standard Turkish and different regional and diasporic varieties of Turkish as well as Kurdish. These inequalities are reproduced in Turkish complementary school classrooms through the teaching and learning of standard Turkish.

Furthermore, this discourse puts forth a new vision of social mobility. It shifts from the image of the small independent businessman firmly rooted in the 'inter-communal micro economy'[1] of north London where regional and diasporic varieties of Turkish as well as Kurdish are important economic and social resources for many members of the Turkish-speaking communities, to the mobile, bilingual professional who speaks standard Turkish and English. For the small independent businessman, who has provided an enduring symbol of success for many members of the older immigrant generations, upward social mobility has been largely defined within the boundaries of the Turkish-speaking communities. However, for the mobile bilingual professional, social mobility is situated in the larger context of British society and the global new economy. This shift risks undervaluing the rich and complex multilingual repertoires of many Turkish-speaking children of Turkish-Cypriot and Kurdish heritage and inadvertently excluding them from access to higher education and the professions.

Community Languages: The Research and Policy Context in the UK

Research in community languages in the UK has illustrated how complementary schools have become 'safe spaces' outside mainstream education for learning, socialisation and identity development (e.g. Blackledge & Creese, 2010; Gregory *et al.*, 2004; Kenner *et al.*, 2007; Martin *et al.*, 2004; also contributions in Creese & Martin, 2006; Lytra & Martin, 2010). This body of work has documented the rich and complex language ecologies in complementary schools and classrooms. In addition, it has identified two seemingly contradictory positions that co-exist in the ideology and practice of complementary schools. In Turkish complementary school classrooms, these two positions are expressed as follows: language and literacy teaching and learning is accomplished primarily *in* and *through* standard Turkish while English or other regional and diasporic varieties of Turkish as well as Kurdish are dispreferred. At the same time, pupils and teachers may draw upon additional linguistic resources to communicate and learn (e.g. English, regional varieties of Turkish) depending on context and participants, reflecting the linguistic, cultural and ethnic diversity of the Turkish-speaking communities in London (Baraç, 2009; Lytra, 2011; Lytra & Baraç, 2008, 2009).

Standard Turkish is based on the speech of the educated élites of western Turkey. Its use is traditionally associated with social prestige, education, economic mobility and Turkish national identity. The high status of standard Turkish in complementary school classrooms reflects its importance among the Turkish-speaking communities in London, where it has developed into the lingua franca and a symbol of unity (Issa, 2005). While the institutional authority and recognition of standard Turkish cannot be denied, regional varieties of Turkish also enjoy symbolic power by providing affective links between their users and their families' places of origin in Turkey and Cyprus (Lytra, 2012). Moreover, they have socio-economic value in communication and business among members of the Turkish-speaking communities in London (Issa, 2005). Cypriot-Turkish and its varieties diverge from the standard in terms of vocabulary, syntax, morphology and phonology due to long-term contact with Cypriot-Greek and more recently with English on the island of Cyprus. Other mainland Turkish regional varieties have minor differences from the standard, mainly at the level of phonology (e.g. accents) and vocabulary. Kurdish is an Indo-European language. Kurds from Turkey speak the Kurmanji dialect of Kurdish, which was banned until recently. For this reason, levels of Kurdish literacy are very low and Kurdish people from Turkey tend to be literate in Turkish. Nevertheless, Kurdish remains an important marker of Kurdish identity.

Proponents of government policy have started to view languages other than English as a linguistic, educational, intellectual, cultural and economic resource. This understanding of languages has important implications for community languages too. Martin and Sneddon (2012) identify this shift in government rhetoric in the government document *The School Curriculum*, where ethnic minority and immigrant languages are not only seen as a valuable personal, family and community resource for children, but also as a valuable national resource (DES, 1981). More recently, in the introduction to the report 'Positively Plurilingual. The contribution of community languages to UK education and society' (National Centre for Languages, 2006: 1), Sir Trevor McDonald, patron of the National Centre for Languages, notes:

> The predominance of English and its importance for both our nation and as an international lingua franca are not in doubt. But alongside English other languages are becoming increasingly important to the UK as globalisation, international communications and labour force mobility transform economic and cultural life. Building on existing language skills and expertise is of direct benefit to individuals, fosters greater social cohesion, improves skills available to employers, contributes to our national prosperity and makes us better prepared to contribute positively on the global stage. As a nation seeking to play a key role in global trade and diplomacy we need to be able to draw on a diverse range of languages to further our strategic and economic aims, and these are already represented among the languages spoken by our schoolchildren.

This statement reveals how government policy discourses seek to link the acquisition and development of language skills with national prosperity, global diplomacy and economic competition. Moreover, it displays how such discourses attempt to transform the status of community languages by presenting them as an economic asset and valorising them. A similar connection between language learning, marketability and employability is highlighted in the *Languages Review* (DfE, 2007: 6), where proficiency in 'overseas languages' is viewed as 'increasingly relevant to the prospects of our young people in a world of multinational companies where linguistic skills are valued'. In the same report, community languages are described as 'a national asset' (DfE, 2007: 16).

However, the emphasis of government rhetoric on the instrumental value of community language learning for future marketability and employability fails to be supported by concrete action. Martin and Sneddon (2012: 36) take issue with such government rhetoric, arguing that

> although there is some official recognition of the languages of the immigrant population, their status is uncertain; they have traditionally not been given the status of 'Modern Foreign Languages'. These languages have largely been left to fend for themselves.

Indeed, mainstream schools often take credit for their pupils' successful GCSE and A level Turkish results without providing any aid to complementary schools for preparing the pupils for the examinations.

In this chapter, I show how members of the Turkish-speaking élites selectively draw on government rhetoric on the economic value of community languages to construct the institutional discourse whereby learning standard Turkish is seen as having added value.

The Study

The study is part of a larger, comparative, team ethnography of multilingual practices and identity processes in complementary schools across four communities in the UK: Chinese (Mandarin and Cantonese) in Manchester, Gujarati in Leicester, Bengali in Birmingham and Turkish in London. The project was funded by the Economic and Social Research Council and was conducted from March 2006 to November 2008 (Creese et al., 2008). Researchers were paired, with at least one researcher being bilingual in English and the community language in each site. In the Turkish case study reported in this chapter, researchers collected ethnographic observations of lessons, break times, school assemblies and other formal school-sponsored events (e.g. end-of-year and national celebrations) during 10 visits over a period of three months. Five key participant children aged eight to 12 were selected, after four weeks of observations and through a process of student self-selection and teacher suggestion. Audio and, where possible, video-recordings of the key participant children were made inside and outside the classroom setting over a period of six weeks. The key participant children, their mothers, four teachers and four members of the schools' managing committees were also interviewed. Photography and documentary data were collected throughout the project. Informed consent was sought at all stages of the project.

It is estimated that there are around 180,000–200,000 members of the Turkish-speaking communities, mainly concentrated in the Greater London area. According to the *Community Languages Bulletin* (National Centre for Languages, 2009: 9), in England, Turkish is the ninth most commonly spoken language by schoolchildren whose first language is not English. The two Turkish complementary schools in this study were founded in the late 1980s. 'East London'[2] Turkish school attracted children and families living mainly in north, northeast and east London where Turkish-speaking communities have traditionally settled and continue to live. At the time of the fieldwork it had about 250 registered pupils. Most of the children were of Cypriot-Turkish origin, although there were some children whose families came from mainland Turkey. 'West London' Turkish school had a larger catchment area, with families traveling from west and northwest London and its environs.

At the time of the fieldwork, there were about 110 registered children. The majority of the children's families were from mainland Turkey with almost half of the children of mixed heritage. In both schools, most families were from working-class backgrounds, or were small business owners, and some families were on benefits. There was also a very small number of families from educated middle-class backgrounds.

Members of Turkish-speaking Elites

The members of the Turkish-speaking élites who articulated the discourse of the added value of standard Turkish for the younger generation of mainly British-born Londoners of Turkish descent consisted of a small group of bilingual and bicultural first- and second-generation parents and educators. They were college or university educated in Cyprus, Turkey or the UK and had linguistic and cultural fluency in both English and Turkish, thereby acting as language and community brokers for the Turkish-speaking communities. They were actively involved in the management committees of the two schools, and some had been in the past, or were at the time of the fieldwork, also teaching Turkish in the two schools. The interview excerpt with Adem Bey, head of 'East London' Turkish school's management committee and GCSE teacher at the school, is representative of their educational and professional trajectories.

Excerpt 1

Adem Bey: I left Cyprus in '75 and went to university in Istanbul, the Sports Academy, for four years. I graduated in '79 and after two weeks I flew to the UK because of my hip. I came to see a specialist here and since then I'm here. During all those years I worked in different places, local councils, Hackney, Haringey, Islington. My last post was in Islington in the Racial Equality Unit as a centre coordinator. Then, I worked for a refugee organisation. While I was working there I applied to Brunel University to do a Master's degree in physical education. I started in '98 and got my degree in 2000. In January 2001 I started working in the secondary school I'm still teaching, Islington Arts and Media. I started off as a PE teacher, but in the last two years I worked for EMAG [Ethnic Minority Achievement Grants]. This term I'm not teaching PE, only EMAG. I'm also supporting media, BTEC [the Business and Technology Education Council is the British body which awards vocational qualifications] in Media for Years 8, 9, 10 and 11, doing media lessons, doing arts and drama studios.

Interviewer: great, so you're moving from sports to arts and drama

Adem Bey: I'm moving to media and drama, which I'm enjoying. I've got four years' experience working as a journalist for *Toplum Postası* and then *London Turkish Gazette.*

Adem Bey's educational and professional trajectory documents his rich and diverse forms of engagement in education, the media and social and professional services for the Turkish-speaking communities and youth in London. As in the case of others, these forms of engagement intersected with their advocacy for improving educational opportunities for Turkish-speaking youth, including the recognition of Turkish as a community language by the broader mainstream society. The field notes below demonstrate the advocacy role they sought to play. They describe my first encounter with Ceyda Hanim, a qualified Turkish language teacher from Cyprus who taught A-level Turkish at 'East London' Turkish school.

Field notes 1

Classes are about to start and I see some teachers hovering about the teachers' table sipping coffee/tea and chatting among themselves. I join them and greet them. I notice a teacher I hadn't met before and I greet her too. We briefly talk about the project and how welcoming everyone has been. She smiles and then asks me whether the project will have any impact on changing attitudes towards A-level Turkish examinations. She explains that some universities are reluctant to accept Turkish A-levels, claiming that students are native speakers of Turkish and the examinations are too easy for them. This is unfair because it doesn't give Turkish the same status as French, German and other modern foreign languages. It also perpetuates a confusion regarding the status of Turkish A levels among parents and children who are less motivated to prepare for these language qualifications when they see that they may not count towards getting into university. She concludes that although community educators and leaders have repeatedly raised this issue with the educational authorities nothing has been done. There is a sense of urgency in her voice and I feel that I must say something positive to that effect. I say that I totally agree that the current situation is completely unfair and hope that through the project educational authorities will find out about the good work

Turkish schools do and that universities throughout England will accept Turkish A levels. I don't think my answer satisfied her.

The ongoing efforts to consolidate the status of Turkish A levels was reiterated throughout the fieldwork by other members of the Turkish-speaking élites who viewed these examinations as an important incentive for children to continue studying standard Turkish. Their active engagement in improving educational standards for Turkish-speaking youth echoes that of the Turkish 'immigrant élites' in Berlin described by Yurdakul (2006: 435) as 'important political actors to negotiate rights and memberships in the name of th[e] ethnolinguistic group'. As members of the Turkish-speaking élites, they mediated between the other key actors involved in Turkish complementary schooling, namely the UK government, mainstream school authorities, and children from different linguistic, cultural and ethnic backgrounds and their parents.

The Discourse of the Added Value of Standard Turkish

Members of the Turkish-speaking élites in Turkish complementary schools articulated the discourse of the added value of standard Turkish by linking Turkish language learning to the attainment of standard Turkish language qualifications, academic success in mainstream education and access to tertiary education and the professions. The deployment of this discourse has a commodifying effect on standard Turkish. Its use is seen as a form of social and economic capital that can be exchanged for access to university and the job market. Its mobilisation can be situated in the context of government policy discourses that equate community language skills with an economic asset for future employability (see the earlier section on Community Languages), as well as economic, social and political conditions in Turkey and in the diaspora that have opened up new possibilities for economic activity and niche markets locally and globally.

The antecedents to the development of this discourse can be traced in community and government discourses of low academic achievement among many Turkish-speaking youth (see Issa, 2005, 2008; Issa *et al.*, 2008; Mehmet Ali, 2001; Turkish Cypriot Forum, 1999). Although a thorough discussion of this complex issue is beyond the scope of this chapter, the following statement from the most recent report on 'Young people's educational attainment in London's Turkish, Turkish Kurdish and Turkish Cypriot Communities' (Issa *et al.*, 2008: 14) sums up academic achievement among Turkish-speaking youth: 'while all our participants recognised that Turkish, Turkish Kurdish and Turkish Cypriot pupils were achieving below the Local Authority average, there are some very high-achieving pupils within the communities'. Even though this statement does not capture crucial differences based on ethnicity, social class, gender, age and other factors, it reveals the continuing gap between high-achieving and low-achieving pupils. In this context, members of the Turkish-speaking élites in Turkish complementary schools sought to mobilise the discourse of the added value of standard Turkish as part of their ongoing effort to raise academic attainment. In what follows, I examine key components and assumptions of this discourse in more detail.

Ege Bay taught GCSE and A-level Turkish classes in 'East London' Turkish school before his recent appointment as education coordinator at the same school. In the interview excerpt below, he makes the link between Turkish language learning, the attainment of language qualifications and future marketability explicit:

Excerpt 2

Interviewer:	how important is it that children learn Turkish?
Ege Bey:	it's very important because first of all even if they are living in this country for 200 years, they'll still be called Turkish, or Greek, or Jamaican. No matter how many years you've lived in this country, even if you're born in this country, you've got your identity on you. This identity should not disappear. I think it's very important for their self-esteem. Language is the key to culture. So if they don't learn the language, they don't learn much of the culture either. On the other hand, London is quite a cosmopolitan city and I believe if they learn Turkish they get their certificates, A levels or GCSE or whatever that is, they can they've got the chance to get a job easily. In some way because there is quite a big [Turkish-speaking community] in London. When they apply for any job it helps them to speak a second language.

Ege Bey begins by discussing the importance of Turkish language learning in the development of Turkish language, culture and identity. The children's Turkish identity is seen as stable, fixed and homogeneous and their language as expressing identity. He asserts that children need to learn Turkish because they are Turkish. Proficiency in Turkish is, thus, viewed as constituting 'Turkishness', while loss of Turkish language and culture means loss of 'Turkishness' too (cf. Lytra, 2012). This emotional reaction that offers a moral justification to learning Turkish is followed by a practical one: Turkish language learning is linked with obtaining language certificates and improving access to the professional job market where bilingualism in standard Turkish and English is regarded as an asset. He claims that, in the case of Turkish in particular, the demand for Turkish language skills is compounded by the significant size of the Turkish-speaking communities in London. Adnan Bey, head of the 'West London' Turkish school's management committee, voices a similar position, when he discusses the aims of the school.

Excerpt 3

Interviewer: What would you say are the aims of the school?
Adnan Bey: The aims of the school are supplementary education. Ensuring that the children learn their mother tongue, Turkish language and culture. As you know most of our students come from mixed marriages. At home, most of them are exposed to English, at home and at school, at mainstream school. So we provide a service really, education for them to learn. Even if they already speak Turkish, they improve it. It [attending Turkish classes] actually prepares them for later education, you know to get their GCSE and A-levels. It helps them in their mainstream education to go to university.

Attending Turkish complementary school is seen as supplementing the children's education by providing a 'Turkish space' to perpetuate Turkish language and culture beyond the home and mainstream schools dominated by English (cf. Li Wei & Wu, 2010 for similar findings in Chinese complementary schools). As in Excerpt 2, this moral justification is complemented by a practical one, where learning Turkish is viewed as preparing children for language examinations, succeeding in mainstream education and facilitating access to higher education.[3]
Adem Bey, head of 'East London' Turkish school's management committee, reiterates a similar argument, when he assesses the success of the school.

Excerpt 4

Interviewer: What do you think is your biggest reward as you've been involved with this school for some years now?

Adem Bey: I believe our school succeeded its target, its aims because we have lots of students in university and some who have graduated already and who like my daughter were in our school. They were here from the first level up to A level and the main aim I believe as Turkish schools was to help these students get through to university level.

Adem Bey evaluates the success of the school based on the number of students who have gone to university. His statement corroborates observations during fieldwork that Turkish complementary schools used significant resources in preparing children for GCSE and A-level Turkish examinations as well as educating the parents about their significance. Indeed, early on in the fieldwork it became clear that the schools' reputation was built around their success rate, as the next interview excerpt with Ipek Hanim reveals. Ipek Hanim was raised in London, where she attended college and had been working as a secretary in an export-import company with close business ties to Turkey. She was actively involved in the 'West London' Turkish school's managing committee, particularly in initiating and running the school's Turkish book club. Prior to this excerpt, she explained how the idea of the book club came about.

Excerpt 5

Interviewer: how successful has the book club been?
Ipek Hanim: it's only successful if you have parents that really push the children. If parents don't push the children to do their homework, to read, it won't be successful because the teachers only have three hours to teach the children. You know with the children this year they have had 6–7 children who took their GCSEs and 5 of them got A* [the top mark] which is a very good result which means that those children are doing something right either they are being pushed at home or they are sitting here and learning
Interviewer: or both
Ipek Hanim: exactly or doing both which is a great example which is a great thing for the school, but most of the other children are not doing that. I think we're also learning from our mistakes so every time we have a meeting with parents we keep bringing it up so I think parents are taking that in now. They are more relaxed as well as. But now I can see a lot of determined parents who want their children to succeed.

Ipek Hanim discusses the children's Turkish language skills as measured through tests. Turkish language learning is reflected in the children's success in achieving high examination scores, which she attributes to high parental expectations and the children's own motivation to succeed. By placing an emphasis on individual success, however, this line of argument seems to ignore factors such as the low teacher expectations, marginalisation and racism experienced by many Turkish-speaking youth in mainstream schools, which past research has shown to contribute to school disaffection (cf. Issa, 2008; Turkish Cypriot Forum, 1999).

By mobilising the discourse of the added value of standard Turkish, members of the Turkish-speaking élites seek to increase the access of Turkish-speaking youth to higher education and redress low achievement and underrepresentation in the professions. Nevertheless, the emphasis on standard Turkish seems to consolidate dominant language hierarchies inside and outside Turkish complementary schools, to which I now turn.

Consolidating Dominant Language Hierarchies

Recent research in Turkish complementary schools in the UK illustrated the complex range of linguistic resources, including standard Turkish, standard English, instructed foreign languages, regional and diasporic varieties of Turkish, regional and classed varieties of English and youth varieties circulating in complementary schools and classrooms. However, literacy teaching focused on reading, writing and speaking in standard Turkish, or 'temiz Türkçe' [clean/correct Turkish]. As I have discussed elsewhere (Lytra, 2012), the use of the metaphor of purity identifies standard Turkish with 'temiz' [clean/proper] Turkish, and implicitly positions regional varieties of Turkish as potentially 'unclean' and 'contaminated' by traces of other linguistic resources (cf. Heller, 2007). Linguistic boundaries were further policed during literacy teaching by pedagogic practices, such as the overt correction of regional accents and the avoidance of the use of Turkish-Cypriot vocabulary, as well as sanctioning the use of English (Lytra & Baraç, 2008, 2009; Lytra et al., 2010). Most teachers, parents and school administrators supported these linguistic practices during literacy teaching and regarded Turkish complementary school classrooms as key sites for the spread and promotion of standard Turkish (Lytra, 2012).

Set against the backdrop of these beliefs and practices, the discourse of the added value of standard Turkish seems to consolidate the institutional authority of standard Turkish and marginalise regional and diasporic varieties of Turkish as well as Kurdish in the Turkish language classroom.

The following field notes bring the privileging of the standard into sharp focus. They are from a GCSE class where the teacher, Melisa Hanim, is practising with the children for the GCSE oral examination. Part of the oral examination consists of the children choosing three topics and the teacher asking them questions.

Field notes 2

The teacher is asking questions and the pupils are taking turns to respond:

Teacher: Peki evde annene yardım ediyormusun?
Pupil 1:   Evet yemek yapıyorum.
Teacher: Başka biri. Ailede en çok anlastığın kişi kim?
Pupil 2:   Annem bana arkadaşım gibi davranıyor.
Teacher: OK. Do you help your mother at home?
Pupil 1:   Yes I cook at home
Teacher: Another person. Who do you get on well with most in your family?
Pupil 2:   My mum treats me like a friend.
I am struck by the proficiency of the pupils in Turkish. It's very good only with a bit of a London accent.

The running commentary by the researcher, who is of Cypriot-Turkish background, on the children's oral performance reveals the expectation that the children's responses should be in standard Turkish. Moreover, the expected standard Turkish seems to be based on some 'ideal native' speaker norm that may not bear phonological or lexical traces of English, Kurdish or regional Turkish varieties. These traces seem to be regarded as 'a problem', hindering the examinee from achieving a very good performance in the mock oral examination.

The focus of GCSE and A-level examinations on performing and being assessed in the standard seems to privilege children who are proficient standard speakers of Turkish over those who may be speakers of Turkish-Cypriot or other regional and diasporic varieties of Turkish. By failing to perform in 'correct/clean' Turkish, the linguistic competences of the latter seems to be less valorised. On this issue, Issa (2005: 17) comments that 'while the importance of learning standard Turkish is recognised, it is criticised by some educators who argue that the path to achieving this should be through recognition of the language varieties spoken by the children'. He cautions that 'when reminded to speak the "correct" form of Turkish, children begin to doubt their own Turkish variety and this can undermine their self-image and seriously affect their learning' (Issa, 2005). Consequently, while seeking to raise educational attainment, the discourse of the added value of standard Turkish may in fact be excluding part of the first-, and in particular second- and third-generation Turkish-speaking youth of Cypriot-Turkish and Kurdish heritage who may not have high competence in standard Turkish. This appears to lead to the following paradox: while one of the aims of Turkish complementary schools is to reduce inequalities in access to education and the professions, by focusing on teaching and learning standard Turkish without integrating the children's other Turkish varieties and Kurdish into the learning process, Turkish complementary schools seem to be inadvertently accentuating linguistic inequalities within their settings.

Language and Social Mobility: From *kebapçı;* to Professional

In his historical account of the economic development of the Turkish-speaking communities in London since the early 1950s, Issa (2005) describes how the first Turkish-Cypriots sought employment in small businesses (e.g. factories and shops) and how within a decade they went on to buy many of these small businesses. As migration from Cyprus slowed down, it was replaced by mainland Turks from the 1970s onwards and then by Kurds from Turkey who came as asylum seekers in the 1980s. The constant supply of labour resulted in the following pattern of economic development: once immigrants established themselves and set up their own businesses, they employed newly arrived immigrants from their own communities. Issa (2005: 34) argues that 'this close network of support generated community based economic activities which grew stronger with each new arrival, and became a thriving domestic economy'. In the context of these historical and socio-economic processes, 'the independent businessman' emerged as one important model of upward social mobility within the communities for many members of the older immigrant generations, reflecting attitudes from the countries of origin, Cyprus and Turkey, where 'having your own business' was highly valued (Issa, 2005: 38–39).

Through the discourse of the added value of standard Turkish, members of the Turkish-speaking élites seem keen to promote a new vision of upward social mobility for the younger generation of mainly British-born youth. They associate this new vision of social mobility with joining the ranks of an increasingly mobile, bilingual, professional workforce. The following field notes trace aspects of this new vision of social mobility. They report on a meeting between members of the 'East London' Turkish school's managing committee and a group of mothers and children attending the GCSE and A-level classes. The purpose of the meeting was to inform mothers and children about the GCSE and A-level examinations, but also to provide input about the British educational system more generally. In the excerpt below, the discussion led by Ege Bey, the school's education coordinator, turns to ways of improving children's educational opportunities.

Field notes 3

Ege Bey emphasises the need for children to know what he calls their 'mother tongue' referring to Turkish. He points at us [the researchers sitting in the audience] and references our work when he tells the audience that bilingual children can be more successful in their studies provided they are equally proficient in both languages. He then recounts his experiences as a mainstream schoolteacher where he observed that almost no Turkish child took part in extracurricular activities organised by the school [...] Ege Bey expresses his disappointment and says: 'There are about 30,000 Turkish children in mainstream school. Why don't we care about them? Why can't we produce artists, musicians, swimmers and sportsmen? Are we all going to make and sell kebabs? Don't get me wrong I'm not putting down this profession but we need to encourage our children to take part in sports, music and art activities.'

In his talk, Ege Bey refers to the instrumental value of languages associated with becoming proficient in both standard Turkish and English to ensure academic and future professional success. The new vision of social mobility he outlines proposes a move from the career path of the kebapçı [a person who makes and sells kebabs, or owns a Kebab shop] to a professional career, for instance, in sports, music and the arts. Unlike the kebapçı who tends to have few, if any, educational qualifications and works long hours in the family business to ensure economic advancement, the professional is envisioned to have high socio-economic capital, bilingual linguistic skills, and employment beyond the inter-communal micro economy of north London.

These two visions of success are premised on different approaches to social mobility. Portes and Zhou's (1993: 82) discussion of the different paths to social mobility for second-generation immigrant youth in the US can provide useful insights. They postulate:

we observe today several distinct forms of adaptation. One of them replicates the time-honored portrayal of growing acculturation and parallel integration into the middle-class; a second leads straight in the opposite direction to permanent poverty and assimilation into the underclass; still a third associates rapid economic advancement with deliberate preservation of the immigrant community's values and tight solidarity.

Broadly speaking, the career path of the small business owner largely situates upward social mobility within the boundaries of the Turkish-speaking communities, while that of the professional orients children towards middle-class aspirations that are shared by the broader British society and towards economic opportunities that straddle the boundaries of the Turkish-speaking communities and beyond, both nationally and globally.

These two visions of social mobility have important implications for the role of language, too. In the inter-communal micro economy of north London, regional and diasporic varieties of Turkish are valued as important linguistic resources by many members of the Turkish-speaking communities, whereas in the national and global economy proficiency in Turkish is measured according to GCSE and A-level examination results in the standard. Thus, while linguistic competence in regional and diasporic varieties of Turkish and Kurdish may contribute to economic advancement in the inter-communal micro economy of north London, these linguistic skills do not seem to be transferable in the national and global markets. Indeed, from the global markets' perspective, as Turkey's economy continues to grow and its geopolitical position continues to strengthen, demand for bilinguals in standard Turkish and English is likely to grow too, lending further support to the discourse of the added value of standard Turkish. However, packaging aspirations for upward social mobility with learning standard Turkish risks excluding many Turkish-speaking youth of Turkish-Cypriot and Kurdish descent who may not have high competence in standard Turkish and undervaluing their existing linguistic resources.

Conclusions

In this chapter, I examined how members of the Turkish-speaking élites in Turkish complementary schools mobilised the discourse of the added value of standard Turkish to raise educational attainment among many Turkish-speaking youth. I demonstrated how learning standard Turkish was seen as supplementing standard English and was linked to academic success in mainstream education, the attainment of Turkish language qualifications and access to higher education and the professions. While Turkish language and literacy learning continued to be associated with maintaining

Turkish language, culture and identity, the development of this discourse seemed to suggest a re-investing of standard Turkish as 'ethnic capital' (Francis *et al.*, 2010). This reinvestment, however, raised important questions about what counts as commodifiable language and whose linguistic resources count as legitimate in accessing university and the workplace (cf. Heller, 2010).

As I argued, the institutional discourse of the added value of standard Turkish reinforced dominant hierarchies in Turkish complementary school classrooms and the Turkish-speaking communities in London more broadly. It reproduced the institutional recognition of standard Turkish over regional and diasporic varieties of Turkish and Kurdish, thereby inadvertently devaluing the linguistic resources of Turkish-speaking youth of Cypriot-Turkish and Kurdish heritage. This discourse also put forth a new vision of social mobility for the younger generation of mainly British-born Turkish-speaking Londoners associated with the mobile bilingual in standard Turkish and English professional. Unlike previous models of upward social mobility situated within the boundaries of the Turkish-speaking communities, this new model was located in the broader British society and the global new economy. However, this vision was not all-inclusive as it was preconditioned on high competence in standard Turkish.

At the time of the fieldwork, the discourse of the added value of standard Turkish was articulated by a small élite in the two Turkish complementary schools who participated in the study. Although the two schools had different pupil populations and catchment areas (see section on 'The Study'), it is important to acknowledge that the sample was relatively small, particularly when one takes into account that according to the Turkish Language, Culture and Education Consortium UK there are currently about 30 Turkish complementary schools operating in the Greater London area with an estimated pupil population of 3000 children (http://www.turkishschools.co.uk/membersc.html). Future research could examine whether this discourse has indeed spread and evolved, by whom and in what ways. Moreover, the findings on language and the economy discussed in this chapter emerged during the ethnographic fieldwork. A study with an explicit focus on language and images of personhood in the globalised new economy would illuminate specific aspects of this discourse further. In particular, one important component of this discourse is the link between successful GCSE and A-level examinations and access to tertiary education and the professions. Although there is anecdotal evidence to this effect, there has not been any systematic research investigating this link. Another area for future research could examine whether Turkish-speaking youth and their families are adopting the new vision of social mobility, who and in what ways and how it may be affecting their language use, attitudes and values towards standard Turkish as well as regional and diasporic varieties of Turkish and Kurdish in complementary schools and at work.

Acknowledgements

The author gratefully acknowledges the financial assistance of the Economic and Social Research Council, UK for the project *Investigating Multilingualism in Complementary Schools in Four Communities*, upon which this chapter draws its data. She is grateful to Angela Creese, Adrian Blackledge, Arvindt Bhatt, Shehila Hamid, Li Wei, Chao-Jung Wu and Dilek Yağcıoğlu-Ali and, in particular, Taşkin Baraç, for insightful discussions at different stages of the project. She also wishes to thank Alexandre Duchêne, Melissa Moyer, Celia Roberts, Tözün Issa, Isil Erduyan and the anonymous reviewers for their very helpful comments. All shortcomings are of course the author's own.

Notes

(1) I thank Tözün Issa for suggesting this term in lieu of 'ethnic economy' to capture the variability within the Turkish-speaking communities and their economic ties with other communities in North London.
(2) The names of schools and participants are all pseudonyms.
(3) This link was repeated in a recent article published by the North London Turkish daily *Haber*, entitled 'Turkish A level opens door to University' (23 October 2010). In this article, the Youth and Education spokesperson of the Federation of Turkish Associations, a current mainstream and former complementary school Turkish language teacher, dispels misconceptions about the acceptance of Turkish A levels by universities, and a group of new university students discuss how their successful Turkish A level results allowed them to go to university. I thank Taşkın Baraç for bringing this article to my attention.

References

Baraç, T. (2009) Language use and emerging ethnicities among London born youth of Turkish descent. Unpublished MA thesis, King's College, London.
Blackledge, A. and Creese, A. (2010) *Multilingualism: A Critical Perspective*. London: Continuum.
Creese, A. and Martin, P. (2006) Interaction in complementary school contexts: Developing identities of choice. An introduction. *Language and Education* 20 (10), 1–4.
Creese, A., Baraç, T., Bhatt, A., *et al.* (2008) *Investigating Multilingualism in Complementary Schools in Four Communities: Final Report*. Birmingham: University of Birmingham.
DES (1981) *The School Curriculum*. London: HMSO.
DfE (2007) *Languages Review*. London: Department of Education. https://www.education.gov.uk/publications/standard/publicationDetail/Page1/DFES-00212-2007.

Francis, B., Archer, L. and Mau, A. (2009) Language as capital, or language as identity? Chinese complementary school pupils' perspectives on the purposes and benefits of complementary schools. *British Educational Research Journal* 35 (4), 519–538.

Francis, B., Archer, L. and Mau, A. (2010) Chinese complementary school pupils' social and educational subjectivities. In V. Lytra and P. Martin (eds) *Sites of Multilingualism. Complementary Schools in Britain Today* (pp. 85–96). Stoke-on-Trent: Trentham.

Gregory, E., Long, S. and Volk, D. (eds) (2004) *Many Pathways to Literacy: Young Children Learning with Siblings, Grandparents, Peers and Communities*. London: Routledge.

Heller, M. (ed.) (2007) *Bilingualism: A Social Approach*. London: Palgrave/Macmillan.

Heller, M. (2010) The commodification of language. *Annual Review of Anthropology* 39, 101–114.

Issa, T. (2005) *Talking Turkey. The Language, Culture and Identity of Turkish Speaking Children in Britain*. Stoke-on-Trent: Trentham.

Issa, T. (2008) Multiculturalism and inter-group dynamics: Language, culture and the identity of Turkish-speaking youth in the UK. In V. Lytra and N. Jørgensen (eds) *Multilingualism and Identities Across Contexts: Cross-disciplinary Perspectives on Turkish-speaking Youth in Europe* (pp. 151–177). Copenhagen Studies in Bilingualism 45. Copenhagen: University of Copenhagen.

Issa, T., Allen, K. and Ross, A. (2008) Young people's educational attainment in London's Turkish, Turkish Kurdish and Turkish Cypriot communities. Report for the Mayor of London's Office. Institute of Policy Studies in Education. London Metropolitan University, London.

Kenner, C., Gregory, E. and Ruby, M. (2007) Developing bilingual learning strategies in mainstream and community contexts. Final Report ESRC R000221528. Goldsmiths, University of London, London.

Li Wei (2006) Complementary schools, past, present and future. *Language and Education* 20 (1), 76–83.

Li Wei and Wu, C.-J. (2010) Literacy and socialisational teaching in Chinese complementary schools. In V. Lytra and P. Martin (eds) *Sites of Multilingualism. Complementary Schools in Britain Today* (pp. 33–44). Stoke-on-Trent: Trentham.

Lytra, V. (2010) Investigating discourses on language and the economy: The case of Turkish complementary schools in the UK. Paper presented at the AILA Language and Migration Seminar, University of Fribourg, Fribourg.

Lytra, V. (2011) Negotiating language, culture and pupil agency in complementary school classrooms. *Linguistics and Education* 22 (1), 23–36.

Lytra, V. (2012) Discursive constructions of language and identity: Parents' competing perspectives in London Turkish complementary schools. *Journal of Multilingual and Multicultural Development* 33 (1), 85–100.

Lytra, V. and Baraç, T. (2008) Language practices, language ideologies and identity construction in London Turkish complementary schools. In V. Lytra and N. Jørgensen (eds) *Multilingualism and Identities Across Contexts: Cross-disciplinary Perspectives on Turkish-speaking Youth in Europe* (pp. 15–43). Copenhagen Studies in Bilingualism 45. Copenhagen: University of Copenhagen.

Lytra, V. and Baraç, T. (2009) Multilingual practices and identity negotiations among Turkish-speaking young people in a diasporic context. In A-B. Stedström and A. Jørgensen (eds) *Youngspeak in a Multilingual Perspective* (pp. 55–78). Amsterdam/Philadelphia: John Benjamins.

Lytra, V. and Martin, P. (eds) (2010) *Sites of Multilingualism. Complementary Schools in Britain Today*. Stoke-on-Trent: Trentham.

Lytra, V., Martin, P., Baraç, T. and Bhatt A. (2010) Investigating the intersection of multilingualism and multimodality in Turkish and Gujarati literacy classes. In V. Lytra and P. Martin (eds) *Sites of Multilingualism. Complementary Schools in Britain Today* (pp. 19–31). Stoke-on-Trent: Trentham.

Martin, P. and Sneddon, R. (2012) Alternative spaces of learning in east London: Opportunities and challenges. *Diaspora, Indigenous, and Minority Education* 6 (1), 34–49.

Martin. P., Creese, A., Bhatt, A. and Bhojani, N. (2004) Complementary schools and their communities in Leicester. Final Report ESRC R000223949. University of Leicester, Leicester.

Mehmet Ali, A. (2001) *Turkish-speaking Communities and Education. No Delight.* London: Fatal Publications.

National Centre for Languages (2006) *Positively Plurilingual. The Contribution of Community Languages to UK Education and Society.* Reading: CILT.

National Centre for Languages (2009) *Community Languages Bulletin* 24.

Portes, A. and Zhou, M. (1993) The new second generation: Segmented assimilation and its variants. *Annals of the American Academy of Political and Social Science* 530 (Interminority Affairs in the US: Pluralism at the Crossroads, November), 74–96.

Turkish Cypriot Forum (1999) Turkish Cypriot children in London schools. Report by the International Centre for Intercultural Studies and the Culture, Communication and Societies Group, Institute of Education, University of London, London.

Yurdakul. G. (2006) State, political parties and immigrant elites: Turkish immigrant associations in Berlin. *Journal of Ethnic and Migration Studies* 32 (3), 425–453.

Part 3

Sites of Resistance

8 'Integration hatten wir letztes Jahr'. Official Discourses of Integration and Their Uptake by Migrants in Germany

Werner Holly and Ulrike Hanna Meinhof

The continuing influx of migrant populations into European societies is widely perceived as one of the major challenges of the 21st century. Although the European Union has set a very general legal and social framework for all partner states, there is considerable diversity in the ways in which this translates itself into national, regional and local practices. The political science literature has clearly advanced our understanding of European cultural diversity at the more general and abstract level (Delanty & Rumford, 2005), but remains largely silent as to the more everyday discourses and practices, the paradoxes, prejudices and confusions arising among the people themselves. And yet it is specifically at local and personal level that everyday discourses about identity and integration, about who does and who does not belong and about what 'belonging' actually means can be studied and compared.

The main emphasis of our chapter focuses on a particularly prevalent discourse, which shapes current debates about migration in the official channels of politics and in the media: namely that of 'integration'. Integration discourses in Germany have largely replaced the earlier more polarised debates about a 'Leitkultur' – usually describing positions on the political right – and those of 'multiculturalism' and 'cultural diversity', more associated with the political left (Kiwan & Meinhof, 2006). Integration by contrast offers a typically vague compromise formula for addressing and critiquing the ways in which migrants are perceived to accommodate or not to their new society and ways of life. As a result it has become *the* formula, which everyone invokes and needs to engage with, but with different emphases, inflections and evaluations.

The relationship between integration discourses as they filter top-down from European and national policy discussions to the more regional and local levels, and their eventual uptake 'bottom-up' by those who are mainly targeted – namely ordinary people of migration background – offers an interesting spectrum for studying what we would like to describe as 'discursive resistance'. In the second section of this chapter we will argue that such resistance discourses are not consciously or strategically formulated as an outright protest *against*, or a subversion or rejection *of* official discourses and policies, but rather articulate themselves in more subtle, often unconscious reconfigurations of the grammar and of the lexical field of integration, where questions of who does, or is supposed to integrate with whom, into what, and by which means, are continuously posed. We argue that it is through individual migrants' discursive modifications of the hegemonic but ultimately vague and paradoxical policy discourse of integration that they retain or reclaim their personal agency and cultural capital within a society that invariably places them at the margin.

Our chapter is thus not focusing on institutional discourse in the classical sense of official rules and norms through which public bodies or administrations articulate migration policies and laws, nor on the institutional discourses of migrant organisations. Instead we aim to give a voice to the bottom-up view of ordinary members of those ethnic minorities who need to engage with the effects of policy discourses as they appear and are mediated through the communication agencies in the public sphere and are often re-articulated by popular and often racist majority society opinions. We show how those at the receiving end manage to come to terms with both, the vague integration formulas of top-down institutional communication about migration *and* the discriminatory language and behaviour of sections of the public. The discursive strategies of migrants, identified here as resistance discourses, appear in the direct and highly localised context of everyday communicative action and not at the institutional level of organisations at either end of the public spectrum.

The Larger Setting: *Sefone* and the Dynamics of Mental and Geopolitical Bordering

In the first section of this chapter we will briefly introduce the larger context of our work within the Sefone project, leading to an analysis of the ways in which official discourses of integration are constructed at national and local level. Our chapter is based on our fieldwork at two sites – the eastern German town of Chemnitz in the federal state of Saxony, and the western German town of Bayreuth in Upper Franconia. This research formed part of a much larger project: the multi-sited 7th EU Framework research project *Sefone*[1] or, to give it its full name, *Searching for Neighbours: New Dynamics of Geopolitical and Mental Borders in Europe*. Our project inter-related two often quite distinct research areas, namely border studies with studies of migration, race and ethnicity, since it defined and compared bordering and neighbouring activities in different sites of multicultural co-existence. Not only did it bring into a comparative frame 'bordering' or 'neighbouring' activities across political borders, which in the case of Cyprus were ethnic divisions, whereas in some Hungarian borderlands as for example on the Hungarian–Slovacian border were divisions between ethnic Hungarians as a majority and a minority population on either side of the border. It also compared these to other sites in and across Germany and Italy without a political border, where 'borders' between majority and minority populations of different ethnicities had no material but a purely mental and symbolic character.

Our overall aim was to search out various forms of good neighbouring practices across these geopolitically and ethnically defined borders, and to do so by participant observation of everyday life practices, extensive ethnographic interviews on which the extracts in this chapter are based, and the analysis of both official and personal discourse. Seen through this complex prism, it became obvious early on that integration discourses were not only prevalent in the macro-discussion of how different European states and its nationals would integrate with one another at the supranational level, but they also permeated the different debates about multicultural co-existence at national and subnational levels. In this second context, integration became the central policy aim as a means of achieving social cohesion in light of the steadily growing number of citizens with migration backgrounds.

Given the large number of German policy papers at national level of which the *Zuwanderungsgesetz* (Immigration Law) in 2004 and the *Nationale Integrationsplan* (National Integration Plan; see Beauftragte der Bundesregierung für Migration, Flüchtlinge und Integration, 2007) in 2007 are just two of the most important cornerstones, and in light of the dense clusters of migrants in metropolitan cities, it may at first sight seem surprising that this chapter focuses on integration discourses in two German provinces and their medium-sized administrative centres. The majority of work in migration studies focuses on concentrated diasporic communities in *metropolitan* cities, such as the North Africans in the banlieues of Paris or the

Turkish populations of Berlin, to name just two obvious examples. Provincial towns and regions are rarely discussed in this context.

In basing our discussion on interviews and participant observations with migrants and policy makers in two *provincial* German towns we can show, in exemplary form, the extent to which migration and multicultural neighbourhoods have long ceased to be a purely metropolitan phenomenon. Both towns have minority populations that echo to some extent the political and economic allegiances of the (former) GDR and FRG before unification, as well as its post-1990 shared immigration policies.[2] This manifests itself, for example, in quite a sizeable Vietnamese population in Chemnitz as against the strong Turkish presence in Bayreuth, as well as in both towns the so-called 'contingency refugees' (Jews from the former Soviet Union) and 'ethnic Germans/Spätaussiedler' (from former socialist countries), who were granted citizenship on the basis of 'ius sanguinis' (ethnic origin) rather than 'ius soli' (place of birth).[3]

National and regional policy context

Let us now briefly turn to the general context in which the integration debate is framed at national level. Following years of heated parliamentary battles, the efforts of the first national red-green coalition government (1998–2005) finally achieved a modification of Germany's strict immigration laws in 2004 with the so-called *Zuwanderungsgesetz*, which gave limited citizenship rights to long-term residents of migration background. Thus, formally at least, an element of closure had been achieved. However, the controversies around the whole complex of migration and citizenship are far from completed but move back and forth in continuing discursive waves between assent and dissent, liberalisation and retrenchment, with opinions – though overall polarised between red/green and liberal/conservative – often cutting right across the party-political spectrum, with successive politicians entering the fray in search of the popular vote.

The most spectacular recent debate, in 2010, was sparked by a highly polemical book by a Social Democrat politician, Thilo Sarrazin, a former Berlin senator in charge of finances, who in 2009 had just taken up an influential post on the Executive Board of the German Federal Bank. The book, with the inflammatory title *Deutschland schafft sich ab* [Germany Abolishes Itself] (Sarrazin, 2009), attacked German immigration policy and multiculturalism, focusing in particular on the presence of Muslims, who by their ideological make-up and supposed existence in their own 'parallel society' were accused of endangering the future of Germany and its peaceful existence. The ensuing outcry cost Sarrazin his position in the Federal Bank and briefly even threatened his membership of the Social Democratic Party (SPD). The exclusion from the party did not, however, happen in the end, probably because the SPD was not willing to risk disapproval from some sections of the public, including some of its own members, and some of the right-leaning media, who rallied behind Sarrazin. Dressed up in the mantle of the democratic right for free speech, arguments were widely aired that he had only dared to express the views of a silent majority and that bringing the debate out in the open was a necessary and worthy democratic principle.

Similarly, in 2010, when the newly elected President of Germany, Christian Wulff[4] – a former Christian Democrat (CDU) politician, then widely seen as a potential rival and successor for the chancellorship of his party colleague Angela Merkel – declared in a major speech at the anniversary of German unification that 'Islam is a part of Germany',[5] he aroused sharp opposition from the CSU, the more right-wing Bavarian sister party of the Conservatives. Angela Merkel, in turn, while agreeing with Wulff about the positioning of Islam, also appeared to jump on the Sarrazin bandwagon in a speech where she claimed that 'multiculturalism was a failure'.[6]

Several months later, in 2011, on taking up office in the National Parliament, the new Minister of the Interior, Hans-Peter Friedrich from the CSU, reopened this debate. In a direct recall of Wulff's speech he declared that 'Islam does not belong to Germany', a Germany with a 'Leitkultur' of Christian traditions and the German language, adding his own populist call for a 'preventative council' (*Präventionsgipfel*) against the terrorist threat.[7] This link and the implication that prevention of terrorism was the CSU's special policy – a view subsequently praised by CSU party leader Seehofer – rather than a shared perspective of Muslims and Christians alike, in turn offended the Council of Islam, who had already themselves made prevention of extremism one of their targets in their work with young people.

What all this wrangling shows is that the new immigration policies, which finally seemed to have achieved a broad consensus after decades of political disagreement, are by no means so securely anchored in the political discourse nor in the opinions of the general public that they do not offer themselves as useful tools to ambitious populist politicians. In trying to capture or retain the votes of the extreme or even just the broad right, the topic of immigration is far from losing its rhetorical potential to gather votes.

Integration politics

It is against this context that the ubiquitous buzzword of integration has to be understood, since it allows a compromise between the positions on the right and on the left, between Leitkultur and multiculturalism. After the demise of the red/green government, the subsequent Great Coalition between CDU/CSU and SPD continued the emphasis on integration politics, culminating in 2007 in a National Integration Plan (*Nationaler Integrationsplan*) with a double focus on providing training in German language and culture for resident migrants as well as improving their occupational skills (see also Stevenson & Schanze, 2009).

Two reasons, in particular, may explain why even conservative politicians have begun to embrace immigration as an undeniable feature of contemporary Germany: on the one hand, the growing awareness that the low and declining birth-rate of native Germans would make economic growth and international competition unlikely unless demographic figures were boosted by migrant populations; on the other, the reaction to the results of the OECD's PISA Studies (Programme for International Student Assessment, 2000, 2003, 2006) which showed that in international comparisons between OECD countries, German pupils underperformed in the three skills tested – reading, mathematics and science. This embarrassing outcome was widely blamed on children of migration background and the insufficient support given to them in the school system.

Integration thus offered a convenient compromise term for developing policies that would take note of the undeniable fact that more than 15 million people in a population of 81 million in Germany have a migration background, making them a social, cultural and economic reality. With the Integration Plan, a whole series of new offices, policies and conferences were unleashed which made integration neologisms grow like mushrooms. The following are just a few examples of the framing of the official discourse, cutting right across from the national to the regional to the town level: there are, for example, the new offices, officers, councils and integration summits (*Integrationsbehörde, Integrationsbeauftragte, Integrationsbeirat, Integrationsgipfel*), but there are also terms which describe people's willingness and ability, or unwillingness and inability to integrate (*Integrationsfähigkeit/Integrationsverweigerer*). The latter in particular offer themselves as convenient scapegoats for all kinds of problems so that criminality, youth violence, child poverty, unemployment, educational failure and other social evils particularly prevalent in big cities with large migrant populations can be explained away not as a failure of public policies but as problems caused by non-integrated migrants and their 'parallel societies'.

Although, at the level of political rhetoric, integration is often declared to be not just a one-way street but a mutual task for majority and minority populations alike, such awareness is rarely evoked in settings where conflicts of whatever kind are foregrounded. Hence, if we want to go beyond the clichéd phrases of integration politics, we need to understand the ways in which people experience these top-down formulas and work them into their own discursive repertoire and social practices (see also Carstensen-Egwuom & Holly, 2011).

Why Provincial Towns Matter as Research Sites for Multicultural Neighbourhoods

Integration at local level: Bayreuth and Chemnitz

Before we show in detail the ways in which integration does or does not enter the everyday language of ordinary citizens, let us explain why provincial towns provide such intriguing settings for studying integration discourses. Not only are they rarely studied in migration research but, more importantly, municipal policies in the provinces echo the developments and shifts in national policy, yet need to translate these into local measures and initiatives directed at their specific migrant populations. Since the origin of migrants in these two provincial towns also offers an interesting contrast numerically and ethnically in their demographics, reflecting not only recent or contemporary migration flows but also the different recruitment histories and cultural predispositions of the two German states prior to unification, integration practices in Bayreuth and Chemnitz share certain features but differ in others. Let us look at just a few of these.

Bayreuth, which has quite a high percentage of people with a migration background, boasts an 'Integration officer' (*Integrationsbeauftragte*) with his own newsletter and high visibility on the town's website, but his office was transferred from the centre of town's main town hall to a much less central older building and a smaller office. Many of the officers involved are either part-time or voluntary. By contrast, the *Ausländeramt* (Foreigner office), infamous with migrants for its harsh policy of deportation and lack of understanding of their problems, has remained in the main building.

Integration policies in Chemnitz have a firmer institutional grounding. These include the Integration Network (*Integrationsnetzwerk*), which brings together all the organisations dealing with immigration issues and the Foreigners' Advisory Council (*Ausländerbeirat*), which is appointed by the city council every four years and interacts directly with the city council, thus helping to strengthen the voice of the immigrant residents. The *Ausländerbeauftrage* (Officer for foreigners) publishes regular reports on the situation of foreign citizens (*Ausländerbericht*) and in 2008 the city council voted for a 'Rahmenplan zur Integration von Migrantinnen und Migranten' (Masterplan for the integration of migrants).

Whereas in Bayreuth several of the official integration activities take place with major support coming from the Lutheran and to a lesser extent the Catholic Church, Chemnitz follows a more secular route. In both towns the 'Intercultural Week(s)' is one of the flagships of the respective annual integration activities, but it has a somewhat different flavour, as well as a different duration, in each. Dorsch (2011) has shown the ways in which the 2008 Intercultural Week in Bayreuth was marked by absences, with many associations either not participating at all or – as was the case with the groups of Germans from the former Soviet Union in the 2007 event – dominating the event through 'performing their identities to themselves' rather than following the spirit of the event and mingling across the multicultural spectrum. Hence the whole idea of celebrating cultural diversity became overshadowed by divisions between different groups and a general lack of interest from the general public. In Chemnitz a whole month of activities ('Interkulturelle Wochen') is a well-established cultural event with a 20-year tradition; in 2010, it presented more than 60 single events (but see Carstensen-Egwuom, 2011, for a critical account of one of the African entries).

In both towns, a large contingent of recent – that is post-*Wende* – newcomers are the so-called *Spätaussiedler* – ethnic Germans from the former Soviet Union and other socialist countries – who are not officially listed as foreign because of their German passports, but who are widely perceived as major problems for integration. Also present in both towns are the so-called 'contingent refugees' – Jewish people usually from the former Soviet Union. They are not perceived as problem immigrants, at least not in the official discourse, and major efforts are made to accommodate their religious needs by building new synagogues. But this is where the similarity between the two towns stops, since other migration streams often pre-date German unification.

In Bayreuth, with an immigration history dating back several generations to the guest-worker recruitment of the late 1950s and early 1960s, people of Turkish origin, many of whom are Muslims, make up the largest contingent of 'foreigners'. In spite of their long-established residency and the involvement of many in the cultural and civic life of the town, the perceived cultural and religious differences between Muslims and non-Muslims continue to dominate discussions about integration, with special events devoted to better integration supported by the town council, but also the churches and mosques. Both the Lutheran and Catholic churches are equally active agents here. Commentaries by key officials filmed, edited and pasted on YouTube[8] during a Christian–Muslim peace initiative of 2008 show how integration terminology is used by all concerned as a way of bridging the perceived cultural differences between 'us' and 'them'. Filmed as part of an 'open door' day where the local Mosque, the Islamic Centre as well as

Christian Churches of both denominations invited those of other beliefs to pay a visit, the clip featuring comments made by two official representatives – the deputy chair of the Turkish-Islam community in Bayreuth and the deputy mayor of the town – and one practising Muslim from the Islamic Centre, shows how all three implicitly as well as explicitly engage with integration rhetoric as a means for imagining co-existence. Yet in all three comments there is also an underlying distinction between 'us' and 'them', albeit from the different positions of 'Muslim' or 'German'/'Bayreuthian'. But at least in targeting the Germans and Bayreuthians as the ones who should step in and learn, they also implicitly critique the integration discourses of the CSU that place the onus entirely on migrants.

Isolation and prejudice

Another reason for an interest in provincial towns is that migrants perceive themselves to be much more isolated and observed here. This is particularly strongly felt in Chemnitz, which has a much smaller percentage of migrants than Bayreuth. Time and again discrimination was raised as a particular feature of life in the provinces. One of our informants, a German mother of an Afro-German family, told us that her black friends from Cologne felt really uncomfortable on their visit to Chemnitz:

als der nach C kam, sagt er: was isn hier los, s is ja wie im Zoo, dass sich eben dann jeder umdreht und kuckt[9]

When he came to Chemnitz, he said: what's going on here, it's like in a zoo, everyone turns around and stares at you

Later in the conversation she mentions the Saxonian town of Pirna (near Dresden), where a report showed that local people were complaining that foreigners took their work. She rejects that attitude, pointing out that there were no foreigners in Pirna and, besides, no work was to be had there in any case. She sees much better opportunities in the more relaxed atmosphere of bigger cities with more foreign workers:

Dort, wo die Ausländer arbeiten, da sind die eigentlich viel mehr akzeptiert, also zum Beispiel in München, da sacht mein Mann ooch, das is locker, also da kommt er sich ne komisch vor, hier kuckt jeder komisch, aber da isses eben nich so, oder in Berlin.

Where foreigners do work they are much more accepted. In Munich, for example, my husband says that it is relaxed there, he doesn't feel funny there, but here everyone looks at you in a weird way, but there or in Berlin, it's not like that

Such comments are not only made by blacks who feel that they face discrimination because of the colour of their skin, but also by others who look a bit different for other reasons. Thus a young Jewish woman from the Ukraine complains about being asked by a female doctor whether she came from Georgia because of the colour of her hair and her more exotic looks, and feels like dyeing her hair to become less visible. All of this shows that provincial towns are by no means unproblematic places for migrants, in part and precisely because of their relatively smaller numbers. There is a certain paradox here: as individuals, in their everyday life, they are much more visible in their 'foreignness' and thus easy prey for prejudices against them, whereas on the institutional level it is much harder for them to make their voices heard.

Integration Discourses and Strategies of Resistance

What we will now show, in the second part of this article, are the ways in which ordinary people from different backgrounds who live in or at the outskirts of Bayreuth and Chemnitz engage with the discursive cluster of integration in their everyday narratives as social practices. This section demonstrates how, in the process of appropriation, forms of discursive resistance can be identified through the different ways in which the clichéd formula of integration is critiqued, modified, varied and/or strategically used.

We present these extracts as eight discursive strategies, from the most straightforward strategy of avoidance of the formula altogether to increasingly subtle forms of modifications and adaptations and, finally, to the point where it is used as a means of self-empowerment. Obviously these strategies are not hard and fast distinctions but merely an attempt to identify a range of discursive manoeuvres on a sliding scale.

(1) Avoidance

The first extract typically shows the ways in which integration discourses tend to be evoked in situations where the relationship between minority and majority populations is problematised in politically correct modes and avoided or even rendered redundant in situations where ethnic background is irrelevant as a marker of difference. Our informant Michael is a young German who lives in a small town (Speichersdorf) where a large number of 'Germans from Russia' (*Spätaussiedler*) were housed and where they are perceived as a major problem. Unconnected to this, and due to his engagement with young skateboarders in Bayreuth, Michael was offered by the town council the old derelict chocolate factory as a site to build a skate-park for the youngsters. What was striking in our conversation with him was the contrast in his own linguistic labelling preferences.

In the first context, when he talked to us about the integration efforts in Speichersdorf, he used the politically correct label 'Germans from Russia', listing the many different ways in which the commune was engaging in various integration activities with them, with some moderate success but nevertheless with continuing problems. In the second context, when talking about the kids who came together in the skatepark, he used the much more frequent but officially (and by the people themselves) rejected label 'die Russen' (the Russians), but in a crucial linguistic twist avoids the label of 'integration', replacing it by the individually motivated word 'to become friendly with'. Asked about the children with a migration background involved in the skatepark, this is how he puts it:

da kamen alle Schichten mit vorbei, die einfach mal Spass haben wollten und auch von jedem Landesteil, den man sich so vorstellen kann, auf einmal kamen auch viele Russen auf dem Skateboard, die haben das einfach mal ausprobiert, das war toll, des is irgendwo normal geworden.

And [kids from] all social classes came along, who just wanted to have some fun, and from every part of the country [...] all of the sudden quite a lot of Russians came with their skateboards, who just wanted to have a go, that was great, somehow all that became quite normal.

What this quote suggests is that, in everyday life contexts where a hobby or activity of whatever kind is truly shared between different individuals, the labels of integration are no longer appropriate or are even unconsciously avoided because of their problematising associations. 'Russians' with their skateboards can be normal co-skaters, whereas Germans from Russia in Speichersdorf are approached and marked by the top-down efforts of integration politics (see also Meinhof, 2011).

(2) Rejection

In the debate about migration and integration, nearly any topos, any discursive element, is somehow controversial, so that it is not astonishing if one of these elements is simply rejected by one or the other of those involved. Rejecting aspects of an unacceptable proposition is an obvious strategy besides the mere avoidance of the whole problem. It is a first step in the process of resisting those parts of a prevalent discourse which cannot be associated with one's own position. Our material is full of examples of such discursive rejections, either by the explicit denial of a controversial claim, or by more implicit means. The following extract offers one such example concerning the topic of the school success of migrant children.

As we pointed out before, the less-than-promising results of the PISA Studies for schoolchildren in Germany, blamed in part on migrant children's poor performance and a general perception of linguistic deficiencies in long-term migrants, became central in the rethinking of fundamental attitudes and practical measures for migrants and their children, with the acquisition of linguistic competences as one of the key pathways towards integration. For several years now, the conviction that 'language does matter' has become one of the mantras of German integration policies.

Against this background, Vietnamese migrants – here from our Chemnitz sample – without being specifically asked, stress the remarkably good school results of their children:

> unser kINder die in der SchUle sin ich kann auch schon stol sein [...]
> das (--) mit der lEIstung (-) das kann man nicht sagen dass wir unsere
> vietnamesen kinder schlecht sind (-) im allgemeinen sagen fat neunzig
> prozent oder über neunzig prozent (-) deh: vietnamesen kinder die
> lernen in (-) gymnasial gymnasium (2.0) u:nd von dort hER dass
> fast zu hundert prozent die gehen auf e stu zum studium

> *Of our children who are in school I can be proud – and regarding their*
> *achievement there one cannot say that our Vietnamese children are bad – in*
> *general one can say nearly 90 per cent or more than 90 per cent of Vietnamese*
> *children learn in a grammar school, grammar school, and of those nearly*
> *hundred per cent go to university*

In this extract a leading member of the Vietnamese Association declares in his own broken German his pride in the good school performances of Vietnamese children, and explicitly denies the frequently aired assumption about their educational failure. In stating 'You cannot say that our Vietnamese children are bad' in school, he directly rejects an underlying but unspoken discourse about the educational failure of migrant children.

After this general assertion, he offers detailed information about school type and numbers, listing the continuing and increasing success of Vietnamese children, claiming that 90% go to grammar school and of those 100% continue to universities. In the following part (not transcribed here), he even proposes to conduct a study into the reasons for these successful school careers, in order to be able to make recommendations for better ways of integrating children from other migrant groups into the education system.

Earlier on in the conversation, his denial of another current assumption about the Vietnamese community, namely that they are 'isolated', is a further example for the ways in which he rejects prevalent discourses:

die kontakts zwien vietnamesische kinder und deutsche kinder (.) ist (1.0) ich kann sagen es gibt keine keine keine hemmungen oder keine äh keine isolierungen oder keine keine underschIEd ne (.) =weil unsere kinder die lernen (.) in der schule (.) =die lerne mit deutsche kinder (.) un die haben auch sehr gute kontakt

The contacts between Vietnamese children and German children is – I can say – there are no no inhibitions or no eh no isolations or no no differences cause our children they learn in school they learn with German children and they have very good contact

The way in which the term *isolations* (sic) appears in this narrative is somewhat surprising. Wedged between lack of 'inhibitions' and lack of 'differences' – two terms which fit the context of describing the good contact between Vietnamese and German children, the reference to lack of isolations is quasi 'inserted' as a phrase from the general discourse level. In the assertion that Vietnamese children are not isolated from German children, an implicit accusation echoing the debates about migrants' parallel societies and their wilful isolation from majority society is specifically brought up and rejected.

(3) Regrammaticalisation

The next example makes it even clearer that typical discourse elements are regrammaticalised to fit a different semantic. As before, the key reference is an implicit accusation that migrants keep themselves to themselves:

ist nicht dass wir nur AB!seits sin [nur isoLIERT sin is NICHT ne hm sonnern (--) wir haben zum BEIspiel (1.5) (bei Trung Thu FEST)(---) ich kann au (---) au diese (.) AN!dere (-) AUS(sch)ländische (.) MITbürger oder ANdere (-) migrantn (.) AUCH (-)JA. Hm EINgeladen (--) äh EINgeladen und (-) ja (.) und mit un MITzufeiern oder weil (.) ja (-) (wir) (--) bei (inteGRAzon) in die geSELLschaft ham wir auch (.) EINgeladen (--) oder

it's not (the case) that we're only marginalised only isolated, it's not (like that) but for example for Trung Thu festival we have invited , uh invited these other foreign fellow citizens or other migrants -- also (them) and -- well and to celebrate with us or because, well, we -- at the integration in the society we have also invited them

This extract raises the question whether the non-standard grammar 'we have invited them at the integration' should be interpreted as a grammatical error for the verb and noun of the process words 'to integrate' and 'integration', or as a semantic shift. On its own this would be difficult to decide. But in the context of the same informant's further reference to their festival and an accompanying invitation poster, 'Integration with traditional full-moon festival 2008' on the wall of the hall where the integration party was supposed to be held, it can be seen that there is indeed a semantic shift. The process of integration has become an event with a reversed direction: migrants are not seen as people in need of integration into majority society; instead, people from the majority society are invited to integrate with the Vietnamese and their traditions:

> da is eine schiene da is ((integration)) in de gesellschaft und äh wir sin ((viellei)) au stolz darauf dass wir wie gesaht seit zwounneunzig şogar((leichtes lachen)) au sehr aktiv sin. hh ja das zweite ((schiene)) das ((unser)) pflege un verbreitung unser tradidition das is = da haben wir au regelmäßich unsere ((gebräune))verbreitet un organisIErt für unser lansleute für unser kinder(--) nicht zu erzähln ((dass)) ich vergesse niht dass wir(--) fast (--) ((sejes)) jahr eine ((tutu))fest(-)äh((vollsmond))fest mittelherbsfest ((vollsmondmittelherbsfest)) dat is immer am fümfzehnte august ((nach)) mondkAlender(---) un da is äh(-)das fest für(-)der k[in]der

> *there is one strand and that is integration into the society, and perhaps we are a bit proud that since 92 -- as I already said -- we have even been very active ourselves (laughing), well, the second strand is that we care for and disseminate our tradition ... so we regularly have disseminated our customs and organised – for our compatriots for our children - I don't want to forget to tell that almost every year we organise a full moon festival -- a mid-autumn festival -- a full moon mid-autumn festival, that is always on the 15th of August according to the moon calendar and that is the festival for the children.*

(4) Resignification

The following example also involves the keyword 'integration', but here the shift is not concerning a shift in grammatical structure, but the official meaning is challenged because the informant's own convictions do not conform with it. The informant is the mother of a large Afro-German family, a German who is married to a Mozambiquan with whom she has six children of her own plus an adopted child from Mozambique. In the extract below, she links her discussion of 'integration' to a media text where – so it must be inferred – the possibility of the competing model, that of 'Multikulti', a common short version of multiculturalism, has been denied:

das is eben mit diesen ganzn:= ä::hm (1.0) th: (.) inte!GRIERN! immer so ne SAche; also ich hab letzens n artikel gelesn in ner zeitung- (-) wo das ooch darum ging:,= dass dieses (.) multiKUlti und dass das (.) nicht mehr:(.) geht, also dass (.) das das eigentlich nich (-) STATTfindet. (---) also dass das nicht nich n DING is:- was irgendwie: (2.0) mh::: na EINS is sondern das sind dann viele nebenANDER; (2.0) und so is zum beispiel- sind die mosambikANer unter sich- (---) un und erZÄHLN sich- (.) hast schon gehört? (.) der und DER, (.) in berlIN is einer gestorben: und (--)SO- (-) was keen DEUtscher eigentlich dann mitkriegt, (-) das ist deen ihr (--) DING. (--) die sin aber natürlich jetze integriert- die gehn hier arbeiten- die sprechen DEUtsch

Well, there's this whole business of integrating. I've recently read an article in a newspaper where they also discussed that this kind of multikulti stuff doesn't go any more, that it doesn't really happen, that it isn't a thing of all into one, but many alongside each other. And so for example the people from Mozambique are amongst themselves and they tell each other – did you hear such and such has died in Berlin and no German knows anything about that, that is their thing and they are of course integrated here, they work here, they speak German

It is interesting to note here how she references the two key terms: integration and multiculturalism. Her sceptical distance to these is expressed by several means which are impossible to render into English: pejorative demonstrative articles, in one case reinforced by *ganz* (*mit diesen ganzn integriern, dieses multikulti*), a colloquial predicate to express strong doubts (*das is eben ... immer so ne sache*). Her everyday paraphrase of both notions uses a very simple illustration: *nich n ding was eins is, sondern viele nebenander: it isn't a thing of all into one, but many alongside each other*. This is then followed by a narrative about Mozambiquan people sharing news that Germans do not understand. Her example underlines that both cultures are quite separate. The point of her argument is that, of all people, these are migrants who are seemingly 'integrated' in relation to the two main official criteria: they have work and they speak German. We want to suggest that her statement that something does not work (*dass das eigentlich nich stattfindet*) is about the impossibility of integration; not even those officially 'integrated' persons are 'really integrated'.

What she constructs here is a difference between an 'official' and an 'authentic' notion of *integration*. As a member of a multicultural family with a personal stake in the integration model, she is still not willing to accept the official version but has a different daily and more authentic version with her own Afro-German family (see extract in the next section). The pattern of resistance she uses in these utterances is thus a 'resignification' of a very central discursive element.

(5) Modification

Whereas the former examples suggested various strategies of resignification of the current German migration discourse, the next extracts offer examples where migrants modify a standard topic associated with integration and multiculturalism: namely that of discrimination, especially against black or mixed-race migrants. The next extract comes again from the same German mother of the Afro-German family. Here she offers a narrative from her own experience that underlines discriminatory practices:

naja. (-) aber es is (,) halt auch HIEr so geWEsen (.) am Anfang (--) sowas hört dann immer mein MANN; (.) isch hÖr des gar nisch=isch hab mir das ABgewöhnt sowas zu hÖrn (.) der hat gesagt da kamen KINder (-) (andn') also hat=mer noch keen zaun hier ans GRUNdstück un ham gesAgt (--) solln mer euch erSCHIESSen oder verBRENNen

Well, it was like this here as well. It's the kind of thing my husband gets to hear all the time. I don't listen to this any more, I've given up listening to that. He said that there were children – it was at the time when we didn't have a fence around our plot and they said, shall we shoot you or burn you

The story she relates here highlights a racist discourse that has spread even to children and that regularly affects her husband. Yet even here – and quasi in parenthesis – she shows her own resistance by not taking any notice of such behaviour. 'I don't listen to this any more, I've given up listening to that.' Later she returns to the topos of discrimination by giving the example of the notorious town of Pirna near Dresden that we mentioned earlier, but balances this against her own experiences of her own rural area. Thus she opposes those areas where discrimination is bad with others – here her own village of Altendorf – where it is not so bad.

also <<laut> HIER gEHts ja ne?> ( ) grade wenn ma in so ner LÄNDlischen gegend is=das war schon in ALTENdorf so (.) das heeßt nisch umsonst ALTENdorf wenn ma da beKANNT is- is das alles okEE (.) da gibts dann wirklisch vIEle leute die grÜßen:, oder (.) s kInd war vorneweg gerannt da ham die gesagt ja, ihre kleene is schon dUrsch

oder <<schmunzelnd> irgendwie so> =ebend wie im dORF. und das is
hier Och ganz schnELL so gewesen (.) wenn ma alle grÜßt und SO: (--)
wird ma eigentlisch och angenOMMn (2.5) aber dort des=isch weeß
nisch=isch kann mir das überhaupt ni vorstellen dort zu wohn' (--) also
dass die dort überhaupt noch w!OHNEN! kann i' das kann isch mir (.)
!DA! würd isch (.) DAs wär für misch ne NO-go-area (.) wo die leute
aufm bahnhof verDROschen werdn <<leiser und schneller> und so
was ma dort alles schon gehört hat>

*Well here, it's ok, especially if one lives in a rural area. It was like that in
Altendorf, it's not for nothing that it is called Altendorf (village of the old); if
you're known there it's ok; there are plenty of people who greet you. Once my
child was running ahead and they said, your little one has already run past or
<she smiles> something to that effect, typically village that. And it was like
this pretty early on, if one always says hello to people and so on, then you get
accepted. But there <reference to Pirna> I don't know, I can't even imagine
what it would be like to live there, that there are still people <she means
migrants here> living there at all, I can't I can't, I would..for me that would be
a no-go area, where people get beaten up at the railway station and <speaks
faster and softer> all that stuff one hears from there*

In setting her own friendly village against the other place where people
get beaten up – a reference to Pirna – she not only constructs a safe space for
herself and her family, but she also asserts her own agency and control over
the situation. Being friendly and polite oneself (*wenn ma alle grÜßt und SO*) is
shown as an active survival strategy that allows her to get on well in one
locality that is not so markedly racist as the other. Hence, in spite of the
obvious factor of genuine discrimination, she also refuses to be oppressed
by it. In this way a modification of the topos of discrimination is achieved
by a positive experience and a helpful lesson which can be taken from it.

(6) Adaptation

The next strategy we have identified is what we want to define as 'adaptation'. As before, a discursive element is captured and modified, but here the
element is adapted to the informant's own experiences and, although not
explicitly stated, ends up stating the opposite of the original argument. The
topic is again the question of school performance, which in this case is more
delicate, because children from the Afro-German families, which are the
focus of the next extract, are often less successful. Fortunately, the 17-year-
old daughter (D) does not fit this stereotype. Being quite a tough and
self-confident girl she avoids potential discrimination scenarios by a pattern

of self-stylisation as a rather intimidating young punk lady. In contrast to the many Vietnamese children in her grammar school, she is one of the few Afro-Germans there, a situation which she somewhat provocatively explains by asserting that Afro-German kids are simply too stupid for the grammar school. Her mother (M) initially criticises her for saying so, but then together they adapt and co-construct a more acceptable shared version, namely that the mothers of these children are responsible for their bad school results:

D:	[die komm auch nich auf's gymnasium (.) die sin ja einfach dumm (-) die meisten (-) 's kommt vom umfeld ((lacht)) –
M:	<<enttäuscht> das is (--) schlecht (.) wie du das sagst.>- [also
D:	[na aber das sin (.) wenn ich das (.) das is aber so (.) dass (.) dass die meisten halt auf de fröbel- schule [secondary school] geh'n(-) das sin wirklich viele (.) die auf der fröbel-schule sind (.) da sind mehr schwarze als bei uns anner schule ; (4.0)
Interviewer:	woran liegt das ⸮
D:	na also ich denk (.) das liegt daran (.) dass (.) dass halt ooch wirklich viele von den (.) a(l)so von den müttern (-) so e bissch'n ;
M:	nich intelligent [sin;
D:	[nich intelligent sind (.) ja.;
M:	und das nich vererben könn ;
D:	ja (.) nich so wie meine mutter (.) die (-) hochintelligent is und (.) studiert hat ((lacht));
M:	auch kein Abitur (h)hat , (--) hm. (-) nee's is

D:	*they don't get as far as the grammar school, they're just too stupid – most of them – it's their background*
M:	*<frowning> that's bad how you put that*
D:	*well yeah, but it's like that that most of them go to the Froebel school <a secondary modern> there are plenty of them in the Froebel school. there are more blacks than in our school*
Interviewer:	*and what's the reason for that⸮*
D:	*well I think the reason is that many of their mothers they're a bit*
M:	*unintelligent*
D:	*unintelligent, yes*
M:	*and they can't pass it on*
D:	*not as my Mum who's highly intelligent and who studied at university <giggles>*
M:	*and who has no A-levels either*

Here they pick up racist clichés about the lack of intelligence of migrant children, a prejudice that is also omni-present in the public discourse, with blame being shifted onto the mothers. The mother colludes with this reasoning that the other German mothers from whom she has already distanced herself several times before are simply not intelligent enough. However, at this point her daughter teases her with an ironic reminder of her own lower school degree, thus reducing the genetic explanation to absurdity.

This somewhat embarrassing situation is saved by the interviewer who provides a better reason for lack of school success, namely that of missing support for such children. This reasoning allows a way out of their discursive dilemma.

M: bei den kindern ISSes vielleicht gar nich so: (-) aber die ELTern, (.) also s gibt schon einige die auch der förderschule [special school] besucht ham (--) die MÜtter, und: (--) die sinn nur nich in der LAge dann (-) da viel (3.0) zu fördern (-) selber (5.0) obwohl s auch welche gibt die sich GROße mühe Geben

M: *perhaps it's not the case with the kids: but the parents, there are several who only visited a Foerderschule <special school for those who don't manage basic schooling> the mothers and they can't give much support even though there are many who make a lot of effort*

In short, what we have shown here is the ways in which a highly controversial discursive element is seemingly adopted, but then – and here is one point of resistance – inverted from an argument against the foreigner to an argument against the own group, which is split into two – the educated and the uneducated faction. Thus the discourse is mitigated to better fit the personal situation. The risk of sliding into an equally controversial genetic argument is brought into ridicule by the daughter – another resistance strategy – and finally avoided with the help of a third. The example shows how difficult it is for the individual not to fall into the usual traps of the prevalent discourse patterns.

(7) Transference

The above example could also have been described as a case of transference with one discursive element being passed along from one group to another. This seems to be quite a frequent mechanism if one deals with discriminatory statements, as a means to protect oneself against allegations of prejudice. It is not denied that there is something wrong, but the allocation of guilt is displaced to another group or person.

In some cases the problem is one of socially positioning oneself in a range of vertical stratifications, where one tries to find someone else who is less prestigious, with the aim of not getting oneself the most unfavourable place. The following extract – again from the Afro-German family – reverses the common praxis of discrimination, which normally affects black people, by just turning the tables and showing that it works also against a group of white persons. The daughter distances herself from some young people who, having been banned from all other clubs, come to an African club called 'Palanca'. When the interviewer asks if these youths are Afro-Germans too, the daughter denies that and calls them 'real Germans':

D: neenee nee DEUTsche nur- RICHtig deutsche (.) ja. (-) das sind halt
die; (.) das sind halt dann die EINzigen clubs,=wo die noch
HINdürfen, weil die in die anderen clubs schon (-) verBOT
haben,=dann gehen die in der palanca, und kriegen dort AUCH
irgendwann verbot-=weil sie sich irgendwo (.) RUMkloppen;
jaja: (-) naja (-) keine Ahnung. (--) komische leute halt (.) und das
is aber ha:lt (.) OFT so;=dass dann halt; s=so (---) wo=wo ich sage (.)
w=w=UNterklasse UNterschicht;=dass die dann halt (.) dann
halt in diesem CLUB sind;=deswegen (.) gehe ich da auch NICHT
gerne hin

D: *no only Germans – real Germans, yes, these are the only ones these are
the only clubs where they're allowed to go, because the other clubs have
already barred them – so they go to the Palanca and at some point they'll
get thrown out there as well because they get into all sorts so fights; yeah
yeah no idea, funny people they are; it's well what shall I say a kind of
lower class, underclass who goes to this club and that's why I don't
go there*

At this point the mother steps in and criticises this attitude as repeating the same pattern of exclusion that the blacks have undergone themselves. The daughter earlier on had called this group 'Kloppies' (= 'Bekloppte' = stupids, weirdos) and had described them as 'such people' who begin to drink at five in the afternoon and steal in the adjacent drugstore. She frames them by an overt social classification: they are underclass, lower class ('Unterklasse, Unterschicht'). Against this, the mother draws a parallel between that specific praxis of exclusion and the exclusion of black people, arguing also that only this mechanism of exclusion is the reason for the process of group formation ('dadurch kommen die auch zusammen').

M: ja das hat aber was mit AUSgrenzung zu tun. das is genau das THEma. dass (.) das das LEUte sind, die ooch alle über (.) überall woanders NISCH mehr HINdürfen; genau wie die schwarzen; = die in andre discos nisch REINdürfen. und dadurch (--) KOMmen die auch zusammen

M: *yes but that's something to do with discrimination, that's exactly the topic, that's the people who aren't allowed to go anywhere else, exactly like with blacks who're not allowed into the discos and that's how they group together*

From the perspective of the daughter, a first step to avoid discrimination and being excluded is to switch her allegiances to the other side where the excluders are. She has to struggle against an overall discriminatory situation and to work her way through the restrictive frames set in advance by a powerful public discourse where she, as a black person, is commonly associated with the outsiders. Hers can be seen as a desperate attempt to resist the attacks from outside by switching allegiances.

(8) Self-empowerment

The above example shows already how this 17-year-old girl prefers to be on the side of the aggressor rather than that of the victim. Hence one last strategy of resistance that we want to discuss is what we want to describe as 'self-empowerment'. In the extract below, she dissociates herself from aggressive performances by right-oriented hooligans in the context of football games. Whereas her mother worries about 'no-go-areas' (see paragraph 5), the daughter emphasises her own power:

M: DAs wär für misch ne NO-go-area (.) wo die leute aufm bahnhof verDROschen werdn <<leiser und schneller> und so was ma dort alles schon gehört hat>=

D: =kannste auch (nemmer) nach(=eh=)nach AUe gehn; weeßte wie oft=ISCH in AUE bin?

M: <<leise>naja>

Interviewer: is aue schlIMM,

D: ja schon also s=is=ja (.) schon durschn FUSSball sin = da vIEle die da (.) bissl (.) hOOliganmäßich drauf sin und es is halt ooch so dass da (-) also rischtung ERZgebirge (-) schon: (.) mehrere sind so die bisschen rechts sind so

M: *that would be a no-go area for me, where people get beaten up at the railway station and <speaks faster and softer> all that stuff one hears from there*

D: *then you can't go to Aue no more either; do you know how often I*
                am in Aue
M: *well, yes*
Interviewer: *Is it bad in Aue?*
D: *yes it is, the football alone means that there are quite a number of*
                sort of hooligany people and it is also true that towards the
                Erzgebirge <Ore Mountains> there are quite a number of pretty
                right wing people

The daughter who with her punk look already asserts a self-confident image challenges her mother's fear of no-go areas by mentioning her frequent visits to a nearby town in the Ore Mountains called Aue, which has become famous for a rather successful football team. She puts this to her mother as a rhetorical question: 'Do you know how often I am in Aue?' This underlines her fearless attitude, because 'going to Aue' means having enough courage to face possible threats from the local hooligan scene. The more subdued and defensive reactions of both the mother and the interviewer are in contrast to her self-presentation as a 'cool' girl. The style of her answer to the interviewer's question ('Is it bad in Aue?') is a display of 'coolness': a hedged (*schon*) confirmation, a downgrading of numbers from *many* (*viele*) to *several* (*mehrere*); the predications *sort of hooligany people* (*bissl hooliganmäßig drauf*) and *pretty right wing* (*bisschen rechts so*) have the laid-back and also downgraded quality of a youth slang variety. All of this is further tuned down by a whole range of particles in a lower key (Abtönungspartikeln) (*schon, ja, schon, halt ooch, schon, so, so*). By confirming, but verbally minimising, the dangers coming from this hooligan scene, she increases the amount of her own courage.

In this way a very realistic threat is downplayed not only by her visual self-presentation but also by linguistic means. To what extent this is a bravado performance rather than inherent self-confidence cannot be inferred from the texts alone. But in any case her technique of self-empowerment is a strong expression of resistance against a discourse of male-dominated right-wing oppressors (Ellerbe-Dueck, 2011).

Conclusions

In this chapter we have presented the analysis of a series of interview data from two provincial German towns so as to show the ways in which ordinary people are addressed and framed by the dominant discourses of integration politics in mainstream society and how they cope and resist these in their own everyday conversational practices.

Our fieldwork was conducted under the aegis of a larger EU framework project, Sefone, between 2007 and 2010, which included ethnographic interviews as one of the key methods of data collection and brought into one comparative research frame bordering and 'neighbouring' practices of majority and minority groups on national borders, as well as minorities marked by ethnic and racial divisions in non-border or former border regions in smaller towns and provinces (Armbruster & Meinhof, 2011). This chapter is based on one of the sub-strands of this larger project with our own research in Chemnitz, Saxony in eastern Germany and Bayreuth, Upper Franconia in western Germany.

In a brief review of the German policy debate about migration in the last decade we have highlighted a particularly prevalent discourse that frames policy papers and discussions: namely that of integration. We have shown that integration discourses have largely replaced the earlier more polarised debates about a 'Leitkultur' – usually describing positions on the political right, and those of 'multiculturalism' and 'cultural diversity', more associated with the political left. We have argued that integration by contrast offers a typically vague compromise formula for addressing and critiquing the ways in which migrants are perceived to accommodate or not to accommodate to their new society and ways of life. Hence it has become *the* formula which everyone invokes and needs to engage with, but with different emphases, inflections and evaluations.

The main empirical part of our chapter uses extracts from our interviews so as to exemplify a range of different ways and strategies used by ordinary people of, or associated with, migration background: how they are engaging discursively and practically with these 'top-down' policy discourses, how they mould them in various ways to fit their own experiences, and how by these means they manage to resist some of their undesirable implications. We have identified eight overlapping strategies of such discursive resistances through which individuals reassert their own agency in a number of social contexts. By focusing on individuals living in smaller towns and provinces where they often feel more isolated and more noticed in their 'otherness' we were able to add a largely under-researched new dimension to the understanding of the daily lived reality of life in multicultural societies.

Notes

(1) Sefone is a 7th FP research (STREP) project coordinated between 2007 and 2010 at Southampton University by Meinhof and co-directed by Armbruster, with six partners altogether: Southampton, Chemnitz, Bern, Budapest, Catania and Nikosia. See http:www.sefone.soton.ac.uk. For a key publication see Armbruster and Meinhof (2011).

(2) For statistical information about migrant populations see Statistische Ämter des Bundes und der Länder (2008, 2009).
(3) Modification of 'ius sanguinis' legislation in 1999/2000.
(4) Wulff resigned in 2012 following corruption allegations and has been replaced by Joachim Gauck as the new President of Germany.
(5) See http://www.tagesspiegel.de/politik/wulff-islam-gehoert-zu-deutsch-land/1948760.html, accessed 1 February 2012.
(6) See http://www.spiegel.de/politik/deutschland/0,1518,723532,00.html, accessed 1 February 2012.
(7) See http://www.spiegel.de/politik/deutschland/0,1518,770379,00.html, accessed 1 February 2012.
(8) See http://www.youtube.com/watch?v = B0_c1akLwqo, accessed 1 February 2012.
(9) Original German transcriptions follow GAT (see Selting *et al.*, 1998). The English translations (in italics) did not use a transcription system.

References

Armbruster, H. and Meinhof, U.H. (eds) (2011) *Negotiating Multicultural Europe. Borders, Networks, Neighbourhoods*. Basingstoke: Palgrave Macmillan.
Beauftragte der Bundesregierung für Migration, Flüchtlinge und Integration (ed.) (2007) *Der Nationale Integrationsplan: Neue Wege – Neue Chancen*. Berlin: Presse- und Informationsamt der Bundesregierung.
Carstensen-Egwuom, I. (2011) Representing an 'authentic ethnic identity'. Experiences of Sub-Saharan African musicians in an eastern German city. In N. Kiwan and U.H. Meinhof (eds) *Music and Migration. Special Issue of Music and Arts in Action* 3, 3. http://www.musicandartsinaction.net/index.php/maia/article/view/subsaharanmusicians.
Carstensen-Egwuom, I. and Holly, W. (2011) Integration, post-Holocaust identities and no-go areas: Public discourse and the everyday experience of exclusion in a German region. In H. Armbruster and U.H. Meinhof (eds) *Negotiating Multicultural Europe. Borders, Networks, Neighbourhoods* (pp. 94–118). Basingstoke: Palgrave Macmillan.
Delanty, G. and Rumford, Ch. (2005) *Rethinking Europe*. London: Routledge.
Dorsch, H. (2011) Integration into what? The intercultural week, mental borders and multiple identities in the German town of Bayreuth. In H. Armbruster and U.H. Meinhof (eds) *Negotiating Multicultural Europe. Borders, Networks, Neighbourhoods* (pp. 119–140). Basingstoke: Palgrave Macmillan.
Ellerbe-Dueck, C. (2011) Networks and 'safe spaces' of black European women in Germany and Austria. In H. Armbruster and U.H. Meinhof (eds) *Negotiating Multicultural Europe. Borders, Networks, Neighbourhoods* (pp. 158–184). Basingstoke: Palgrave Macmillan.
Kiwan, N. and Meinhof, U.H. (2006) Perspectives on cultural diversity: A discourse analytical approach. In U.H. Meinhof and A. Triandafyllidou (eds) *Transcultural Europe: Cultural Policy in a Changing Europe* (pp. 57–81). Basingstoke: Palgrave Macmillan.
Meinhof, U.H. (2011) Introducing borders, networks, neighbourhoods: Conceptual frames and social practices. In H. Armbruster and U.H. Meinhof (eds) *Negotiating Multicultural Europe. Borders, Networks, Neighbourhoods* (pp. 1–24). Basingstoke: Palgrave Macmillan.
Sarrazin, T. (2009) *Deutschland schafft sich ab. Wie wir unser Land aufs Spiel setzen*. Stuttgart: Deutsche Verlags-Anstalt.

Selting, M., Auer, P., Barden, B., Bergmann, J., Couper-Kuhlen, E., Günthner, S., Meier, C., Quasthoff, U., Schlobinski, P. and Uhmann, S. (1998) Gesprächsanalytisches Transkriptionssystem (GAT). *Linguistische Berichte* 173, 91–122.
Stadt Chemnitz (ed.) (2011) *Die Ausländerbeauftragte informiert: Berichtsjahr 2009/2010. Daten und Fakten*. Organisationen der Migrationsarbeit.
Statistische Ämter des Bundes und der Länder (eds) (2008) *Bevölkerung nach Migrationsstatus regional*. Ergebnisses des Mikrozensus 2008.
Statistische Ämter des Bundes und der Länder (eds) (2009) *Bevölkerung mit Migrationsstatus*. Ergebnisse des Mikrozensus 2009.
Stevenson, P. and Schanze, L. (2009) Language, migration and citizenship in Germany. In G. Extra, M. Spotti and P. Van Avermaet (eds) *Language Testing, Migration and Citizenship: Cross-national Perspectives on Integration Regimes* (pp. 87–106). London: Continuum.

9   Language as a Resource. Migrant Agency, Positioning and Resistance in a Health Care Clinic

Melissa G. Moyer

Introduction

This chapter focuses on how language is used as a resource by migrant patients from various national origins seeking health care at a primary health clinic in the city of Barcelona. Access to health for many migrants crucially depends on language and the concrete ways interactions are enacted and negotiated (Waiztkin, 1986). Language in this sense is considered a valuable resource with serious consequences for a migrant's physical wellbeing, especially when communication is problematic. As Blommaert (2005: 72) points out, the differential access to linguistic and communicative resources results in differing capacities to position oneself, to act linguistically and to contest or resist health institution categorisations. Not all communicative resources are the same; they depend on the language modalities (oral and written), for whom a given language constitutes a resource and what gets accomplished through the communicative act that takes place in the medical encounter. A shared language that is used in the negotiation of the medical encounter is one way of understanding how language constitutes a resource that shapes the medical encounter (Roberts *et al.*, 2004, 2009; Sarangi & Roberts, 1999), but there are other ways in which language emerges as a resource. For migrants in the context of this study, the degree of competence in institutional languages (Spanish or Catalan) or whether a third person mediates the medical encounter has important consequences for the way patients express agency, position themselves and resist institutional categorisations. At the same time, for medical doctors and staff, computerised medical records and medical reports brought along to the consultation by patients contribute to the negotiation of the medical encounter by providing valuable information that helps physicians establish the motive for the visit to the clinic. This written information to which the medical staff has access also categorises and thus positions migrant patients in specific ways that they cannot always contest because this medical history information is not available to them or because they may not have the language skills to understand through talk how they are so positioned. The analysis of interactions between physicians and four migrant patients from different language and cultural backgrounds and with differing linguistic resources and communication capacities shows how language is a resource for negotiating agency, positioning and resistance in two communicative events that involve (a) establishing the motive for the visit to the surgery, and (b) expressing dissatisfaction and resistance to pre-scribed medical treatment. This focus on a migrant perspective in medical encounters complements Moyer's (2011) analysis of ideologies and agency taken up from an institutional point of view.

An ethnographic study of the services connected to the provision of health provides a window to look at the way key institutional organisations of the public sector and society at large are coping with the arrival of persons from the developing world who seek work and life chances that are better than those existing in their country of origin. The data analysed in this chapter were obtained over an extensive period of fieldwork involving participant observation that was carried out between 2001 and 2007. More than 100 hours of audio-recordings involving mediated and non-mediated doctor–patient interactions as well as in-depth interviews with key representatives from the primary health clinic make up the data corpus. A detailed analysis of the interactions with four patients from Argentina, Pakistan, Bangladesh and Tunisia seeking medical attention illustrates what happens when: (a) no language is shared with the physician; (b) when language is mediated by a third person; (c) when there is a limited linguistic competence in one of the institutional languages; and lastly (d) when a migrant patient has fluent or native-like competence in the language spoken by the physician.

The present introduction is followed by a section that frames the medical encounters with migrant patients in terms of their agency, positioning and resistance, as well as the way these notions are understood in the analysis undertaken. Ethnographic information on the context and relevant background information on each one of the patients is presented in the next part.

A detailed analysis of interactions with patients having differing language resources is then examined in order to establish the ways agency and position are negotiated in connection to the motive for the patient's visit to the clinic. The next section complements this previous discussion by examining the role of computers in connection with imposed institutional positioning or categorisations and how patients' language resources are used. The role of a cultural mediator as a language resource is critically examined in the penultimate section, in connection with resistance and positioning and how a third party represents patient meanings. Finally, the conclusions argue for a critical approach to multilingual medical encounters where attention is dedicated to the question of what it means to claim language as a resource. The focus on the detailed ways language constitutes a valuable resource for expressing agency, positioning and resistance in medical encounters gives a better understanding of the ways health inequality gets (re)produced, with serious consequences, in some cases, for the migrant patient.

Agency, Positioning and Resistance

The concepts of agency, positioning and resistance analysed in this chapter must be situated in the context of the health clinic located in the city of Barcelona. Primary attention in the analysis is given to the patient perspective but, in fact, much of what patients can say or do is constrained by the institution and the medical staff who talk and act in its name.

The notion of power provides a way of understanding the relations of asymmetry and control of physicians over the medical encounter but also, as Blommaert (2005: 2) points out, looking at power shows how inequality gets (re)produced and the ways it gets taken up to differentiate, select, as well as to include and exclude, in our case, migrants seeking medical attention. Power at the health clinic studied is primarily based on specialised professional knowledge, competence in Spanish and Catalan, and also on the fact that medical staff are acting on behalf of a public institution of the nation-state (Foucault, 1973). The framing of the interactions in terms of relations of power and domination that are analysed by looking at how migrant patients negotiate agency, positioning and resistance provides a link with social process and with the way Spain and Catalonia through their public institutions are coping with migrants and their social needs.

Ahearn (2001: 130–131) defines individual agency as the socioculturally mediated capacity to act. She holds that social action and its realisation through language is co-constructed where both text and context are intertwined. The meanings and the range of possible social actions are constrained or limited. In the context of the health clinic, language and linguistic form are the key resources examined for expressing agency and, when they are lacking, or not available through a cultural mediator, migrant patients' agency is sharply constrained with consequences for that person's treatment.

From an institutional perspective, medical doctors are invested by the very nature of their employment in making sure that the institutional order is produced and that it continues to get reproduced (Foucault, 1973; Waitzkin, 1986). The linguistic mechanisms of how this is done from both a conversation analytic and an interactional perspective have been extensively studied (Atkinson, 1995; Heritage, 2005; Heritage & Maynard, 2006; Pomerantz *et al.*, 1997; Rehbein, 1994, 2000; Sarangi & Roberts, 1999). In addition to the negotiation and structured nature of medical encounters, it is relevant to recognise that physicians also have agency that can shape the way patients are able to interact.

The notion of positioning – in the case of the health clinic interactions – is understood as part of the dialogic and ongoing dynamic construction of meaning (Baynham, 2011) between patients, doctors and cultural mediators. Du Bois (2007: 163) defines positioning in terms of stance and as

the public act of a social actor, achieved dialogically through overt communicative means, of simultaneously evaluating objects, positioning subjects (self and others), and aligning with other subjects, with respect to any salient dimension of the sociocultural field.

Position, also referred to as alignment or stance, confirms social actor roles in the medical encounter but it is also open for negotiation and, as Jaffe (2009: 4) points out, 'it is a productive way of conceptualising processes of indexicalization that are the link between individual performance and social meaning'. It is also connected to Goffman's (1981) notion of footing and the connection of footing to the shifting of frames or the re-framing of social and cognitive relationships. With respect to positioning, it is important to consider particular cases that involve both *self-positioning* which is linked to forms of agency, and *imposed positioning* or categorisation by health staff at the institution which patients with language resources may try to resist. Categorisation, a form of imposed positioning, when practised by powerful individuals (physicians or other medical staff) within institutions, can go uncontested either because migrant patients choose not to respond or as a result of the fact that they are unable to pick up the differences in cultural, linguistic or contextualisation cues because they do not have sufficient language resources to understand or challenge the way they are being positioned. Several interactions presented show this in connection to the sort of information written in the medical histories of migrant patients who are categorised in medical but also moralistic ways. Forms of disagreement and resistance and the way they are made verbally explicit (and observable to the analyst) by the migrant patient directly or via the cultural mediator are also analysed.

About the Context and the Participants: *Anam, Enrique, Jasmin* and *Rohan*

The primary health clinic analysed is located in the city of Barcelona, in an area which has the highest density of migrant population and also some of the most socially marginal Spanish nationals who live in the neighbourhood.[1] This clinic provides primary health care but it also offers administration services to obtain a national health card, consultations with specialists such as paediatricians, and professionals caring for psychiatry, gynaecology and maternal health, radiology and tropical medicine, among others. It is a clinic of reference that is taken as a model for other primary health clinics in the rest of Catalonia which attend to patients from different linguistic and cultural origins. The clinic accepts medical interns working towards their degree to become a practitioner so that they can gain professional experience with migrants. It is also one of the first clinics in Catalonia to implement new health policies approved by the Catalan Health Department (ICS). The institutional language of the clinic is Catalan but Spanish is used by some of the administrative staff and nurses. Doctors mainly speak Catalan among themselves. The linguistic and cultural diversity at the clinic poses a practical challenge for health professionals who have to cope the best they can with delivering health care to patients with whom they have difficulty communicating. Patients themselves often provide practical solutions to the problem of communication. For example, mothers bring their Catalan-Spanish speaking children, friends or family, or sometimes another patient from the waiting room who has the necessary language skills is invited to interpret. Professional cultural mediators are sometimes available by previous appointment, and there is also a telephone hotline that according to doctors takes too long to prove useful during medical consultations. In addition, the institution offers doctors printed materials and documents with pictures, but this also is a time-consuming method for negotiating meaning and furthermore a good many of the patients do not have basic readings skills in the local language (and see Collins & Slembrouck, 2006).

It is also useful to bear in mind that one of the institutional efforts to overcome inequalities in access to health care that may be attributed to the limited linguistic resources of patients is addressed by organising the presence of a cultural mediator whose goal it is to work both as a language and a cultural broker. In the case of this clinic, cultural mediators are trained and employed by a privately funded non-governmental organisation (NGO) that is an entirely separate entity from the public health clinic. The NGO provides the human resources, hence filling a gap for translators not provided for by the public administration. Furthermore, the lack of official recognition of interpreters from different language and cultural origins reflects the Catalan government's official non-recognition of this professional figure. This institutional position is further supported by the lack of any certified degree in cultural mediation approved by the Catalan government. Many medical doctors' mistrust of cultural mediators expressed verbally in personal interviews may stem to a great extent from this lack of official recognition. The health clinic organises appointments for patients or doctors who have special communication requirements and who request a mediator beforehand. The services provided by cultural mediators at the clinic are limited to three half-days a week and they include native speakers of Arabic, Romanian, Russian, Urdu and Chinese at the time this study was carried out. As a resource for migrant patients, this service is insufficient and furthermore it is not available to all those patients who have communication needs.

The audio recordings were obtained with explicit permission from the institution and the medical staff. The participants in the interactions include three medical practitioners, Doctor Guasch (a male who was highly motivated to be working at this particular clinic), Doctor Capmany (a woman who had many migrant patients assigned to her surgery) and Doctor Sanz (a woman who was aided in the extracts presented by a cultural mediator, Karim, a young man in his twenties from Pakistan who spoke Panjabi, Urdu and Spanish as well as a limited knowledge of spoken Catalan).[2] Four patients, Anam, Jasmin, Enrique and Rohan, accompanied by his friend Ismail, illustrate differing communicative and linguistic resources and the various ways agency, positioning and resistance get negotiated. All names are pseudonyms.

Interaction with Anam from Pakistan

Examples 1 and 6 are taken from an interaction involving Anam, a woman from Pakistan who is 47 years old, Karim a 24-year-old man also from Pakistan who works as a cultural mediator at the health clinic, and Dr Sanz. The entire encounter lasts 10' 46". Anam's native languages are Panjabi with some Urdu. In the interaction she does not appear to understand either Spanish or Catalan, hence the presence of Karim who interprets between the doctor and Anam. Dr Sanz is a middle-aged woman whose native language is Catalan, but she speaks Spanish with the mediator. The interaction begins with Karim gaining Anam's oral consent on behalf of the researcher to undertake the recording, followed by Karim's questioning in order to find out the motive for Anam's visit to the doctor that day. Once he has determined the reason for her visit he is able to fill the doctor in on the motive for Anam's visit which has to do with a pain in her neck that extends up to her head. Throughout the medical encounter, Anam lists a number of very different symptoms, which has the effect of annoying the doctor. Furthermore, she has a medical condition involving anaemia and hyperthyroidism for which she needs to take medication. At the end of the encounter Anam brings up her difficult economic situation and the fact that she cannot afford to buy all the medication that is prescribed.

Interaction with Enrique from Argentina

Example 2 comes from an interaction between Enrique and Dr Capmany which lasts for 14' 52". The researcher is present. Enrique is a man in his early forties from Argentina who seems quite concerned with his physical appearance. He is a habitual consumer of cocaine and a smoker. He has a friendly relationship with Dr Capmany which has been established from his previous visits to the surgery. The doctor is a woman in her mid–late thirties and a native speaker of Catalan. Enrique is a native speaker of Argentinean Spanish and the purpose of his visit is primarily for the doctor to go over the results of his most recent electrocardiograms. The visit with the doctor lasts for what is considered a long time at that primary health clinic. The average time doctors dedicate to patients at the clinic is nine or 10 minutes, maximum. The topics dealt with during the consultation are Enrique's plans to move to Madrid, the stressful time he is currently experiencing, an allergy, and a request for his current weight and height since he is trying out for a movie casting and needs to report these personal measurements. Other topics that come up in the exchange include a request for a prescription for his hair which is thinning. Politics and the economic situation in Argentina are also discussed.

Interaction with Jasmin from Tunisia

Example 3 is taken from an interaction between Jasmin and Dr Guasch and it lasts 10' 11". The researcher is present and occasionally she intervenes to facilitate communication. Jasmin is a woman in her mid-fifties from Tunisia. She first says she has been in Spain for 10 months and later claims that it is 12 months. Her native language is Arabic and she does not under-stand either Spanish or Catalan and only knows a bit of French. This is Jasmin's first visit to this clinic and with this physician. The purpose of her visit is to get more medication for her heart condition. Dr Guasch is a man in his thirties and a native Catalan speaker and general practitioner who chose to practice at this health clinic because he felt a strong personal commitment to working with migrants and more marginal populations who live in the neighbourhood where the clinic is located. He tries unsuccessfully to obtain information for her medical history but this verbal negotiation becomes dif-ficult. Jasmin is asked to wait after she is given a written prescription, so she can continue providing information to the nurse for her medical history, but she leaves the clinic before the nurse had a chance to meet with her.

Interaction with Rohan from Bangladesh

Example 4 is from an interaction with Rohan, a Christian from Bangladesh in his early thirties, and his flatmate Ismail, also in his thirties, who has pre-sumably joined him at the surgery to help interpret, even though his Spanish does not seem much better than Rohan's, and Dr Capmany. The researcher is present during this encounter. The exchange lasts a total of 7' 23". Both Rohan and Ismail have lived in Spain for about three years. They have some knowl-edge of Spanish but their understanding is not fluent and Dr Capmany uses baby talk or an infantilising style of speaking in Spanish involving diminu-tives and simplified language to communicate. This style was not observed when she spoke, for example, with Enrique from Argentina. The purpose of Rohan's visit has to do with small blisters on his tongue that he describes as quite painful. This is his second visit to the doctor for this health problem because it has not improved with the treatment he was first given. At a point in the interaction that is not analysed, his flatmate intervenes with the doctor on his behalf to ask if she can give him some medication for anxiety that he is experiencing that keeps him awake at night with an intense feeling of fear.

Agency and Positioning in Communicating the Motive for the Visit to the Surgery

In the goal-oriented negotiation of communicating the motive for a visit to a primary health clinic I focus on language as a resource for com-municating patient agency. Other researchers (Roberts et al., 2004: 167) examine the orderliness of self-presentation of patients' symptoms and doctors' interactional work in 232 video-recorded interactions. They conclude that patients who have learned British institutional discourse routines do in fact follow the interactional orderliness described in the literature (Gill & Maynard, 2006; Heath, 1981; Heritage & Maynard, 2006; Heritage & Robinson, 2006). However, this orderliness is challenged in patients with a limited communicative competence in English. The authors further conclude that doctors are not trained for the communicative uncertainty and challenges posed by linguistically and culturally diverse patients. The angle on doctor–patient interactions taken up in this chapter builds on these observations about the orderliness of how migrant patients communicate their health problems, but with a view on the consequences for patient agency and positioning when they have different but also more limited communicative resources. The concern with how the motive for the visit gets established and patient agency is afforded or not here assumes Ahearn's idea (2001: 112) that we need to look at communicative practices in order to gain a better understanding of how and what meanings in an interaction get constrained and by whom.

There are several ways in which the motive for a visit to the surgery can get established. Example 1 involving Anam (the patient), Karim (the cultural mediator) and Dr Sanz illustrates a typical way in which it is done at the health centre studied when communication is mediated by a third person. The recording in Example 1 begins at the point transcribed in line 1 and it takes place in time before any information regarding the motive for Anam's visit is given to the doctor. Anam is negotiating her position as a patient with Karim, who is directing the interaction with questions oriented towards eliciting the information he considers Dr Sanz will need in order to establish the reason for the visit. The mediator does not have the medical training in order to make a diagnosis but he is following a questioning protocol typically carried out by physicians (lines 2, 4, 6) in order to determine why the patient is at the consultation. By taking on the physician role here, Karim positions himself to Anam as a medically knowledgeable participant in the encounter who is aligned with the institution.

Example 1 The motive for Anam's visit to the surgery

1 ***ANA:** hā(n) bimārī diyā(n) gallā(n) vich parniyā(n) tu.
   %tra: OK, you're only going to record about the illness.
2 ***KAR:** M□P dasso kis vajah te āyo doctor nu(n).
   %tra: tell me for what reason have you come to the doctor?
3 ***ANA:** vajah ai vai, ai mere dard ai aithe ai tund de vich, aithe badā ai, dekh ai zabān sukh jāndi ai, mu(n) sukh jandā ai, te pher.
   %tra: the reason is, I have a pain here, here in my neck it is a lot, look my tongue gets dry, my mouth gets dry, and then.

4   *KAR: kitne din to dard ai ji?
    %tra: for how many days have you had pain?
5   *ANA: ai somvār nu(n) āyā
    %tra: it started on Monday.
6   *KAR: sirf aisi jagah te?
    %tra: only in this place?
7   *ANA: ā
    %tra: yeah
8   *KAR: xxx (unintelligible)
9   *ANA: aitho aithe vi ā jandā ai ki itnā sakhat, pher aithe zyādah
            aitho chal ke aithe jāndā vich aithe. ai age vi ā jandā ai, hun
            age nālo chokhā ho gayā ai hun ai ...ai jadi ai hadi.
    %tra: it also comes from here to here, it's so strong, and then more
            here, it moves from here and goes in here. it also comes
            forward, and now it's got sharper than before, now it ...
            this bone (here).
10 *KAR: hmm
    %tra: hmm
11 *ANA: ai hadi vich te is bāzu vich āndā ai
    %tra: it comes in this bone and this arm.
12 *KAR: M☐D le empezó un dolor aquí en el cuello, se le pasó a la
            cabeza, luego le bajó a la clavícula.
    %tra: a pain started in her neck and went to her head and then
            down her collar bone.

To establish the purpose of a patient's visit is one of the key goals in a
medical encounter. Karim is quite skilled at getting the information Dr
Sanz needs, as we can see by his questions asking about: the reason of
Anam's visit (line 2) and listening to the symptoms; the amount of time
she has been feeling pain (line 4); and the location of the pain (line 6)
which he finally begins to translate for the doctor in line 12. This first
example focuses on obtaining key information in order to make a diagnosis. For the purpose of communicating basic medical information Karim
serves as an important language resource for Anam to gain access to the
proper treatment. The particular manner in which this 'information-get-
ting event' unfolds is not successful at achieving a more patient centred
medical encounter where a rapport can more easily get established between
doctor and patient.

Karim actively positions himself with the medical staff and the institutions by the questions he asks. This way of mediating for patients has also
been reported in the Italian context and it has been characterised by Baraldi

(2009: 127) as an instance of 'dyadic separation', where a third person in practice is constraining direct interaction between doctor and patient, thus preventing instances of patient agency where meanings of conflict or resistance could get expressed. Another reason that is also given for this way of interpreting is to save time, as doctors are overloaded with patients they must attend to. In Example 1 a doctor–patient rapport would have been more easily accomplished if Karim had positioned himself differently by favouring the interlocutor role between patient and doctor rather than adopting for himself the role of addressee with whom Anam interactionally engages. Davidson (2000, 2001: 173) also critically discusses this form of mediation in his own data where he proposes that mediators are acting as co-diagnosticians and institutional gatekeepers, a point that is also brought up in Maryns' (2006) work on asylum seekers.

The particular mechanisms of Karim's alignment with the institution are also accomplished by the choice of third-person pronouns to represent Anam to the doctor (line 12). The organisation of the medical encounter illustrated in Example 1 shows how Anam's agency and Karim's role are mixed. As a person who elicits and translates key information for the doctor to be able to determine the motive for the visit, Karim is a very important help but the particular positioning of the mediator as Anam's addressee takes away part of her agency to negotiate a rapport with Dr Sanz, who is the person who wields the power to decide the line of treatment and give the patient medication.

Example 2 illustrates how Jasmin's limited linguistic resources to express the motive for her visit and negotiate her agency and positioning as a patient shapes the interaction in very specific ways. Before the medical encounter can even get underway a language negotiation sequence in lines 14–26 (Auer, 1984) is carried out. The trying out of several languages in search of a shared language/code is unsuccessful. As a result, communication in this medical encounter turns out to be problematic and it ends up with a multilingual negotiation in French, Spanish and Catalan. Before attempting to establish the motive for the visit, Dr Guasch tries to obtain basic facts in order to create Jasmin's medical history. He only manages to elicit limited information that he needs, such as the amount of time Jasmin has been in Barcelona and her country of origin (line 27–45), but he was unable to determine whether or not she has had any major illnesses or surgical interventions. He gives up the task of completing the patient's medical record and in line 44 we observe that he has just read the medical report brought by Jasmin and which describes her chronic heart condition. The report was produced by the Department of Tropical Medicine. The report also contains the type of medication she was prescribed but the motive for the visit does not get fully established until Dr Guasch explicitly asks in line 61. Jasmin replies in lines 62 and 64 that she needs medical attention and a prescription for (heart) medication.

Example 2 The motive for Jasmin's visit to the surgery

1	**DOC:**	vale.
	%tra:	ok
	%com:	reading something.
6	**DOC:**	bueno # Jasmin # yo soy el doctor guasch.
	%tra:	good, Jasmin, I am doctor Guasch
7	**DOC:**	doctor.
8	**JAS:**	doctor guasch *ici.*
	%tra:	doctor Guasch here
9	**DOC:**	yo.
	%tra:	i
10	**JAS:**	*oui.*
	%tra:	yes
11	**DOC:**	doctor Guasch.
12	**JAS:**	*oui # ça va bien* ¿
	%tra:	yes, how are you doing ¿
13	**DOC:**	*ça va.*
	%tra:	alright.
14	**DOC:**	Jasmin # tu hablass # castellano¿
	%tra:	Jasmin, do you speak, castillian¿
15	**DOC:**	no¿
16	**DOC:**	frances¿
	%tra :	french¿
17	**JAS:**	frances # *un peu.*
	%tra :	french, a little.
18	**DOC :**	y castellano # español ¿
	%tra:	and castillian, spanish¿
19	**UH1 :**	no.
20	**DOC:**	nada # perfecto.
	%tra:	nothing, perfect.
21	**JAS:**	frances.
	%tra:	french
22	**DOC:**	solo frances.
	%tra:	only french
23	**DOC:**	yo no hablo frances Jasmin.
	%tra:	i do not speak french Jasmin

24	**DOC:**	tu hablas frances [%INV]¿
	%tra:	do you speak french¿
25	**RES:**	yo hablo un poquito # si.
	%tra:	i speak a little, yes
26	**DOC:**	un poquito.
	%tra:	a little.
27	**DOC:**	la Jasmin es de **Maroc # Maroc #** o no¿
	%tra:	jasmin is from morocco, morocco, no¿
28	**RES:**	vous êtes du Maroc¿
	%tra :	are you from Morocco ¿
29	**DOC:**	*ou d' Algérie*¿
	%tra :	or from Algeria
30	**JAS:**	*tunisienne # tunisienne.*
	%tra :	tunisian, tunisian
31	**DOC :**	Tunisia # muy bien.
	%tra :	Tunisia, great.
32	**UH1 :**	*tunisienne.*
	%com:	laughs.
33	**JAS:**	*tunisienne.*
34	**DOC:**	y cuanto tiempo aqui Jasmin¿
	%tra:	and how long have you been here Jasmin¿
35	**RES:**	*ça fait combien de temps # temps*¿
	%tra:	how long, long ¿
36	**JAS:**	ahh # *dix mois.*
	%tra:	ten months
37	**DOC:**	vale.
	%tra:	ok
38	**RES:**	diez meses.
	%tra:	ten months
39	**JAS:**	Tunis.
	%tra:	Tunis
40	**RES:**	Tunis.
	%tra:	Tunis
41	**DOC:**	Tunis.
42	**JAS:**	*c'est bien Tunis.*
	%tra:	Tunis is nice.
43	**RES:**	*c'est bien Tunis.*
	%tra:	Tunis is nice.
44	**DOC:**	aviam # aixo es de tropical.
	%tra:	let's see, that is from tropical (medicine department)

45	**DOC:**	Jasmin # en # a Tunis # alguna +...
	%tra:	Jasmin, in Tunis, some
46	**DOC:**	com es operació pre +...¿
	%tra:	how do you say operation pre...
47	**RES:**	ehhh # *vous avez quelques operations* +...
	%tra:	have you had some kind of operation ¿
48	**DOC:**	operation.
	%tra :	operation
49	**INV :**	+ ... <en Tunisie> [<] ¿
	%tra :	in Tunisia
50	**JAS:**	<noon> [>].
	%tra :	nooo
51	**RES:**	*quelques fois à votre vie*¿
	%tra :	at any point in your life¿
52	**DOC:**	*maladie*¿
	%tra:	illness¿
53	**DOC:**	*maladies* no¿
	%tra:	no illnesses¿
54	**RES:**	*quelques maladies*¿
	%tra:	any illness¿
55	**JAS:**	no.
	%tra:	no.
56	**DOC:**	vale.
	%tra:	ok.
	%com:	types.
57	**DOC:**	bueno # puees +...
	%tra:	good, then...
58	**JAS:**	*ça va*¿
	%tra:	ok¿
59	**DOC:**	*ça va.*
	%tra :	ok
60	**RES:**	*qu'est-ce que* +...
	%tra :	what do...
61	**DOC:**	*qu'est-ce que vous voulez* ¿
	%tra :	what do you want ¿
62	**JAS:**	xx # ehh # *d' attention.*
	%tra :	attention.
63	**DOC:**	*d'attention.*
	%tra :	attention
64	**JAS:**	*pour les medicaments*
	%tra:	to get medication treatment

Jasmin's agency is severely constrained by her lack of linguistic competence. Reliance on a written medical report must be taken with her answer to Dr Guasch's inquiry in line 63–64 to finally determine the motive for the visit. She depends entirely on the doctor making the right inferences about why she is there. Another consequence of Jasmin's limited linguistic resources is that she did not understand the doctor's instructions to wait (after having obtained the prescription) in the waiting room to be seen by the nurse in order for the clinic to complete her medical history and get her contact information. Any medical follow-up – which is strongly recommended in persons with chronic heart disease – is impossible without this information.

Example 3 shows an alternative strategy for communicating the motive for a visit to the doctors when a migrant patient, Enrique, has native-like linguistic competence in an institutional language (in this case Spanish). The way this interaction involving the negotiation of agency and positioning is constrained contrasts with the previous two examples analysed of Anam and Jasmin who have limited communicative resources. This example starts off with the doctor and patient establishing an interactional relationship that gives the migrant patient more interactional chances to express agency. This is also the case with Jasmin and Dr Guasch who do not even share a common language (Heritage & Maynard, 2006: 14). The greetings in lines 1–5 of Example 3 serve this purpose precisely. This is a successful medical encounter where language competence is not a constraint and where the patient communicates early on in the interaction, line 6, the motive for his visit, which is for the doctor to go over his most recent electrocardiograms. Furthermore, Enrique, as discussed in the previous section *About the Context and the Participants*, is able to negotiate a whole set of topics (i.e. his plans to move to Madrid or the economic situation in Argentina), which are not even directly related to the motive for his visit to the surgery. It is also a smooth and even successful medical encounter because it follows what Roberts *et al.* (2004: 163–165) discuss as fulfilling the doctor's expected goal-oriented frame where the patient makes clear the motive for his visit.

Example 3   The motive for Enrique's visit to the surgery

1	*ENR:	hola
	*%tra:	hello
2	*DOC:	hola
	*%tra:	hello
3	*ENR:	buenas tardes
	*%tra:	good afternoon

4	*DOC:	que tal¿
	*%tra:	how are you¿
	*%com:	DOC closes door
5	*DOC:	como estas¿
	*%tra:	how are you¿
→ 6	*ENR:	bien # traje el +...
	*%tra:	good # I brought the +...
7	*DOC:	ah@i # el electro¿
	*%tra:	oh # the electro
8	*ENR:	si.
	*%tra:	yes
9	*DOC:	ah@i es verdad # ya me acuerdo.
	*%tra:	oh, that's right # now I remember

Enrique's interaction with Dr Capmany shows how language competence in a shared institutional language is a key resource for sustaining a direct interactional relationship with the doctor and being able to communicate the motive for his visit, as well as for following and confirming the physicians' understanding of his verbal contributions to the interaction and being able to negotiate position and non-medical topics of conversation vis-à-vis with Dr Capmany. Another element concerning Enrique's positioning in the medical encounter above is his use of Argentinean Spanish. In Catalonia, language choice (i.e. Spanish over Catalan) has simultaneous social meanings that situate speakers (whether intended by the speaker or not) with respect to Catalan institutions. In the case of Enrique, he is being situated by the institution both medically but also as a member of a separate cultural and linguistic background.

A comparison of the three medical encounters with Anam, Jasmin and Enrique shows how a patient's linguistic resources shape the structure of the interactional order (Goffman, 1981) and the different ways the motive for the visit gets communicated (or not as in Jasmin's case). Research on medical encounters carried out by Angelelli (2004), Waitzkin (2000) and Candib (1995) highlights the importance of communication in a patient-centred relationship with healthcare providers as key for enhancing patient agency. Greater patient agency that gets produced through language reduces discordant relationships and has overall therapeutic benefit for the patients.

Language, Computers and Patient Agency

Computerised medical records were already being implemented at the health clinic in Barcelona at the time that the fieldwork was being carried out in 2001. The use of these new information technologies began to change the way physicians working for the Catalan health service were delivering health care. Research on the adoption of computers raised many important questions about how this technology affects communication with patients in the medical encounter (Greatbatch *et al.*, 1995; Ridsdale & Hudd, 1994). It also raises questions about access to reading and writing the information in the electronic records, patient privacy or new ways medical information is managed. Swinglehurst *et al.* (2011), building on the work of Scott & Purves (1996), take the presence of the computer in producing the electronic patient record as a third silent voice (Bahktin, 1981) that shapes the interaction in important and sometimes contradictory ways. In the multimodal analysis that the authors carry out, attention is paid to the micro-analytic dimensions, in order to show how information about the results to medical tests on electronic patient records cannot be interpreted as a medical fact used to make a diagnosis unless information provided by the patient is also included in the joint construction of the medical encounter. In the present section, I am also concerned with the role of patient electronic records and how they are used by the physician to determine the motive for a patient's visit when their language resources are too limited. The information in the computerised medical histories, which has been recorded by healthcare staff other than the attending physician (for example, the results to medical tests or visits to the emergency room), plays a key role in communication in the medical encounter and in determining the motive for the patient's visit. Physicians rely on the information they see on the screen for multiple purposes. In the case illustrated in Example 4, we see that it is an essential tool for Dr Capmany in order to determine the motive for Rohan's visit to the clinic. At first the physician thinks Rohan has come to get the results of medical tests (line 9). This information is based on what she is reading on the computer screen. As Dr Capmany continues to read the screen she discovers that she is wrong and that he has already been back for the results of the tests (line 11), and that after collecting his medical test results he returned to the clinic for an emergency appointment (not with Dr Capmany). Rohan's linguistic skills are limited but he understands enough Spanish to ratify or disagree with the information on the computer as it is presented by the physician in lines 9, 11, 12, and 18 and 19.

Example 4 Computers in the medical encounter

1	**DOC:**	Rohan XXX¿
2	**DOC:**	hola.
	%tra:	hello

3	**INV:**	hola.
	%tra:	hello
4	**ROH:**	puede pasar ¿
	%tra:	can he come in¿
5	**DOC:**	si el quiere si.
	%tra:	if he wants to yes
6	**ROH:**	tu quieres # si¿
	%tra:	do you want to¿
7	**ISM:**	hola.
	%tra:	hello
8	**RES:**	hola # como estamos¿
	%tra:	hello how are we doing¿
9	**DOC:**	como estas Rohan # teniamos un analisis # no # para mirar¿
	%tra:	how are you Rohan, we had some analyses, no¿ to see¿
10	**ROH:**	sssi # ehh # no +...
	%tra:	yyyes, uh, no.
11	**DOC:**	no # ya vino para mirar...
	%tra:	no, you already came to see...
12	**DOC:**	ah@i no # vino de urgencias.
	%tra:	oh, no, you came to emergencies.
13	**ROH:**	si # urgencias.
	%tra:	yes, emergencies
14	**DOC:**	ah2i.
15	**ROH:**	porquee # ehh # sale de ampollas.
	%tra:	because, ehh, blisters come out
16	**DOC:**	unas ampollas.
	%tra:	some blisters
17	**ROH:**	si # de lengua.
	%tra:	yes, of tongue
18	**DOC:**	vino el dia veinte # no # por lo mismo # micropapos en la base de la lengua.
	%tra:	you cameo n the 20th for the same reason, micropapas on the base of the tongue.
19	**DOC:**	le dio para hacer # una doctora le escribio una cosa para grrr # para hacer enjuagues no¿
	%tra:	she gave to do, a doctor wrote you something to , to do a mouth wash, no¿
20	**ROH:**	si.
	%tra:	yes

21   **DOC:**   y no esta bien¿
     %tra: and you are not better¿
22   **ROH:**   no # no # no esta bien.
     %tra: no, no no it is not good

This example shows how information from the computerised medical record can replace the need of the patient to provide detailed language-based explanations about the motive for his visit. Rohan's understanding of Spanish allows him to follow step by step how Dr Capmany is constructing the motive for his visit. The source of Rohan's agency relies on his ability to agree or disagree with the physician. When patient and physician do not share a common language, the computer can be useful to determine the patient's reason for attending the consultation (Hsu, 2005; Stewart, 2005). So the written language on the computerised medical record is another type of language resource for patients with some linguistic skills in the institutional languages and doctors for communicating relevant health information. The interaction in Example 4 supports the view of the computer as a sort of third party that enhances Rohan's agency in the medical encounter. This example also shows how written information gets brought into oral interactions in a three-way negotiated effort to determine the motive for the visit.

Patients in Spain are typically not given free access to the information that has been recorded by different health professionals on their electronic health records unless it is somehow revealed in the verbal interaction by the physician at the consultation (see Greatbatch *et al.*, 1995; Ridsdale & Hudd, 1994). Example 5 shows how information that is not strictly medical and which in fact implies a moralistic judgement (i.e. *I have seven messages* saying she is not taking her medication) of Anam as a problematic patient has been added to her medical history. She is unaware of this information and the implications that categorise her in this rather negative way. Even when this information is revealed by Dr Sanz in the interaction, the cultural mediator does not translate it.

Rather than investigate the reasons why the medication is not being taken, Anam's behaviour is recorded in a reprobatory manner which could negatively influence the way she gets positioned in the present interaction but it can also have consequences for future medical encounters with staff who have access to those messages in her records. In the exchange, Anam explains that she has stopped taking the medication for anaemia because it upset her stomach and made it feel swollen, but that she has continued taking the medicine for her thyroid. All this gets explained by the cultural mediator to the physician in the present interaction; however, we do not have information about whether a cultural mediator was present to ensure such information was communicated in all the previous visits where medical staff recorded that she was not taking her medication.

Example 5 Individual categorisation based on computer information (interaction with Anam)

1 ***DOC:** que sí, que sí ((LF)). tiene una anemia que debería tratar con hierro y tiene un hipotiroidismo, pero tengo aquí en el ordenador como siete notas diciendo "no se está tomando las pastillas".

  *%tra: that's right. she has an anemia that should be treated with iron and she has hypothyroidism but here in the computer i have seven messages saying 'she is not taking her medication'.

This example raises questions about computerised medical records that categorise patients in medical terms based on information that counts as facts that are used in the delivery of health and the chances a person has of contesting or resisting such categorisations, especially when they are not familiar with the languages of the clinic (Swinglehurst et al., 2011). Patient agency is constrained by not knowing what is in their medical records but also by not having the language resources to understand the direct and implicit ways physicians reveal information that is contained in a medical history. When the three-way negotiation of the medical encounter (patient, doctor and computer) is impaired by a patient's limited language skills, there may be serious consequences, as observed in the case of Jasmin in Example 3 who disappeared from the consultation before the institution could get her contact information and complete her medical history.

Mediating Patient Positioning and Resistance

Research on interpreter-mediated medical encounters is extensive (Angelelli, 2004; Baraldi, 2009; Bolden, 2000; Buhrig & Meyer, 2004; Cambridge, 1999; Candlin & Candlin, 2003; Davidson, 2000, 2001; Hale, 2007; Roberts et al., 2009; Tebble, 1999; Wadensjo, 1998; Wadensjo et al., 2007). It has been concerned with how the linguistic acts of the interpreter (whether professionally trained or not) shape the course and content of interactions between migrant patients who are not familiar with the institutional languages, and physicians (Davidson, 2001: 170). One of the issues that has been raised is interpreter neutrality. Proponents of neutrality typically argue that professional interpreters should limit themselves to translation word for word (see, for example, Hale, 2007: 62; Tebble, 1999; Valero Garcés, 2003). Furthermore, they call this a direct approach and claim that it closely resembles the more desirable monolingual doctor–patient interactions. Underlying this perspective is the assumption that meaning in interpreting in medical encounters typically consists of translating linguistic forms. Mediated communication from this perspective should not be influenced by asymmetric roles and social relations of power and inequality (Hale, 2007: 52–53). An objectified view of language and meaning contrasts with research that departs from the notion of neutrality by recognising how interpreting is also shaped by social meanings, context and relations of power that get negotiated and enacted in the doctor–patient interaction (Baraldi, 2009; Cicourel, 1992; Roberts et al., 2009). Furthermore, as Davidson (2001: 177) points out, different types of alignment or positioning are represented and communicated by different types of interpreters (for example, a family member, friend, non-acquaintance or professional interpreter or mediator). The extent to which the medical encounter with an interpreter is doctor or patient centred is also relevant for understanding alignment, as Baraldi (2009: 123) points out. In more patient-centred consultations, the voices and perspectives of the migrant patients have some influence over the institutional order and the cultural presuppositions associated with a Western medical system.

This section analyses how interpreters, who represent a particular kind of language resource for migrant patients, manage (or not) to represent patient positioning and their acts of resistance to the attending physician. Angelelli (2004: 15–18) argues for a patient-centred approach since a rapport and a collaborative relationship with the physician, she claims, increases patient autonomy and promotes responsibility towards her/his illness. The question of whether a truly collaborative relationship can be accomplished across cultures with the intervention of an interpreter is raised in Example 6, where we can see what gets accomplished by the way Anam positions herself and expresses her disagreement with the medical treatment she has received up to the point of this visit to the clinic.

There are two key reflections that are relevant for understanding the particular way Anam's interactional role in Example 6 gets shaped. The first has to do with the doctor- or institution-centred approach to the delivery of health care to patients. Information based on extensive participant observation at the health clinic and explicit evidence from this interaction (line 4), where Dr Sanz claims she is a doctor and if she (Anam) has a problem she should go to the social worker, serve to reinforce the doctor's position of a medical authority who is not responsible for patients' other life concerns. The second reflection has to do with Karim, an educated young man in his twenties, and how he is positioned with respect to Anam, who is a woman in her forties from a rural area of Pakistan. While there is a cultural and national origin affinity with the patient, there are gender, educational, social status and age differences. As we see (lines 3, 6, 8, 10) Karim chooses to align himself with the institution. This is illustrated by the choice of third-person pronouns (line 3), a laugh (line 8) that is complicit with Dr Sanz's rather mocking words that are meant to be funny about how she is going to perform a miracle by placing his hands over Anam and curing her, or (line 10) confirming the doctor's previous words that a miracle pill for Anam does not exist.

Anam addresses Karim. She refers to Dr Sanz in the third person (line 1) *'the first time I came to* her'. Anam is positioning herself interactionally with Karim, hence recognising his role as the interpreter of her words, but the information and the tone Anam is expressing is intended for Dr Sanz who has the authority and medical knowledge to provide a solution to her problems. Anam also positions herself in disagreement with the medications prescribed and the treatment she has received which have not helped to improve her health (lines 1, 2, 5). An additional positioning is as a person with economic difficulties, hence having problems with purchasing the medication that the doctor has prescribed. So, to what extent and in what ways does Karim constitute a language resource for Anam? How does the way he positions himself and how and what he decides to interpret reflect on the way the doctor replies to Anam?

Example 6   Anam's position vis-à-vis medical practices

1   ***ANA:**   ā pehle aide kol āiyā(n) do rang diyā(n) [she coughs] goliyā(n) khāiyā(n). pher hun utle doctor kol gai, pher do khāiyā(n). te o aitni te pakki nai honde tankhāh ai na mere 'marido' sat sau (700) rupaiya, at sau te chāli (840), te assi che sau (600) vich deneā kirāyā, te o khāiye keh roz goliyā(n), mai(n) kitho(n) lā(n)? ai hun satā(n) dinā vich do varā khāiyā(n), che che 'euro' dā divāi.

    %tra: the first time i came to her i ate/took pills of two colours. then i went to the doctor upstairs and had two again. and my husband's salary isn't very certain, seven hundred rupees, eight hundred rupees, and we pay a rent of six hundred rupees, and to take pills every day, from where do i bring (money)? and now within seven days, twice i've taken medicine at six rupees each.

2   ***ANA:**   vāyā(n) changi divāi den jide nāl 'well' ho jā(n), menu (n) koī roz paise dene dā shāu(n)k te nai xxx xxx xxx.

    %tra: give me some good medicine with which i'll get well, i'm not fond of giving/spending money every day.

3   *KAR: ahora me está hablando de temas económicos, que su
             marido no cobra mucho y que tiene problemas.
     %tra: now she is telling to me about financial matters, that
             her husband doesn't earn very much and that she has
             problems.
4   *DOC: dile que yo soy el medico y que si tiene algun problema que
             vaya a la asistente social y que entonces veremos.
     %tra: tell her i am a doctor and that if she has any problem
             she should go see the social worker ... and then we
             will see.
5   *ANA: vāyā(n) changi divāi den jide nāl 'well' ho jā(n), menu (n)
             koā roz paise dene dā shāu(n)k te nai xxx xxx xxx.
     %tra: give me some good medicine with which i'll get well, i'm
             not fond of giving/spending money every day.
6   *KAR: dice que cada dia compra muchos medicamentos y que no se
             cura, dice que tiene que hacerle receta de una medicación
             que vaya muy bien.
     %tra: she says that she many medications each day and she
             doesn't get better, she says that you have to write a prescrip-
             tion for a medication that will cure her.
7   *DOC: D□M sí, claro. dile que mejor le voy a imponer las manos y
             la voy a curar.
     %tra: tell her that there is something better, i will place my hands
             over her and cure her.
8   *KAR: ((LF))
9   *DOC: dile que si va al médico cada tres días, que es lo que hace
             ella, pues claro, le vamos dando medicación. que yo le
             cambio las pastillas porque el paracetamol no le ha ido bien,
             le doy el hierro que ya se tomaba porque se lo tiene que
             tomar para poder curarse, le doy el protector de estómago y
             le doy la pastilla del dolor porque ella ha venido a la consulta
             con un cuadro de dolor. o sea, que los médicos curamos con
             pastillas y que sin pastillas no sabemos curar y que ésto lo
             tiene que entender.
     %tra: tell her that if she goes to the doctors every three days, which
             is what she does, of course, we will be giving her medication.
             that i change her pills because paracetamol didn't work well
             for her, i giver her iron which she was already taking because
             she has to take it in order to get better, i give her a stomach
             protector and i give her a painkiller pill because she came to
             see me about a pain. in other words, doctors cure with pills

and without pills we do not know how to cure anyone, and
she has to understand this.

10   *KAR: y que tampoco hay una pastilla que sea milagrosa.
      %tra: and no miraculous pill really exists.
11   *DOC: y que si hubiera una pastilla milagrosa ya se la hubiéramos
                dado el primer día, vale¿
      %tra: and if it did exist we would have given it to her on the first
                day, ok¿

Karim (line 3), when addressing Dr Sanz, leaves out Anam's account at
the beginning of line 1 and line 2 of her previous experience at the clinic
and the previous prescriptions she was given of various medications. At the
point that is highly relevant for understanding why she is worried about
her economic situation, Karim selectively translates just the part where she
claims that she is talking about her husband not earning enough money
and that she has economic problems. Dr Sanz's response (line 4) to Karim
(line 3) disengages from Anam's economic problems, suggesting that she go
to the social worker as this is not a medical problem and thus she cannot
take care of it. The implicit disagreement and criticism of previous medical
attention received at the clinic expressed by Anam (lines 1 and 2) is simply
not translated; nor is the doctor's response that Anam should go and see
the social worker relayed back to her. Karim's decisions on what to translate and what not to translate not only explains Dr Sanz's reply (line 4) but
it is also consequential for the limited empathy and rapport between doctor
and patient. Anam's disagreement about the treatment and medication she
received can be taken as an expression of resistance – a form of resistance
that Karim does not translate at first (line 3) and when he eventually does
(line 6) the doctor replies to him jokingly (line 7), an exchange that does
not get conveyed to Anam. Anam's attempts to resist institutional medical
practices are met with certain sarcasm by both the doctor and Karim, a
position she cannot contest as she is unaware of what is being said. Anam
is being delegitimised by the cultural mediator. Her objections are ridiculed
because she is not familiar with standard Western and medically informed
ways of delivering health care. Example 1 showed how interpreter-mediated talk facilitated establishing the motive for the visit because what was
key to that communicative event was the translation of key information.
In Example 6, where objections to medical treatment and positioning may
be conflictual, the cultural mediator intervenes to reduce tension and make
the medical encounter flow, but Karim's choice not to translate all of
Anam's and the doctor's words has consequences for Anam's chances of
negotiating alignment with her doctor, an alignment that can be achieved

in monolingual medical encounters by joint unmediated negotiation. The cultural mediator's position vis-à-vis the doctor and the health clinic, as Example 6 shows, works against migrants' access to health care in ways that are available to patients who have the language resources to express their objections and negotiate their position directly with medical professional and not through a third person who often ends up fulfilling his/her own face needs.

Conclusions

The present analysis of migrant patient and doctor interactions in the institutional context of a health clinic shows the ways language works as a valuable resource for persons with differing linguistic skills in the languages of the institution. It seeks to understand the detailed ways in which public institutions of the health sector are dealing with communication to a culturally and linguistically diverse clientele and the consequences these practices may have for persons seeking access to medical care.

Not all modalities of language are equally useful for migrant patients, as we have seen. Patient agency, the negotiation of meaning and key medical information, positioning and resistance can best be accomplished with the knowledge of an institutional language, as in the case of Enrique who was able to align himself with the physician and engage in a conversation about personal and other life matters. A patient's limited linguistic skills put the focus of the medical encounter on the exchange of key information in order to establish the motive for the visit to the clinic. Computerised records of patients' medical histories provide physicians with some of the information that a patient cannot explain. However, the information in the computerised records can categorise patients (both medically and morally) in ways they are unable to contest because they just do not have the language skills to pick up on the information revealed (often in indirect ways) in the interaction by the physician, or they simply are unaware of the negative categorisations that have been written in their medical histories as in the case of Anam. It is in this respect that agency or the chance to renegotiate one's position or identity is limited on account of language. When language is mediated by a third person, such as a cultural mediator trained to bridge the communication gap between doctor and patient, we see how the exchange of key information about symptoms and treatment is accomplished. However, a patient's agency and positioning vis-à-vis the physician is complicated by the mediator who brings in his own concerns of agency and positioning which end up limiting the patient's chances of expressing agency and resistance to institutional categorisations that get expressed in the interaction.

For researchers concerned with language and understanding wider social processes about how institutional practices account for the (re)production of inequality, the focus on a public health clinic showing how migrant agency, positioning and resistance is negotiated in doctor–patient interactions provides a detailed account of how social structuration is accomplished in our locally rooted everyday talk.

Transcription conventions

The transcription conventions used for the examples are as follows:

D☐M	**D**octor is looking at **M**ediator/**P**atient
M☐P	**M**ediator is looking at **P**atient
//xxx//	Utterance unintelligible
Text in bold	Utterance in Catalan
Text in italics	Utterance in French
Regular text	Utterance in Spanish
%tra	Translation of utterance
%com	Comments
<>	Overlapping utterances
// //	Intervals within and between utterances
#	Short pause
:	Lengthening of preceding sound
(...)	Long pause
Intonation	
.	Stopping fall in tone
¿	Rising intonation, not necessarily a question
Transcription doubt (words)	Words enclosed in single parentheses are in doubt
XXX	Word not retrievable from recording
XXX	Words not retrievable from recording

Acknowledgements

This research was funded by the Spanish *Ministerio de Economia y Competitividad* Grant FFI2011-26964 and the Salvador Madariaga Mobility Grant PR2011-0574, at Birkbeck, University of London, and Cardiff University where this chapter was written. I am also grateful for the detailed comments from Celia Roberts, Gabriele Budach, Alexandre Duchêne and Mike Baynham.

Notes

(1) The district of *Ciutat Vella* had the highest percentage, 19.51% (47.984 inhabitants) of foreign population in 2007 in the city of Barcelona. See the Statistical Institute of Catalonia, consulted in May 2012 at http://www.idescat.cat/poblacioestrangera/?res=e19&b=10&lang=en&t=2007&x=10&y=3 .

(2) The interaction with Dr Sanz was recorded by Dolores Ruiz from the CIEN research team and the transcription and translation was carried out by Naresh Sharma from the Department of the Languages and Cultures of South Asia at SOAS, London. All other examples in the paper were recorded by myself and the transcriptions were carried out with the help of Maria Rosa Garrido from the CIEN research team.

References

Ahearn, L.M. (2001) Language and agency. *Annual Review of Anthropology* 3, 109–137.
Angelelli, C.V. (2004) *Medical Interpreting and Cross-cultural Communication*. Cambridge: Cambridge University Press.
Atkinson, P. (1995) *Medical Talk and Medical Work*. London: Sage.
Auer, P. (1984) *Bilingual Conversation*. Amsterdam: John Benjamins.
Bahktin, M. (1981) *The Dialogic Imagination*. Austin: University of Texas Press.
Baraldi, C. (2009) Forms of mediation: The case of interpreter-mediated interactions in medical systems. *Language and Intercultural Communication* 9 (2), 120–137.
Baynham, M. (2011) Stance, positioning, and alignment in narratives of professional experience. *Language in Society* 40, 63–74.
Blommaert, J. (2005) *Discourse*. Cambridge: Cambridge University Press.
Bolden, G. (2000) Toward understanding practices of medical interpreting: Interpreters' involvement in history taking. *Discourse Studies* 2 (4), 387–419.
Buhrig, K. and Meyer, B. (2004) Ad hoc interpreting and the achievement of communicative purposes in doctor–patient communication. In J. House and J. Rehbein (eds) *Multilingual Communication* (pp. 43–62). Amsterdam: John Benjamins.
Cambridge, J. (1999) Information loss in bilingual medical interviews through an untrained interpreter. *Translator* 5 (2), 201–219.
Candib, L. (1995) *Medicine and the Family: A Feminist Perspective*. New York: Basic Books.
Candlin, C. and Candlin, S. (2003) Healthcare communication: A problematic site for applied linguistics. *Annual Review of Applied Linguistics* 23, 134–154.
Cicourel, A. (1992) The interpenetration of communicative contexts: Examples from medical encounters. In A. Duranti and C. Goodwin (eds) *Rethinking Context* (pp. 291–310). Cambridge: Cambridge University Press.
Collins, J. and Slembrouck, S. (2006) 'You don't know what they translate': Language contact, institutional procedure, and literacy practice in neighborhood health clinics in urban Flanders. *Journal of Linguistic Anthropology* 16 (2), 249–268.
Davidson, B. (2000) The interpreter as institutional gatekeeper: The social-linguistic role of interpreters in Spanish–English medical discourse. *Journal of Sociolinguistics* 4 (3), 379–409.
Davidson, B. (2001) Questions in cross-linguistic medical encounters: The role of the hospital interpreter. *Anthropological Quarterly* 74 (4), 170–178.
Du Bois, J.W. (2007) The stance triangle. In R. Englebretson (ed.) *Stancetaking in Discourse: Subjectivity, Evaluation, Interaction* (pp. 139–182). Amsterdam: John Benjamins.

Foucault, M. (1973) *The Birth of the Clinic*. London: Tavistock.

Gill, V.T. and Maynard, D.W. (2006) Explaining illness: Patients' proposals and physicians' responses. In J. Heritage and D.W. Maynard (eds) *Communication in Medical Care* (pp. 115–150). Cambridge: Cambridge University Press.

Goffman, E. (1981) *Forms of Talk*. Philadelphia: University of Pennsylvania Press.

Greatbatch, D., Heath, C., Campion, P. and Luff, P. (1995) How do desk-top computers affect the doctor–patient interaction. *Family Practice* 12 (1), 32–36.

Hale, S.B. (2007) *Community Interpreting*. New York: Palgrave Macmillan.

Heath, C. (1981) The opening sequence in doctor–patient interaction. In P. Atkinson and C. Heath (eds) *Medical Work: Realities and Routines*. Aldershot: Gower.

Heritage, J. (2005) Revisiting authority in physician–patient interaction. In M. Maxwell, D. Kovarsky and J. Duchan (eds) *Diagnosis as Social Practice* (pp. 83–102). New York: Mouton de Gruyter.

Heritage, J. and Maynard, D.W. (2006) Introduction: Analyzing interactions between doctors and patients in primary care encounters. In J. Heritage and D.W. Maynard (eds) *Communication in Medical Care* (pp. 1–20). Cambridge: Cambridge University Press.

Heritage, J. and Robinson, J.D. (2006) Accounting for the visit: Giving reasons for seeking medical care. In J. Heritage and D.W. Maynard (eds) *Communication in Medical Care* (pp. 48–85). Cambridge: Cambridge University Press.

Hsu, J. (2005) Health information technology and physician–patient interactions: Impact of computers on communication during outpatient primary care visits. *Journal of the American Medical Informatics Association* 12 (4), 474–480.

Jaffe, A. (ed.) (2009) Introduction: The sociolinguistics of stance. In Alexandra Jaffe (ed.) *Stance: Sociolinguistic Perspectives* (pp. 3–28). Oxford: Oxford University Press.

Maryns, K. (2006) *The Asylum Speaker. Language in the Belgian Asylum Procedure*. Manchester: Saint Jerome.

Moyer, M. (2011) What multilingualism? Agency and unintended consequences of multilingual practices in a Barcelona health clinic. *Journal of Pragmatics* 43 (5), 1209–1221.

Pomerantz, A., Fehr, B.J. and Ende, J. (1997) When supervising physicians see patients: Strategies used in difficult situations. *Human Communication Research* 23 (4), 589–615.

Rehbein, J. (1994) Rejective proposals: Semi-professional speech and clients' varieties in intercultural doctor-patient communication. *Multilingua* 13 (1–2), 83–130.

Rehbein, J. (2000) Intercultural negotiation. In A. Di Luzio, S. Gunthner and F. Orletti (eds) *Culture in Communication: Analysis of Intercultural Situations* (pp. 173–199). Amsterdam: John Benjamins.

Ridsdale, L. and Hudd, S. (1994) Computers in computation: The patient's view. *British Journal of General Practice* 44, 367–369.

Roberts, C., Sarangi, S. and Moss, B. (2004) Presentation of self and symptom in doctor–patient communication in linguistically diverse settings. *Communication and Medicine* 1 (2), 159–169.

Roberts, C., Sarangi, S. and Jet-Bekkers, M. (2009) Third party insurance? Role and alignment in interpreter and mediated primary care consultations. Unpublished manuscript.

Sarangi, S. and Roberts, C. (eds) (1999) *Talk Work and Institutional Order: Discourse in Medical, Mediation and Management Settings*. Berlin: Mouton de Gruyter.

Scott, D. and Purvis, I.N. (1996) Triadic relationship between doctor, computer and patient. *Interacting with Computers* 8 (4), 347–363.

Stewart, V. (2005) Clinician style and examination room computers: A video ethnography. *Family Medicine* 37 (4), 276–281.

Swinglehurst, D., Roberts, C. and Greenhalgh, T. (2011) Opening up the 'black box' of the patient electronic record: A linguistic ethnographic study in general practice. *Communication and Medicine* 8 (1), 3–15.

Tebble, H. (1999) The tenor of consultant physicians. Implications for medical interpreting. *Translator* 5 (2), 179–199.

Valero Garcés, C. (2003) Una visión general de la evolución de la traducción e interpretación en los servicios públicos. In C. Valero Garcés (ed.) *Traducción e Interpretación en los Servicios Públicos. Contextualización, Actualidad y Futuro.* Granada: Editorial Comares.

Wadensjo, C. (1998) *Interpreting as Interaction.* New York: Longman.

Wadensjo, C., Englund Dimitrova, B. and Nilsson, A.L. (2007) *The Critical Link 4. Professionalization of Interpreting in the Community.* Amsterdam: John Benjamins.

Waitzkin, H. (1986) Micropolitics of medicine: Theoretical issues. *Medical Anthropology Quarterly* 17 (5), 134–136.

Waitzkin, H. (2000) *The Second Sickness. Contradictions of Capitalist Health Care.* Lanham: Rowman and Littlefield.

10 Informal Economy and Language Practice in the Context of Migrations

Cécile B. Vigouroux

Introduction

When I started my research on French-speaking African migrants in Cape Town in 1997, I often got in answer to my question, 'What kind of job do you do here?' the recurrent answer, 'I don't work'. In such cases I ventured a follow-up question about how the person earned money to sustain their basic needs such as food and accommodation, and was surprised when I heard 'I am a *security*' [security guard] or a *car watcher*. I realised then that there was a clear discrepancy between what I was defining as work, 'a way to make money in order to sustain oneself', and what my interlocutors were considering as work. Actually, I don't know exactly how they constructed the category 'work', since I never asked them. I can just infer from the answers I received that the activity of earning money they were referring to was typically low paid, at the bottom of the socio-economic ladder, and not clearly defined institutionally. Such a discrepancy between the researcher's categories and those of his/her subjects is not new; it has been amply documented in the literature. Yet it calls for an investigation of how categories are constructed in the social environment in which they emerge and where they are discursively articulated in order to understand, on the one hand, how the subject positions himself/herself and, on the other, how the categorisation lends meaning to her own and others' social practices.

A few months ago, the issue of work came up again in my research as I was trying to explain how Lingala, a Congolese vehicular language, has been spreading among non-Lingala-speaking Congolese migrants in Cape Town. During one of my fieldworks in June 2008, I noticed that some Congolese were acquiring Lingala at the cost of not learning (enough) English, which has been assumed to be the language of symbolic capital and economic promises in South Africa. I was not convinced by the common argument that Lingala or any such language was spreading because of the critical mass of its traditional speakers, because the notion of *critical mass* is a relative one (for instance, when does a population become critical enough?) that needs to be articulated with a multiplicity of other factors such as a population's settlement and growth patterns, and the regularity and types of interaction, to cite just a few. In other words, the fact that there are a significant number of Lingala speakers in Cape Town does not necessarily entail that speakers of other Congolese languages must learn it. The critical mass argument does not explain why they would not learn Xhosa, the local dominant language, which has a far greater critical mass. At that stage of my research, I had hastily assumed that the vast majority of the Congolese migrants, who were in Cape Town simply because they had fled poverty and deprivation at home, would try to improve their economic conditions in the host country by learning English or any local language that is economically important. The fact that many Congolese migrants found it more useful to learn Lingala called for a different kind of explanation. If critical mass is part of the explanation, there must be another reason that can explain why these migrants chose a Congolese language instead. This is where the issue of work comes into the picture.

My intent in this chapter is to articulate the relationship between language practice and labour in the context of migration. In so doing, I particularly focus on the often overlooked dimension of *informal economy*, which, as I argue below, should not always be interpreted as an alternative to people's 'unfitness' for the main national economy. Although this interpretation may indeed apply to some of those who practice informal economy, I argue that for many Congolese in Cape Town it is the rational economic model of choice, in which they strategically engage, for a short or longer period of time. For some it is the only way they know to sustain a living. I submit that because informal economy is based on the social capital that one needs to accumulate in order to survive in the host country (with or without a job), it favours the spread of the migrants' African vehicular language. For reasons explained below, if competition arises between different vernaculars, the 'winner' is likely to be that spoken by the most entrepreneurial group.

Hypotheses and therefore knowledge on the relationship between language practice and labour have usually been grounded on limited cases – observed typically in Europe and North America in particular – which are far from being representative of worldwide economic dynamics (Grin, 1996; Grin *et al.*, 2010). For instance, the fact that the informal economy represents an average of 42% of sub-Saharan Africa's GNP compared to 13% of that of Canada, Australia, New Zealand and the United States combined or 18% of that of western Europe's GNP (Schneider, 2002) calls for caution in generalising a correlation between access to employment and competence in the dominant language of a country.[1]

A close examination of informal economy as social organisation suggests that notions such as *skilled worker* and *cultural capital* need to be understood in relation to the micro social environment in which they are articulated and in which they really matter for the economic actors themselves. Among the issues I wish to address are the following: What counts as competence in informal economy? How are skills assessed? What requirements should individuals meet in order to be hired/employed to work? Although the context-based approach of cultural capital I emphasise here is very much in line with that of Bourdieu's, it needs to be revised relative to the account of the African ecology discussed here, which is very different from the French socio-historical context in which Bourdieu and Passeron (1964) originally articulated it.[2] In the context of this chapter, cultural capital refers to a set of dispositions that the Congolese call *la débrouille*, i.e. 'making the best of one's capacity in the environment in which one evolves', which enables individuals to sustain a living especially in adverse socio-economic environments. Cultural capital can be assessed by its conversion into economic capital; lack of the former triggers exclusion from economic resources and may also prevent access to social networks. An empirically grounded definition of cultural capital helps us better understand how it gets, or does not get, converted into economic capital in a given social ecology. I show below that such a perspective sheds new light on the relationship between geographic mobility and social mobility, because what may be considered as cultural capital in one ecology may not be in another. In the case of migrations, what matters for migrants' social mobility is the *transferability of capital*. For example, some forms of objectified cultural capital such as a university degree may be devalued outside the ecology where it was acquired.[3] We all know of cases of highly educated migrants who cannot have their home degrees ratified by host institutions[4] (see Hawthorne, 1997, in the case of non-English-speaking medical doctors in Australia).

In order to understand the conditions of capital transferability, I suggest developing an integrative approach that factors in both the socio-economic ecology where the migrants' cultural capital is converted into other capitals (social, economic or symbolic) and the environments where forms of cultural capital were acquired (i.e. the migrants' country of origin or other countries on their migratory trajectories). In the case of the Congolese migrants, it will help us understand why Lingala, rather than some other Congolese national lingua franca such as Swahili or Kikongo, is selected in Cape Town.

Before turning to my ethnographic data, I start by articulating the notion of *informal economy*, focusing on its social implications. Among the questions I wish to address is how social capital is acquired in informal economy. How, or to what extent, does it differ from the social dynamics occurring in formal markets? Adopting an 'integrative approach' to the migrants' socio-economic practices, I then turn to the economic system prevailing in Kinshasa, the capital city of the Democratic Republic of Congo. I show how this system is characterised by scholars as a 'fend-for-yourself economy' or an 'economy of predation'. It appears that some of the socio-economic factors that account for the success of Lingala in Kinshasa are similar to those that apply to the migrants in Cape Town. I submit in the conclusions that the transferability of Congolese entrepreneurship and the creation of the relevant economic niches in Cape Town should not be considered as peripheral to the South African economy. Rather, they are a component of it.

The ethnographic data used in this presentation were constructed over 14 discontinuous years of ethnographic field research in Cape Town, involving observations in different settings such as flea markets, internet cafés, churches, ethnic neighbourhoods and interviews. In addition, I was immersed for six months in a predominantly Congolese milieu, sharing a house with a Congolese friend and developing close relationships with my Congolese neighbours. Consistent with the integrative approach I advocate here, I conducted ethnographic fieldwork in Kinshasa (DRC) in June 2010, where I observed various forms of *débrouille*.

Informal Economy and its Social Implications from the Point of View of its Practitioners

The concept of the informal economy, also called *underground, second* or *undeclared economy*, among many others, was born in the 1970 s from a series of studies of labour markets in Africa (BIT, 1972; Hart, 1973). The criteria used to define it remain somewhat fuzzy and researchers do not all agree on the kind of activities the notion encompasses. A definition of informal economy in contrast to formal economy appears quite irrelevant, since the two are often intertwined (Portes & Haller, 2005). Indeed, many formal activities may at some point involve some informality. For example, a construction company paying its taxes and providing social security to its employees may concurrently engage in informal economy as it negotiates markets through bribing key political or economic actors. Conversely, many informal activities also involve formality, as in the case of a trader selling cigarettes and candies on the street who may not pay income taxes nor emplacement fees for her stall but pays taxes on the goods she has bought to resell. As economists have shown, it is also inaccurate to draw a rigid distinction between formal versus informal economic practices since, as shown by Browne (1995) and Lautier (1994/2004), for example, many people draw their incomes from mixed economic activities. Thus, it is not uncommon to see an institutionally employed construction worker renovate apartments in his free time at weekends, to round up his monthly income.[5]

Although the informal economy may involve illegal activities such as drug smuggling, prostitution, the black market and counterfeit, it would be misleading to reduce it to criminal activities. Indeed, the discursive construction of the informal economy as outlaw practices contributes to the criminalisation of migrants and often serves to justify ever harsher immigration policies and/or to explain violence from segments of host populations.

It is less the economic definition of informal economy that matters for us linguists than the social practices that it entails and to which we are turning now. The adjective 'informal' is somehow misleading since it implicitly suggests the lack of social or economic structures. Yet the informal economy relies on highly structured networks such as family, church affiliations or neighbourhoods (Lautier, 1991; Light, 2005), as aptly summarised by Light (2004: 515): 'In an informal economy, people draw upon relationships and networks. The relationship is part of the value exchanged.' Indeed, transactions in informal economy are based on personal relations and reciprocity between social agents; they do not necessarily involve money. For example, on the Green Market Square, a flea market in downtown Cape Town, it is very common during transactions with customers to see migrant traders borrow artefacts from another stall instead of sending the customer to their colleague's stand. From a purely economic point of view, it may appear counterproductive for trader B to enable her competitor A to close a deal with her own goods. Yet by doing so she can expect a favour in return from colleague A which will not necessarily be in the form of money or an equivalent artefact.

This kind of capital is based on *reciprocity transactions* (Portes & Sensenbrenner, 1993: 1324) where transactions are based on 'social intangibles'. Reciprocity in the case of the Green Market Square does not only bind A to B but to all the traders of the market. Failure to reciprocate transactions may be sanctioned by ostracism from other traders. A's compliance with the group expectation ensures her economic viability at the flea market. Portes and Sensenbrenner (1993) define this form of social capital as *enforceable trust,* in which the actor's behaviour is oriented to the web of the entire social network (see also Portes, 1998).

The example of traders' relations at the Green Market reveals some hidden costs of the informal economy, such as obligation to and interdependence between individuals and/or a group. Second, the informal economy is often presented as being more accessible than its formal counterpart. Work on the economics of migration and ethnographic studies of migrants' language practice have convincingly shown how lack of competence in the language of the main economy may prevent migrants from making use of their occupational experience and knowledge acquired at home or from applying for positions within the host society's labour market. Many studies corroborate the language–labour intricate relationship, although the findings provided by sociologists, economists and political scientists must be refined first by approaching language as indexical and not solely as denotational, as they generally do (Bohning & Zegers de Beijl, 1995; Esser, 2006; Remennick, 2003; Zimmerman et al., 2008).[6] Indeed, by pointing out the indexical nature of language, linguistic anthropologists such as Blommaert et al. (2005) underscore the fact that there is no strict fit between mobility of speakers and mobility of their language repertoires. What may be a language resource in one socio-economic environment may become an impediment in another.

Gatekeeping also exists in the informal economy, but it is of a different nature from that in the formal economy. Lautier (1994/2004) mentions *financial and non-financial capitals* as barriers to access the informal economy. Financial barriers apply strongly to independent workers who need to buy goods to set up a small or big trading business, or to purchase tools for performing their activity, as in the case of street hairdressers who need to buy hair extensions to braid hair. Lack of financial capital may be compensated by networks, as is evident from the social organisation of many migrant-based beauty shops in Cape Town. Hairdressers with no start-up capital rent a chair in one of their counterparts' salons and have access to the facility's equipment, tools and products, until they can start their own business. Therefore, workers in the same work environment can be bound by different kinds of socio-economic ties: employer–employee (in the case of hiring), (chair)renter–(chair)owner, or co-workers, as in the case of the employee and the chair renter.

The *non-financial* gatekeeping in informal economy involves primarily access to networks, which may be communicational, commercial or organisational. In the case of wholesale traders in Cape Town, being 'well connected' may mean knowing which South African police or custom officers to bribe to reduce import taxes. For a self-employed walking-trader it may be where to get suppliers or where to find the most affordable Chinese belts and purses to resell, whereas for newcomers it may mean learning where and how to seek employment. Access to networks enables migrants to navigate the host environment's system, legally or illegally.

In the informal migrant activities I have observed in Cape Town, language competence does not typically seem to play a significant role in preventing access to the informal economy. The reason lies in the nature of the process through which workers are selected. Unlike in the formal economy, the process is not regulated by formalised and clearly articulated protocols such as a job interview (Campbell & Roberts, 2007; Gumperz, 1992). However, the Congolese local 'population structure' (Mufwene, 2008) suggests that language may play a covert role, because it determines who can communicate with whom in order to obtain the relevant information. As already discussed in Vigouroux (2008), the Congolese in Cape Town are roughly divided into two groups, according to regional origin. On the one hand are people from the Eastern Congo who speak Swahili as their primary vehicular language and, on the other hand are people from Kinshasa, the capital city, and from the surrounding western areas who are predominantly Lingala-speakers. Those who belong to other linguistic groups such as the Kikongo and Ciluba speakers or who happen to speak both Swahili and Lingala often navigate between these two groups. The social distinctness of the two major groups is well marked by the nicknames associated with them: 'les Allemands' [*the Germans*] in reference to Swahiliphones versus 'les Arabes' [*the Arabs*] in reference to the Kinois and other people from Western DRC associated with them.[7]

Different patterns of socialisation emerge from the above opposition, as is evident from church affiliation (the churches are predominantly Swahiliphone and Lingalaphone; see Vigouroux, 2010) and house sharing, especially for people who have relocated alone to Cape Town. (Similar dynamics are observable among the Congolese in Johannesburg and Durban, as explained by Amisi, 2005, 2006; Mavungu, 2007.) Observations have shown several clusters of Lingalaphones and Swahiliphones in some Cape Town neighbourhoods.

Because the informal economy is mainly based on networks, a Lingalaphone entrepreneur is likely to select his business partner or employee(s) from the pool of his contacts (a neighbour, a church member, a friend of a friend) who is therefore likely also to be Lingalaphone. Although the ultimate criterion in the selection is trust and not simply the sharing of a common language, in migratory situations where people are not family bound and where there is no history of somebody's trustworthiness, language as indexing common origin plays a role in controlling or facilitating access to the job market. In the case of the Congolese, 'common origin' refers less to a mappable geographic entity than to a (perceived) distinctive way of life, as I show in the next section.

As argued by Lautier (1994/2004: 58), one must take into account all the gates someone has to pass through to access the informal economy as an independent worker or employee. This makes it clear that the informal economy is more than just an alternative to the migrants' repeated failures to enter the formal economy, although for some it may well be the case. The point applies to many Congolese in Cape Town whose informal economic activities reflect their successful transfer, in the host economy, of competences they had acquired at home. Transfer does not imply perfect replication, since practices in the host economy are also shaped by the new ecology. I therefore suggest that in order to better understand the relationship between language dynamics and labour in the Congolese diaspora in Cape Town, we need to factor in the socio-economic practices in the Congo and more specifically in Kinshasa, where many of the entrepreneurial migrants have acquired their economic habitus. In light of this comparison, I argue that the socio-economic factors that forged the connection between the informal economy and the use of Lingala in Cape Town are very similar to those of Kinshasa. The integrative approach I am advocating here makes it possible to historicise people's economic and language practices and therefore better understand the impact of the new, host environment on the social and economic habitus acquired prior to migration. Such a perspective implies that the context of migration should be reassessed and not posited a priori as the main (if not the only) explanatory factor in shaping people's practices. Thus, I focus on Kinshasa in the next section so that I may provide the requisite information for the development of my position.

Lingala, the 'Lumpen' Language of Kinshasa

The Democratic Republic of Congo has been declared 'economically dead' by economists for more than two decades. The informal economy has become the principal, if not the only, viable economic system that provides day-to-day subsistence work for millions of people and is practised even by those whose education would normally be associated with the formal economy. According to Meni (2000), in 1990, only 5% of the Congolese's primary source of income came from the formal economy. Ten years later, in 2000, this figure had dropped to 1%. As remarked by MacGaffey (2005), when a lecturer's monthly salary at the University of Kinshasa is just sufficient to buy one phone card, equivalent to $10 in 2001, one wonders why people seek employment at all or continue to perform their professional duties. More than 70% of the Congolese population live on less than $1 a day.

Some people may engage in the informal economy at an early age, selling lipsticks and make-up to their peers in class or in the schoolyard, although such practice is officially prohibited (Kalete Mufwene, pers. commun., December 2009). It is common practice in Kinshasa to bribe the technician who just cut off your electricity so he can have an income that his regular job does not pay. The 'economy of predation', as the practice is characterised by some experts, has pervaded all strata of the Congolese society from the top of the state to the bottom. MacGaffey (2005) reports the following common answers to her questions regarding how people buy clothes, pay for their beer and their children's tuition: *on se débrouille* [we fend for ourselves] or *on vit mystérieusement* [we live mysteriously]. *La débrouille* or *système D*, as it is referred to in Kinshasa, is encapsulated by what is commonly described as the 15th unwritten amendment to the Congolese Constitution: 'fend-for-yourself, you are at home'.

Now daily survival in Kinshasa largely depends on one's ability to secure networks that are no longer exclusively based on family or village ties. The collapse of the formal economy has fostered new forms of social contacts and given rise to alternative and often ephemeral networks of solidarity and collaboration. Needless to say, the fend-for-yourself economy comes at very high social costs, with the quest for individual profit undermining any relationships, even the closest ones.

In such an economy, where nothing works properly from public transportation to running water, one can easily assume that in order to 'function', everyone must learn the 'Kinshasa way of survival'. This includes speaking Lingala, the 'lumpen language' of the city, i.e. the language of the dispossessed, of the economic powerless.[8] As a hub, hosting people from other provinces and also from African countries such as Angola, Kinshasa is highly multilingual with several Congolese lingua francas and ethnic languages (Bokamba, 2008). Yet Lingala remains the 'people's unmarked vernacular and lingua franca for daily interactions' (Bokamba, 2008: 109). This pervasive use of Lingala in Kinshasa generally entails that Congolese from other provinces who resettle there learn it in order to properly function in the city, although their non-native variety indexes them as outsiders, which means that they may be taken advantage of.

The growing pauperisation of the population has been accompanied by a weakening of the urban administration and the concomitant decline of the status of the former colonial language, French, to the benefit of the urban vernacular. The socio-economic emancipation associated with western education since colonial times has faded away and triggered a clear disjunction between symbolic and economic capitals: French no longer elicits social prestige and affluence. Even those who succeeded in climbing the social ladder thanks to the democratisation of the school system now have to adjust to a different socio-economic world order for which they were not prepared. Therefore, there is now grassroots social pressure to acquire Lingala exerted on those who once were considered the pace setters. Irregularly paid teachers and university professors often have to work several jobs to make ends meet. The fact that Lingala has always been the language of popular culture, in which song lyrics have often articulated the plight of the underprivileged, has contributed to this particular ethnographic evolution of Lingala (Salikoko S. Mufwene, pers. commun., January 2010).

Ironically, the values indexed by Lingala in Kinshasa are what also fostered strong resistance to adopt it from Congolese living in other regions. Kinois are often criticised for their ostentatious and superficial ways of life, their lack of education and sophistication. As noted above, this contrast between the Kinois and the other Congolese has been rearticulated in the transnational migration context of Cape Town. Yet despite the negative values associated with the Kinois and their language, the economic capital of Lingala seems to be on the rise in Cape Town, as it has been adopted by growing numbers of Congolese who did not speak it in the homeland.

In order to understand this latter linguistic development, we must approach the Congolese migrations to South Africa from a historical perspective, pointing out its sociological transformations from its beginning in the 1980 s to date. Such an approach will enable us to show: (1) that the pauperisation of the Congolese population both in the Congo and in South Africa has favoured the spread of Lingala; (2) how the pauperisation in the Congo has changed the demographics of Congolese migrations to South Africa over the years, as the later migrants are less educated than their earlier counterparts; (3) how these newcomers have developed entrepreneurial skills that are easily transferrable into the host economy, making them potential sources of economic emancipation for other Congolese; and finally, (4) how the indexicalities of Lingala are changing as it becomes the primary language of the Congolese economic niche in Cape Town.

Congolese Migrants' Language Practice and Labour Experience in Cape Town

The first Congolese migrants to arrive in South Africa belonged to the economically privileged stratum of their society. Highly educated, they were hired by the South African apartheid government for their expertise as engineers, technicians and medical doctors. In the 1980 s, the Congo, then Zaire, was (still) considered a prosperous and stable country, with high educational standards that made its intellectual and scientific elite competitive on a transnational African labour market. Thanks to the professional competence they had acquired at home, the Congolese migrants were integrated into the South African local economy, although they evolved in the social and geographic periphery of the country, as they were employed primarily in the homelands.

Although they were chronologically the first Congolese migrants to settle in South Africa, they do not seem to have paved the way for the Congolese who arrived 10 years later, in the mid-1990s. Social class differences between the highly educated population that blended into the South African urban fabric and the less affluent one that followed and is now struggling to find its place in the host country overshadows any sense of common geographic or national origin between the first and second groups. Several factors triggered the second wave of Congolese migrations, including social upheavals and the worsening economic crisis in the Congo. Although most of the Congolese I interviewed in 1996 had benefited from the last crumbs of an already collapsing education system, they found themselves marginalised on the Cape Town job market. Unlike the earlier migrants, the occupational experience and knowledge acquired at home were not transferable to the host formal economy. In 1999 I met Elise at her workplace, on Beach Street in Sea Point, where she was performing her car-watcher job.[9] Here is what she told me when we talked about her current work:

Elise: je pensais que quand on allait _ dès qu'on a- arrive ici _ ça sera comme chez nous _ vous passez _ vous avez votre diplôme _ vous passez dans dans un hôpital ou dans un département médical _ on vous fait _ vous passez l'examen _ après l'examen si vous réussissez _ vous êtes vous vous vous vous mettez à travailler _ je savais pas que ça devait être si compliqué aller mettre les cachets à Pretoria (…) il faut écrire _ je suis pas encore en mesure d'écrire l'anglais correctement _ tu vois ça c'est le problème

Elise: *I thought that when we came _ as soon as we c- came here _ it will be like at home _ you go _ you have your degree _ you go to to a hospital or to a medical department _ medical _ they make you _ you sit for the exam _ after the exam if you pass [it] _ you are you you you you start working _ I did't know that it had to be so complicated go put stamps in Pretoria (...) you have to write _ I am not able to write English correctly _ you see this it's the problem*

Elise, a Swahiliphone who trained as a nurse in the eastern part of the Congo, rationalises her low-paid job as a car watcher by invoking her lack of proficiency in written English, which allegedly bars her from performing the work she was trained to do.

The data show that the migrants' discourse on the relationship between English competence and job opportunities in South Africa is matched by their hope that French will provide them with the same opportunities. Therefore, being bilingual in English and French would give them a competitive edge. Attitudes toward French and English as economic capital are strongly correlated with the migrants' experience with the local labour market, the duration of their stay in the host country and, to a certain extent, their occupational skills acquired in the home country. Interviewees who tend to see French as an asset in South Africa are mostly self-employed or freshly arrived migrants who have not (yet) been directly confronted with the challenges of the local labour market, such as in the case of Aurélien who is a self-employed Congolese carpenter:

Cécile: c'est un avantage pour un étranger africain de parler français en Afrique du Sud/

Aurélien: un étranger comme moi/ oui un avantage\

Cécile: pourquoi un avantage/

Aurélien: parce que vous allez dans certaines compagnies-là _ dans les hôtels-là _ si vous cherchez un boulot dans un hôtel _ _ on peut vous demander parlez combien de langues _ _ tu peux dire je parle le français je parle anglais c'est déjà beaucoup _ y a des Français qui peuvent venir _ on te présente celui-là il parle français il peut servir de _ catalyseur entre vous et l'hôtel _ voilà pourquoi c'est important de parler _ français et anglais _ deux langues _ _ ça peut t'aider à quelque chose de bien

Cécile: *is it an advantage for an African foreigner to speak French in South Africa/*

Aurélien: *a foreigner like me/ yes an advantage*

Cécile: *why an advantage/*

Aurélien: *because you go to some companies _ to hotels _ if you are looking for a job in a hotel _ _ they can ask you how many languages [you] speak _ _ you can say I speak French I speak English it is already a lot _ there are French people who can come _ they introduce you that one he speaks French it can act as a catalyst between you and the hotel _ that's why it's important to speak _ French and English _ two languages _ _ it may lead you to something good*

As is evident from Aurélien's use of the modal *peut* [can], French as an asset on the Cape Town labour market is more a matter of potential than likelihood. In many migrants' discourse, the value that French may carry on the South African job market is often downplayed by the fact that they are African migrants and therefore will not be hired. As a matter of fact, during my numerous stays in South Africa, I was often asked by working- and middle-class South Africans if Francophone Africans speak French 'well'! Aurélien's self-assessment shows that language attitudes towards French are largely inherited from colonial structures in the migrants' countries of origin, where French carried a lot of prestige. Blommaert (2005) characterises it as a 'transnational hierarchy' in which French becomes a symbolic power in a value system which goes far beyond the South African context (see also Bourdieu, 1979, 1980). Yet the confrontation with the reality of the market leads to a change in the indexical values of the language, as in the case of Christian, who has long been struggling to find employment:

Cécile: et est-ce que tu penses que c'est un avantage pour un étranger ici de parler français/
Christian: ici/ _ de parler français/ _ _ {rire} pas du tout hein/ {rire} _ _ non il faut que je le dise franchement\

Cécile: *and do you think that it is an advantage for a foreigner here to speak French/*
Christian: *here/ _ to speak French/ _ _ {laughter} not at all/ {laughter} _ _ no I must tell it frankly*

Christian's discourse echoes Michel's. As a self-proclaimed businessman after unsuccessful attempts to get a job, he does not consider the command of English as an asset to enter the South African labour market, invoking employment discrimination toward migrants. Here is how he responded to my question about the importance of English for finding work in Cape Town:

Michel: C'est problème ou c'est pas un problème aussi ça ne dérange pas parce que il n'y a pas de boulot pour les étrangers, il n'y a pas les avantages ici en Afrique du Sud

Michel: *It's problem or it's not a problem also it doesn't matter because there are no jobs for foreigners there aren't the advantages here in South Africa*

The second wave, especially that of non-Kinois, has been harshly exposed to the local job market in which they have to compete with newly emancipated local black labour for low-paid jobs.[10] Unlike their fellow countrymen of the first generation, their geographic mobility was accompanied by a social downgrading that caused a reshuffling of their language repertoire. As is obvious from the above, the symbolic and economic capital that French acquired through the migrants' formal education is generally undervalued in the new labour market, making it difficult for them to capitalise on it.[11] Ironically, the fact that the majority of them are educated (though less well than their earlier fellow-countrymen), often holding university degrees, and some of them had stable jobs prior to their migration has proved to be a disadvantage in the host country. They brought with them occupational skills that did not make them competitive on the formal labour market where access is highly regulated by objectified cultural capital and/or English as linguistic capital, as illustrated above with Elise, who trained as a nurse. Many of those who, after repeated failures to find employment, tried to retool themselves as African craft traders, failed in their enterprise, mostly because they lacked experience with self-employment. Interestingly, such social and economic downgrading of these fairly well educated Congolese in Cape Town has not been experienced by many of the most recent migrants from Kinshasa, for reasons I can now elaborate on.

As explained above, many of these young newcomers were school dropouts but had developed skills that were immediately transferable in their new South African ecology. Having grown up in the informal economy of Kinshasa, they had learned from their parents, and in some cases even developed, survival entrepreneurial skills that the Congolese of the second wave lacked. It is the total collapse of the Congolese economy combined with discriminatory immigration laws in Europe that drove this new class of Congolese to South Africa.

The category 'Kinois', as they are dubbed in Cape Town, embodies not just a common origin, Kinshasa, but shared social experiences and way of life. The term also carries a derogatory connotation, being associated, among the Congolese, with fraudulent practices and an adventurous lifestyle, as noted above. Despised on one hand mainly because of the prevalent 'bad reputation' they generally hold (at home and in other African countries), they are also praised on the other hand for their expertise, which could benefit the entire migrant population. For instance, in the late 1990s some of them were experts in providing affordable international communication services thanks to the hijacking of regular telephone lines. However, if the Kinois' entrepreneurship had remained confined to illegal activities, it is likely that Lingala, the language associated with it, would not have spread as widely as it has now among other non-Lingalaphone Congolese.

In the past 10 years, this entrepreneurship has transformed into a burgeoning of visible businesses such as internet cafés, African restaurants and beauty shops. Competing on the same ground as their South African counterparts, as they provide equivalent types of services, these companies have become potential sources of employment for other Congolese who might have been reluctant to be associated with the Kinois in the past. On the other hand, the insertion of the latter into Cape Town's economy was partly eased by some of their Congolese predecessors who had good knowledge of the South African environment and had already established local social networks.

Ethnographic research I conducted in different settings such as Congolese beauty salons (Vigouroux, 2003), internet cafés (Vigouroux, 2009), and African design stores show that employment is often ethnic based.[12] Any Congolese who wish to benefit from the potential work opportunities provided by the Kinois need first to acquire the requisite social capital in order to be informed about the availability of the jobs or to make themself visible. Although Lingala may not be an explicit job requirement, it may help open the first 'hiring gate', especially when the group is divided along regional origins and therefore linguistic lines. The accumulation of some social capital in the informal economy is not only important at the first stage of the selection process but also to migrants' social mobility. The main reason is that, because they are often based on fragile associations, many of the businesses are short lived, leaving employees jobless, often without notice. Because many of the Congolese-run businesses in Cape Town are supported by Congolese patrons (for some more than others), they provide their employees with excellent opportunities to extend their social networks within the community.[13]

Creating an incentive for learning or speaking Lingala, this new economic niche has consequently transformed the indexicalities of the language. Closely associated with *Kinoiseries* (i.e. a fend-for-yourself economy) in the DRC, it has come to index potential socio-economic emancipation in the Cape Town job market, which is not always welcoming to African migrants. Note that the transformation of the indexicalities of Lingala is concomitant of the change in the functionality of the language in the local economic niche.

Yet, the picture would not be accurate without factoring in the migrants' occupational trajectories in the host country. It is important to distinguish those who engage in short-term informal economy from those who experience it as a way of life. As I am about to show, the two entail differing linguistic behaviours.

Migrants who engage in short-term informal economy experience it as a temporary solution until they find more stable and permanent employment. Most of the time, they are relative newcomers with no, or limited, economic

capital but with a degree in higher education or at least some formal education. To them, the economic and social capital they gain in the informal
economy is accumulated at the cost of the linguistic capital, English, which
they think should help them access regular employment in the South African
formal economy. Such a perception is illustrated by Nadine's reaction to a
question addressed to her in Lingala by one of her customers at the internet
café where she works. A Swahili speaker, Nadine raises her voice and exclaims
in French that she came to South Africa to learn English, not Lingala, and if
people keep talking to her in this language she will never make it. This
example points out that formal and informal economies are regulated by
different linguistic markets that might be in competition with each other, at
least as perceived by some speakers. It also highlights the fact that, thanks
to the economic niche created by the Congolese, Lingala and English may be
in competition as vehicular languages giving access to employment in the
Cape Town labour market. This confirms Mufwene's (2008) forceful argument that languages can compete with each other only when they perform
the same communicative functions.

Next to people who experience the informal economy as a transitory
stage are those who are engaged in long-term informal activities. At one end
of the spectrum are successful entrepreneurs such as those discussed above;
at the other end is a population of people epitomised in the self-ascribed
category *aventurier* [adventurer]. Although the *adventurer* is not a new emblem
in the history of African migrations, as shown by scholarly work in history
and anthropology, until now it has not really caught linguistic anthropologists' attention. *Adventure* is a particular form of migratory experience filled
with risk taking and quest for a new valorised identity through acts of brav-
ery and exploits (Bredeloup, 2008). In adventure, acts are driven by individual
profits and a quest for intense experience. Usually adventure represents a
definite period of time in somebody's life until he decides to seek stability by
getting married or by engaging in a more conventional professional career.
Alex defines himself as an adventurer in the following terms:

Alex: bon _ comme un aventurier _ il faut foncer
Cécile: tu te considères comme un aventurier/
Alex: maintenant _ je me considère comme un aventurier _ je me dis
           que je dois gagner _ je ne dois plus perdre _ c'est à dire quand
           j'entreprends une activité _ je dois gagner _ quand je dois perdre _
           je laisse tomber\

Alex: *ok _ as an adventurer _ you have to move fast*
Cécile: *you consider yourself as an adventurer/*

Alex: *now _ I consider myself as an adventurer _ I tell myself I have to win _ I don't have to lose anymore _ it means that when I engage in an activity _ I have to win _ when I have to lose _ I give up*

For migrants like Alex, participation in the informal economy is not a choice by default after unsuccessful attempts to access more formal markets; it is a way of life driven by immediate profit and individual success. On the formality–informality continuum, adventurers are situated at the extreme point of informality.

The Congolese adventurers I met in Cape Town were predominantly young Kinois dropouts, some engaged in illicit activities such as diamond smuggling or other trafficking, usually designated by the fuzzy category of *business*. Preliminary ethnographic work in June 2008 shows a new linguistic trend among this population with a significant number of them speaking a kind of French and favouring Lingala over English. Their socialisation in Cape Town seems to be limited to their fellow-countrymen involved in the same kind of activities, therefore not favouring interactions in English. This recent linguistic development reflects the increasing pauperisation of some of the most recent migrants.[14] Unlike their predecessors, their relocation into a new socio-economic and linguistic environment is inscribed in the continuation of an ongoing struggle to survive, started long before the migratory journey. By capitalising on Lingala, at least for now, these migrants seem to favour local power within the Congolese community, making profit out of the socio-economic skills they acquired at home. The social emancipation experienced by these adventurers does not resemble that of other migrants; it is inscribed in their daily power to overcome whatever obstacles may impede their epic journey. Such migratory journeys and the experience of labour entailed in the Cape Town economy is an additional facet of the already complex picture of the different ways in which labour and language practice shape each other in the specific context of Congolese migration.

Conclusions

The relationship between language practice and labour in the context of migrations has been addressed here through the lens of the informal economy, a domain still understudied and therefore under-theorised in linguistics. Leaving this dimension of labour unexplored prevents us from having a more complete and nuanced understanding of the role and effect of economy on language dynamics. In addition, the informal economy is a significant part of nations' GNPs, as illustrated by Schneider's (2002) figures; it therefore constitutes a substantial source of employment for workers around the world.

We saw that the notion of *informal economy* is hard to capture and its reality on the ground is hard to assess, since there are no hard-and-fast social and/or economic characteristics defining it, nor is there a clear dichotomy between formality and informality. Such theoretical fuzziness entails methodological questions, which I have not touched upon here, on how to conduct ethnographic work on these socio-economic practices. Despite their theoretical opacity, informal economic practices are of interest to us linguists, because they first help us put in perspective the often taken-for-granted correlation between migrants' *integration* into host countries' socio-economic structures and *competence* in the language of their dominant economies. As explained above, Lingala has become the Congolese migrants' language of socio-economic integration in Cape Town – for some by default and for others by choice – if we understand by 'integration' the process whereby somebody fits into a given environment. Discussing integration in this context implies that we don't consider the informal economy as marginal to nations' main economies but as part of them. As convincingly argued by Lautier *et al.* (1991), the informal economy should not be analysed as a state's inability to regulate labour; on the contrary, it indexes intricate relationships between the state, employers and employees. Undocumented migrants' labour is a case in point: loudly decried and officially penalised, it is implicitly encouraged by the state's lenience towards employers or corporations, such as the food industry in the United States, where a significant part of the workforce is made up of illegal underpaid Hispanic workers. By decreasing the labour costs, corporations make additional profits on the products they sell for consumption, with the implicit blessing of the provincial and federal governments. See Kenner's (2008) *Food Inc.* documentary on the food industry in the United States. Because state regulations exist that help decide what practices to tolerate or condemn, the informal economy is neither socially nor economically peripheral to a nation's main economy; it is a component of it.

This leads us to discuss the political instrumentalisation of the relationship between proficiency in the host language and socio-economic integration. I concur with Wallace Goodman (2011), who argues that language requirements as a condition for (legal/official) immigration are used by governments as regulatory processes to control immigration and access to local labour markets. Yet, as noted above, the same regulatory dynamics apply in the informal economy in Cape Town, where Kinois employers implicitly use knowledge of Lingala as an implicit hiring requirement.[15]

Moreover, use of language for gatekeeping access to employment also applies to nationals, as Cornwell and Inder (2008) illustrate in the case of black South Africans at home. Although I have some reservations about the authors' methodology, their findings prompt us to rethink the longstanding dichotomy between *nationals* (or locals) versus *migrants* and the strong correlation between unemployment and racial discrimination. They show, for example, that white Afrikaans-speaking South Africans do not have any advantage on the job market compared to English-speaking Asians. They also argue that, although black South Africans are still overwhelmingly disadvantaged on the local job market, those who speak English have the same employment prospect as English-speaking whites: 'the labour-market experiences of the African who speaks English are more similar to those of an English-speaking white than to the Xhosa-speaking African' (Cornwell & Inder, 2008: 522). Such findings point out that the issue of socio-economic integration goes far beyond the context of migrations and should be investigated without preconceived social categories (e.g. *locals* versus *migrants*) to whom it may apply.

Although, as scholars, part of our responsibility is to unveil the ideology of political discourse on fluency in the host language(s) as the *sine qua non* condition of migrants' access to the labour market, one cannot deny that language proficiency matters on the ground. For people like Elise, the nurse, it appears to do so. This chapter simply shows that it does not matter equally for everybody. In the case of Congolese migrants in Cape Town, those who are the most subjected to labour market language requirements are those from the middle class whose cultural capital's conversion rate in the new economy is very low. At the other end of the scale, those who were disenfranchised in the Congo are the ones who seem to overcome the hardships of the Cape Town labour market relatively better, thanks to the successful transfer of economic skills and language capital, Lingala, acquired at home. In order to understand the forms of capital and the conditions of their transferability to the migrants' new environment, I advocated an integrative approach that may factor in both the socio-economic ecology in which these capitals were acquired and that of where they are being reassessed. Such an approach helps to account for differing language practices within the Congolese diaspora in Cape Town. I believe it can provide new insights into the intricacies and multiplicity of factors that shape the relationship between language practice and labour. Further inquiries will verify this initial conclusion.

Transcription conventions

_	short pause
_ _	long pause
/ \	rising/falling intonation
{laughter}	extralinguistic annotation

244 Part 3: Sites of Resistance

Acknowledgements

The author would like to thank Celia Roberts and Alexandre Duchêne for reading the initial draft of this chapter attentively and critically. Their challenging questions have prompted her to hopefully articulate her positions more clearly and strengthen her arguments. Needless to say that they cannot be held accountable for any remaining shortcomings. She would also like to thank Salikoko Mufwene for serving as a sounding board from the initial stage of this project until its completion.

Notes

(1) Figures on the informal economy are hard to assess and therefore should be taken with caution. The figures point out that this economic style is far from being limited to developing countries.
(2) For a review of the different meanings of 'cultural capital' in Bourdieu's work, see Lamont and Lareau (1988).
(3) Needless to say that such practices are meant to regulate migrants' access to sectors of the host job market as argued later.
(4) Because the conversion rate of objectified cultural capital is often tied to the symbolic and economic capitals of the relevant countries, it is a good indicator of power dynamics on a broader scale.
(5) In agreement with Lautier (1991), I talk of 'informal economy' rather than 'informal sector'. The latter is a misleading notion, since no particular sector can be clearly associated with informality.
(6) For a critical review of economic studies on language competence and access to the labour market, see especially Lebeau and Renaud (2002).
(7) The Kinois are so designated because they are allegedly lazy and perfidious, whereas the Swahiliphones are claimed to be hard workers and well organised. This ethno-linguistic distinction unveils long-term political dissentions inherited from the home country. In the Cape Town migratory context, it also indexes a class distinction between a generally better educated and economically more successful Swahili group and a larger population of young Kinois *aventuriers* [adventurers], victims of the collapse of the Congolese education system and the harsh living conditions in Kinshasa who are 'risking anything' in search of better opportunities.
(8) The Democratic Republic of Congo is characterised by what Bokamba (2008: 100) calls 'pervasive multilingualism' with an estimated total of 214 languages, including four 'national', vehicular languages (Lingala, Swahili, Ciluba and Kikongo) and French as the official language. The other indigenous languages are also typically associated with corresponding ethnic groups.
(9) Car watching on the street aptly illustrates the fuzziness of the distinction between the formal and informal economies. Car watchers are 'employed' by registered security companies from which they daily rent their identifiable jackets. This gives them the right to perform their duties on an assigned portion of a street where they help drivers to park and look after the latter's cars. They make their 'incomes' from the variable tips car drivers are willing to give. Needless to say, incomes are highly unpredictable.

(10) People coming from the Eastern part of the Congo generally do not transit by Kinshasa to come to South Africa. Most of those I interviewed travelled by trucks, buses and sometimes on foot via Zambia and Zimbabwe.

(11) The relevant clientele is primarily European. Few affluent Africans come to Cape Town as tourists. Yet, my most recent trip to Cape Town in January 2011 makes me believe that this situation is changing. I witnessed an increasing number of Francophone Africans working in highly touristic restaurants. I surmise that such a change indexes Cape Town's tourism industry's commodification of French as an 'African language' or as an important international lingua franca. Ironically, this is how the Alliance Française promoted French in 1994, the year of the first democratic elections, with the following motto: 'French: reconnecting South Africa to Africa'.

(12) These businesses are said to belong to the informal economy because of their unregistered business activity and undeclared employment. In addition, adjacent business activities often occur on their premises such as trading of products not associated with the main activities of the stores or money exchange (local money for US dollars).

(13) On the other hand, some well-to-do Congolese told me that they refuse to go to Congolese-run businesses in order to stay away from the potential financial and social pressures that their fellow countrymen may want to exert on them.

(14) On the other side of the Congolese social spectrum in South Africa there is also an increasing number of middle and upper middle-class university students who were sent by their parents to get a 'good' education in English. According to my ethnographic research, the paths of these two populations hardly cross.

(15) As aptly pointed out to me by Alexandre Duchêne (pers. commun., September 2011), in migration contexts, other forms of language instrumentalisation may occur, for instance, when companies capitalise on their 'unskilled' employees' language resources and occasionally ask them to volunteer as interpreters. This has been documented with migrant baggage handlers at Zurich airport (Duchêne, 2011).

References

Amisi, B.B. (2005) *Social Capital, Social Networks, and Refugee Migration: An Exploration of the Livelihood Strategies of Durban Congolese Refugees*. Durban: Centre for Civil Society, University of KwaZulu-Natal.

Amisi, B.B. (2006) *An Exploration of the Livelihood Strategies of Durban Congolese Refugees*. Durban: Centre for Civil Society, University of KwaZulu-Natal.

BIT (1972) *Employment, Income and Equality: A Strategy for Increasing Production Employment in Kenya*. Geneva: International Labour Organization.

Blommaert, J. (2005) *Discourse: A Critical Introduction*. Cambridge: Cambridge University Press.

Blommaert, J., Collins J. and Slembrouck S. (2005) Spaces of multilingualism. *Language and Communication* 25, 197–216.

Böhning, W.R. and Zegers de Beijl, R. (1995) *The Integration of Migrant Workers in the Labour Market: Policies and Their Impact*. Labour Market-paper 8. Geneva: International Labour Organization. http://www.ilo.org/public/english/protection/migrant/download/imp/imp08e.pdf, accessed 2 September 2011.

246   Part 3: Sites of Resistance

Bokamba, E. (2008) The lives of local and regional Congolese languages in globalized linguistic markets. In C.B. Vigouroux and S.S. Mufwene (eds) *Globalization and Language Vitality: Perspectives from Black Africa* (pp. 97–125). London: Continuum.

Bourdieu, P. (1979) Les trois étapes du capital culturel. *Actes de la Recherche en Science Sociales* 30 (1), 3–6.

Bourdieu, P. (1980) Le Capital social. *Actes de la Recherche en Science Sociales* 31, 2–3.

Bourdieu P. and Passeron, J.-C. (1964) *Les héritiers.* Paris: Les éditions de Minuit.

Bredeloup, S. (2008) L'aventurier, une figure de la migration africaine. *Cahiers Internationaux de Sociologie* 125, 281–306.

Browne, K.E. (1995) Who does and who doesn't earn 'off the books'? The logic of informal economic activity in Martinique, FWI. *Anthropology Review* 16 (1–2), 23–33.

Campbell S. and Roberts, C. (2007) Migration, ethnicity and competing discourses in the job interview: Synthetizing the institutional and personal. *Discourse Society* 18 (3), 243–271.

Cornwell K. and Inder, B. (2008) Language and labour market in South Africa. *Journal of African Economies* 17 (3), 490–525.

Duchêne, A. (2011) Néolibéralisme, inégalités sociales et plurilinguisme: l'exploitation des ressources langagières et des locuteurs. *Langage et Société* 136, 81–106.

Esser, H. (2006) *Migration, Language and Integration.* AKI Research Review No. 4. Berlin: Social Science Research Center.

Grin, F. (1996) The economics of language: Survey, assessment, and prospects. *International Journal of the Sociology of Language* 121, 17–44.

Grin, F., Sfreddo, C. and Vaillancourt, F. (2010) *The Economics of the Multilingual Workplace.* New York: Routledge.

Gumperz, J. (1992) Interviewing in intercultural situations. In P. Drew and J. Heritage (eds) *Talk at Work* (pp. 302–327). Cambridge: Cambridge University Press.

Hart, K. (1973) Informal income opportunities and urban employment in Ghana. *Journal of Modern African Studies* II (1), 61–89.

Hawthorne, L. (1997) The question of discrimination: Skilled migrants' access to Australian employment. *International Migration* 35 (3), 395–418.

Kenner, R. (2008) *Food Inc* [Documentary]. Magnolia Pictures.

Lamont, M. and Lareau, A. (1988) Cultural capitals: Allusions, gaps and glissandos in recent theoretical developments. *Sociological Theory* 6 (2), 153–168.

Lautier, B. (1991) Les travailleurs n'ont pas la forme. Informalité des relations de travail et citoyenneté en Amérique Latine. In B. Lautier, C. de Miras and A. Morice (eds) *L'État et l'informel* (pp. 11–76). Paris: L'Harmattan.

Lautier, B. (1994/2004) *L'économie informelle dans le tiers monde.* Paris: La Découverte.

Lautier B., de Miras, C. and Morice, A. (1991) *L'État et l'informel.* Paris: L'Harmattan.

Lebeau R. and Renaud, J. (2002) Nouveaux arrivants de 1989, langue et mobilité professionnelle sur le marché du travail de Montréal: une approche longitudinale. *Cahiers Québécois de Démographie* 31 (1), 69–94.

Light, D.W. (2004) From migrant enclaves to mainstream: Reconceptualizing informal economic behavior. *Theory and Society* 33 (6), 705–737.

Light, D.W. (2005) The ethnic economy. In N. Smelser and R. Swedberg (eds) *The Handbook of Economic Sociology* (pp. 650–677). New York: Princeton University Press.

MacGaffey, J. (2005) New forms of remuneration for labour in Congo-Kinshasa's economy of favours. In S. Bhattacharya and J. Lucassen (eds) *Workers in the Informal Sector. Studies in Labour History 1800–2000* (pp. 141–160). New Delhi: MacMillan.

Mavungu, M. (2007) Social capital, economic performance, and political engagement. A case study of Congolese immigrants in central Johannesburg. MA research report, School of Social Sciences, University of Witwatersrand, Johannesburg. http://wired-space.wits.ac.za/handle/10539/2040, accessed 26 September 2011.

Meni, M. (2000) L'importance du secteur informel en RDC. *Bulletin de l'ANSD* 1, 21–40. http://www.uqac.ca/jmt-sociologue/, accessed 5 January 2010.

Mufwene, S.S. (2008) *Language Evolution: Contact, Competition and Change*. London: Continuum.

Portes, A. (1998) Social capital: Its origins and applications in modern sociology. *Annual Review of Sociology* 24, 1–24.

Portes, A. and Haller, W. (2005) The informal economy. In N. Smelser and R. Swedberg (eds) *The Handbook of Economic Sociology* (pp. 403–425). New York: Princeton University Press.

Portes, A. and Sensenbrenner, J. (1993) Embeddedness and immigration: Notes on the social determinants of economic action. *American Journal of Sociology* 98 (6), 1320–1350.

Remennick, L. (2003) Language acquisition as the main vehicle of social integration: Russian immigrants of the 1990s in Israel. *International Journal of the Sociology of Language* 164, 83–105.

Schneider, F. (2002) Size and measurement of the informal economy in 110 countries around the world. Paper presented at a Workshop of Australian Tax Centre, ANU, Canberra.

Vigouroux, C.B. (2003) Réflexion méthodologique autour de la construction d'un objet de recherche: la dynamique identitaire chez les migrants africains francophones au Cap (Afrique du Sud). PhD thesis, University of Paris X, Paris.

Vigouroux, C.B. (2008) From Africa to Africa: Migration, globalization and language vitality. In C.B. Vigouroux and S.S. Mufwene (eds) *Globalization and Language Vitality: Perspectives from Black Africa* (pp. 229–254). London: Continuum.

Vigouroux, C.B. (2009) A relational understanding of language practice: Interacting times-spaces in a single ethnographic site. In J. Collins, S. Slembrouck and M. Baynham (eds) *Globalization and Language in Contact: Scale Migration Flows, and Communicative Practices*, (pp. 62–84). London: Continuum.

Vigouroux, C.B. (2010) Double-mouthed discourse: Interpreting activity, framing and participant roles. *Journal of Sociolinguistics* 14 (3), 341–369.

Wallace Goodman, S. (2011) Controlling immigration through language and country knowledge requirements. *West European Politics* 34 (2), 235–255.

Zimmerman, K.F., Kahanec, M., Constant, A., DeVoretz, D., Gataullina, L. and Zaiceva, A. (2008) Study on the social and labour market integration of ethnic minorities. IZA Research Report No. 16. IZA, Bonn.

11 Fighting Exclusion from the Margins: *Locutorios* as Sites of Social Agency and Resistance for Migrants

Maria Sabaté i Dalmau

When my boss exploits me, who listens?
Without papers there is no work and without work there are no papers,
the spiral strangerises and I get caught in Spain's net.
What can I do? I breathe hopelessness,
living a bad life in a dark hideout because my salary is not enough,
I go to the locutorio *daily, this is my duty,*
to get to know how my people are, what they will have to eat.[1]
Nach. Tierra Prometida, *Ars Magna – Miradas*

Introduction: Investigating Migrants' Bottom-up Resistance

Today, the current life trajectories, family configurations and work prospects of transnational migrant populations are largely negotiated, maintained and orchestrated by information and communication technologies (ICTs; Castells, 2000[1996]), in particular the mobile phone – the *social glue* for globe-trotting (Vertovec, 2009: 54).

The relevance and impact of ICTs on migrants has already been studied as a powerful source of crucial *social capital* (see, for instance, Alonso & Oiarzabal, 2010; Castells, 2009). However, less importance has been placed on the structural barriers posed to unconnected migrants who, at the bottom of the social ladder, are still experiencing the *digital divide* as 'technology-have-less' in societies that belong to the so-called 'information-rich' states.

Indeed, in the context I wish to present here, the community of Catalonia in the Spanish state,[2] many 21st-century migrants who try to get access to ICTs today find themselves navigating through a series of legal regimes, economic constraints and, above all, communicative and linguistic barriers posed by two extremely powerful institutional fronts: *the Spanish nation-state* and its new techniques of citizenship registration via ICTs, on the one hand, and *the telecommunications sector* and their alienating non-management of migrants' non-elite multilingualism, on the other.

From a critical sociolinguistic perspective (Heller, 2006[1999], 2010a), in this chapter I investigate how migrants articulate bottom-up resistance against the aforementioned barriers and react to situations of social inequality concerning access to ICTs. More specifically, I analyse a very unique *space of resistance and empowerment* whereby migrants collectively get mobilised and establish their own ICT businesses in order to skirt, overcome and combat the nation-state's and the private sector's sociolinguistic orders and market rationalities: the *locutorios*, or migrant-tailored call shops. I argue that *locutorios* are an excellent space in which to analyse informal *alternative institutions of migration* whereby migrants can gain a certain degree of social agency (in the Giddens' sense of the word; Giddens, 1984), from the margins. I show that these ventures are an example of and a window into how migrants, *through language*, mobilise resistance in order to insert themselves into contemporary communicative regimes through their own linguistic capitals and in their own self-regulated discursive spaces.

In order to get to grips with the migrants' resistance spaces, I conducted a *network ethnography* (Howard, 2002; Sabaté i Dalmau, 2012a) of a *locutorio* over two years of fieldwork (2007–2009, although I actually lived in the neighbourhood for three and a half years). This is a 'web-tracking' methodology whereby I could follow, observe and analyse the life trajectories of a very heterogeneous group of 20 migrants who came to organise themselves around a *locutorio* in a very marginal Spanish-speaking neighbourhood at the outskirts of the metropolitan area of Barcelona (in a county called the Vallès Occidental). These informants, men and women aged between 27 and 52, were mostly born in Pakistan, Morocco and Romania (some also came from El Salvador, the Dominican Republic, Bolivia, Guinea, Equatorial Guinea, Cuba and Brazil). With the exception of some who became *locutorio* workers, they were largely unemployed and undocumented.

The data presented in this article basically include *thick description* (Geertz, 1973) of the context, the linguistic ideologies and the systematised communicative practices observed in this migrant space. These were recorded through a very active participant observation, in many different discursive spaces (not only in their *locutorio*, which was my window into the network, but also in their households, the bars and the street). I also include an excerpt of the 14 open-ended interviews involving 17 *locutorio* users and workers that I conducted during the time of my fieldwork, as well as some documentary data, visual materials, and relevant census information. Finally, to show both sides of the coin, I also draw on a second piece of research: an ethnographic analysis of the management of linguistic diversity by the Spanish telecommunications sector; that is, by the 29 multinationals, ICT ventures and migrant-oriented companies operating in Spain at the time of the fieldwork. This second set of data includes a linguistic examination of the languages that the companies publicly employed in (i) their call centres, (ii) official websites and (iii) advertising campaigns (also carried out between 2007 and 2009), on the one hand, and six open-ended interviews with key ICT social agents working for the multinationals operating in Spain, such as mobile phone operator entrepreneurs, automatic translators and call centre assistants, on the other hand (I here present one excerpt; see Sabaté i Dalmau, 2012b, for more details). These two complementary sets of data have proved helpful when linking the migrants' (micro) resistance practices with some of the (macro) social processes occurring in the private world, which I understand to be mutually constitutive (Heller, 2001).

In the next section I first present the context in which transnational migrants find themselves when navigating the Catalan network society. Then, in the third section, I analyse the institutional barriers against which, I argue, bottom-up resistance gets articulated, focusing on how a modern nation-state and a powerful segment of the private sector (the telecommunications market) approach migrant phenomena through marginalising practices today. After that, I move into a *locutorio* to analyse how migrants collectively find an alternative for accessing ICTs and for finding the help required to survive transnationally outside institutional realms. I conclude by stating that migrants have successfully consolidated a subversive space of resistance wherewith to connect the unconnected from below, from within the realm of informality.

The Context: The *Mobile-isation* of Transnational Migrants in Catalonia

One of the most remarkable globalisation processes unfolding in Catalonia is demographic: for the first time, 1,182,957 foreign residents have acquired citizenship and constitute 15.7% of a total population of 7,535,251 people (Generalitat de Catalunya, 2011: 3). The second major process is linguistic. These multilingual newcomers, mainly born in other parts of Europe (30.4%), Africa (26.8%) and South America (25.7%), have challenged, for a few years now, Catalonia's traditionally bilingual Catalan–Spanish complex *soundscape* (a term I borrow from Appadurai, 2001), notably with the incorporation of languages such as Arabic, Tamazight, Romanian, Punjabi, Urdu/Hindi, Ukrainian, Portuguese, Quechua, Wolof, Wu, Russian, Polish and Italian (Generalitat de Catalunya, 2007: 9).

Thirdly, these mobile populations have become key transnational *knowledge providers* and *information switches* of globalisation via ICTs (Katz, 2008), since they show a remarkably higher connectivity rate when compared to that of non-migrants. Approximately 78.9% of migrants (as opposed to 57.4% of non-foreigners) use mobiles, and 44% (as opposed to 26.1% of non-foreigners) choose to communicate via SMS in Catalonia (Castells *et al.*, 2007: 52–53). Moreover, documented migrants aged between 15 and 29 actually make *twice* as many calls, SMS and internet connections as non-migrant youth (Robledo, 2008).

As a reaction to this 21st-century *mobile-isation* (that is, as a reaction to the increased communicative and social capitals that migrants can gain via access to ICTs), I believe that the institutional context in which migrants are welcomed today in Catalonia has also changed remarkably, for two main reasons. Firstly, in the current economic and political context of the information age the Spanish nation-state has become less welfare orientated (or less public or community centred) and more individual- and market-focused, forming strategic alliances with key segments of the private world, in particular with the telecommunications sector. Partly as a consequence of this, I believe that it has become a *technopolitical entity* (Inda, 2006). That is, Spain has become an internationalised nation-state which, on witnessing the failure of its border patrols, has started to play out the real battle concerning migration in the information and communication realm (Ros *et al.*, 2007), making use of the privileged management it has over the ICTs to fight undocumented migration, to regulate access to citizenship and to hinder migrants' *mobile-isations*. (Today, the Spanish constitution states that the central government is the ultimate authority in deciding upon issues which concern *telecommunications*; see article 149.1.21a.)

Thus, whereas other European states have reacted to transnational migration movements by taking other paths and, for instance, setting up citizenship regimes basically in the domain of language as the eligibility criteria for legal residency (through the establishment or modification of new compulsory language entry requirements, for example; see Extra *et al.*, 2009), the Spanish state has chosen not to engage too overtly in migrants' language-testing regimes (Vigers & Mar-Molinero, 2009). Instead, it has decided to foster, as I have just outlined, the implementation of extremely powerful ICT 'dataveillance' systems to contribute to the gatekeeping of migration movements – choosing to institutionalise a Spanish-only monolingual scenario for migrants in more covert ways. This is so because, faced with a complicated linguistic mosaic characterised by governmental struggles to maintain linguistic unity (Spanish-only) while dealing with the demands of 'internal' minority languages (Catalan, Basque and Galician), the state cannot afford to reopen the Pandora's box regarding already highly contested language policies and minority language rights protests.[3] Thus, whereas in most of Western Europe and North America the regulation of technology is just another citizenship-gatekeeping technique (see Rheingold, 2002), I argue that in Spain ICTs are a particularly crucial tool to regulate access to legal residency.

The second globalisation process I want to highlight is that, in a market where language is at the epicentre of economic processes (Duchêne, 2011; Heller, 2003, 2010b), ICTs have also become catalysts for the rise of the information- and knowledge-based economy, where technology itself has turned into a precious resource – the new petroleum (Harvey, 2005). The Spanish telecommunications sector (multinationals, ICT start-ups and the like) is now navigating the economic recession by trying to target migrant customers as the newest lucrative economic niche, thus participating in and competing for the management of what they call *'el segmento inmigrante'* [the 'immigrant' segment]. However, this ICT market is trapped in the following contradiction: it is put in a difficult position because, on the one hand, it is designing commercial tactics to attract highly needed new transnational clients in a messy and aggressive ICT marketplace; on the other hand, it is forced to form an alliance with the nation-state in following the migrants' digital trails and, whether directly or indirectly, in enculturating them into the state-fostered Spanish-only linguistic hierarchy, thus participating in the exclusionary regimes which migrants face today.

In short, the complex intertwined institutional changes of these two social entities (the state and the private sector) have propelled the establishment of a series of legal, economic and language barriers that have become the main yardstick against which, I believe, migrant resistance is articulated today, as I will show in the next section.

Institutionalised Barriers: The State and the Telecommunications Sector

'Migration is not supported anymore by fairly liberal labour policies, like those that characterised Northern Europe during the 1960s [...] and Southern

Europe during the late 1990s', state Extra *et al.* (2009: 3). In this section I will show that ICT can become a unique field for the investigation of how the Spanish state, trying to secure its place amid EU-level authorities and international orders, is not only not supporting current labour migration but is also looking for new ways to regulate migrants' access to communication technology as a way of gatekeeping citizenship.

I will also show that, simultaneously, the Spanish telecommunications sector, which is nearly reaching saturation levels in terms of acquiring new clients,[4] has realised that, as Vegas, head of the 'immigrant' customer department of Orange, puts it, 'immigration in Spain is the most important emerging market'[5] (CiberP@ís, 2007). Ethnic mobile phone operators and multinationals have henceforth invested in market studies that scrutinise migrants' ICT-mediated communication practices to plan new entrepreneurial tactics which attempt to 'integrate' migrant callers into the consumer habits of dominant consumerist cultures and into customer-oriented capitalistic regimes (see Harvey, 2003).

I will argue that, above all, this sector's entrepreneurial tactics are pursued by also asking for legal residency for the purchase of their ICT services, as well as by institutionalising serious communication and language divides. Its public face makes claims of a self-attributed 'multilingual competence', following the global neoliberal rhetoric on the 'proper' management of linguistic diversity and migration phenomena which is characteristic of the 'multilingualisation era' in which we live (Duchêne, 2009: 28). However, in reality, in contrast to this multilingualism-as-added-value rhetoric, its real entrepreneurial practices point towards monolingualism and are geared towards an already connected global technoliterate elite.[6] That is, the sector rests on a Spanish-unified marketplace and on a Western written culture nested in the northern hemisphere that do not suit many of the migrants' actual communicative needs, leaving the vast majority of non-literate or non-schooled clients or those who are not familiar with ICT uncatered for, as I will now explain in more detail.

The state

Following the Directives for ICT data storage approved by the European Parliament and the Council of Europe (Directive 2006/24/CE) as a reaction to the terrorist attacks in New York and Washington in 2001, the Spanish Cabinet issued a bill which revolutionised the Spanish telecommunications landscape and which had a direct impact on migrant populations: *Ley 25/2007* (October 2006). This new regulation obliged any operator to register the identity of each client via personal identification (that is, via proof of legal residency) by 2009, on the grounds that, since telecommunications have become so widespread in the Spanish territory they are currently being used for 'unwanted, if not criminal purposes'.[7]

The Spanish nation-state, before passing this law, had also experienced terrorist attacks such as the Madrid bombings on 11 March 2004, involving 29 people from Morocco, Syria, Algeria, India and Spain, among others, but apparently carried out by three Moroccans (one of whom, Jamal Zougam, had already been convicted for murder, theft and terrorism in 2001 by Judge Garzón) and two Spanish-nationalised Indians who activated the bombs precisely via prepaid mobile phones. Claiming fear of further (supposedly migrant-organised) terrorist attacks, the Spanish Ministry of the Interior stated that with the new law they were attempting to make Spanish cities more secure through controlling access to technology 'for the protection of people and goods and for the maintenance of public security' (Official State Bulletin, BOE, 2007: 42520), because, according to the Spanish mass media, at the turn of the century 'cards are sold without control' (El País, 2009).

This law put special emphasis on the storage of the data from prepaid SIM-card services (in fact it was presented as a 'Compulsory registration plan for prepaid calling card users'; see http://www.mir.es/), which were previously sold without having to provide any proof of legality. Thus, in theory, since November 2009, it has been illegal to own a phone card unless a person is documented. Non-compliance in providing identification for top-ups means deactivation of the already-purchased number and involves automatic disconnection from the network. This, of course, affected many of the undocumented migrants whose only option for owning a mobile phone at that time was using unregistered prepaid cards.

The day after the established deadline (9 November 2009) there were still around 800,000 unregistered mobiles in Catalonia, according to the then-director of the Catalan Consumer Agency, Jordi Anguera. The Spanish Minister of the Interior, under pressure from the three big multinationals (Movistar, Vodafone and Orange) which, trapped in these governmental orders, were risking a loss of approximately 8–9 million euros if disconnection was carried out, decided to give an extension of six more months to the still unregistered clients before cancelling any mobile phone accounts (Avui, 2009). Thus, many unidentified phone users can still use their phones at the time of writing, but it is becoming more and more difficult to access a new line without registration – difficult if not already impossible.

I argue that this law was in fact a *hidden modern migration policy* circulated through a salvationary discourse of national security – the advanced liberal 'prevention through deterrence' strategy (Inda, 2006: 2) – targeting not only terrorists and criminal gangs organised via ICTs but also undocumented 'immigrants' residing illegally in Spanish territory, 'whose initial preference', the Spanish mass media hurried to circulate, 'is a prepaid phone which does not require the giving away of personal data or a bank account number'[8] (CiberP@ís, 2007: 1). The way in which this law was presented, with the imperative '¡*Identifícate!*' [Identify yourself!], together with the fact that it was issued by the Ministry of the Interior (noticeably, *not* by the Ministry of Industry, upon which telecommunications depend) seem to provide further evidence that the state was trying to incapacitate undocumented migrants: this is the first legal barrier that migrants have to overcome if they want to follow the formal circuits of communication.

The telecommunications sector

Following the nation-state's rules, since 2009 the Spanish telecommunications sector has to provide a record of all their clients to the governmental authorities (a '*libro-registro*' ['book-register'], as the new law calls it) and, therefore, it also requires legal residency for issuing phone contracts. However, even with legal status, it is not always easy for non-Spanish nationals to gain access to ICTs via the formal telecommunications sector. Perhaps fearing non-payments (apparently, non-payment for telephone invoices increased by 57% during 2008; GSM Spain, 2009), some of the now well-established telecommunications companies with an already secured large number of national customers have decided to take a further step and now require new migrant clients also to show a work permit or, in some cases, a Spanish ID for nationals (a '*DNI*') to obtain a contract. This was experienced by informant Nicolae,[9] a 27-year-old factory worker born in Romania who talks about the difficult route to obtaining a phone contract in Example 1:

Example 1   Legal barriers

	@Location:	24 September 2008. Bar near the *locutorio*.[10]
	@Bck:	Nicolae (NIC) explains to the researcher (RES) how certain operators only issue telephone numbers to customers who are officially registered as Spanish nationals.
1	***RES:**	vale # <qué te> [//] <te pidieron papeles para la línea> [¿].
	%tra:	ok # <what did they> [//] <were you asked for the papers to get the line> [¿].

2   ***NIC:**   <<sí> [/] <sí> [/] <sí >> [!].
    %tra: <<yes> [/] <yes> [/] <yes>> [!].
3   ***RES:**   <qué te pi:> [≀] # <el pasaporte o> [≀].
    %tra: <what did they:> [≀] # <the passport or> [≀].
→ 4   ***NIC:**   +^ el pasaporte y la residencia comunitaria de aquí.
    %tra: +^ the passport and the European residency permit from here.
5   ***RES:**   vale bueno +...
    %tra: ok well +...
→ 6   ***NIC:**   +^ pero Movistar no lo aceptan [el pasaporte y la residencia comunitaria] # es la única.
    %tra: +^ but in Movistar they don't accept this [the passport and the European residency] # it's the only one.
7   ***RES:**   por qué≀
    %tra: why≀
→ 8   ***NIC:**   +^ es la única compañía que no lo acepta.
    %tra: +^ it's the only company that doesn't accept it.
    [...]
→ 9   ***NIC:**   aceptan la residencia sólo tipo d n i.
    %tra: they only accept as residency the d n i type.
    %com: The DNI is the Spanish identification document for Spanish nationals.
10   ***RES:**   sólo quieren el d n i≀
    %tra: they only want the d n i≀
→ 11   ***NIC:**   sí # no aceptan la residencia en papel # ésta no lo aceptan.
    %tra: yes # they don't accept the residency # this [paper] they don't accept it.
12   ***RES:**   para contratos # <de verdad> [≀].
    %tra: for contracts # <really> [≀].
→ 13   ***NIC:**   ellos sí # no lo aceptan.
    %tra: they yes # they don't accept it.
14   ***RES:**   anda!
    %tra: really!
15   ***NIC:**   intento dos tres días hacer un contrato y <no> [/] no quieren.
    %tra: I try to get a contract two three days and they <don't> [/] don't want to.
16   ***RES:**   no quieren≀
    %tra: they don't want to≀

→ 17 ***NIC:**   ni de autónomo ni nada # no quieren <ni> [/] ni ver
                      papeles # quieren ver el d n i.

    %tra: not even as self-employed nothing # they don't
                      <even> [/] even want to see the papers # they want
                      to see the d n i.

Nicolae explains that he managed to get a contract with a multinational by showing his passport *and* his European residency permit (line 4). When I am about to change the topic, though, he brings it to my attention that informally and non-officially, the largest multinational operating in Spain will not accept these two proofs of legal status (line 6) – an idea which is repeated twice (in line 8). The only document that Movistar (formerly Telefónica) accepts, he states, is the Spanish ID card, the *'DNI'* (line 9). He repeats this twice (in lines 11 and 13) in order to answer my insistent questions, aimed at checking whether the residency permit is acceptable documentation and whether a phone company will refuse to offer a contract to a legal foreign resident. Apparently, the company will only accept a DNI, not residence permits or proof of self-employment (line 17) – indeed, the necessity to be a Spanish national was asserted to me, off the record, by individual agents working for that specific company. Together with the nation-state, then, the market also puts legal barriers upon many documented and undocumented migrants.

The second barrier that migrants encounter is linguistic. The telecommunications sector in Spain manages a particular kind of multilingualism that poses a challenge for many migrants, since rather than fulfilling or understanding their non-elite multilingual and hybrid communicative practices and needs, it is oriented towards an already connected global elite. I will now demonstrate this with an analysis of the language practices of the 29 mobile phone ventures operating in Spain at the time of the fieldwork in: (1) their call centres, (2) their official websites and (3) their advertising campaigns and information provided via leaflets.

Basically, the vast majority of companies in this sector embrace and publicise a post-modern 'multilinguistic model' (Tan & Rubdy, 2008: 2); that is, they claim to offer services such as a 'multilingual support team' for migrant clients (see advertisement in Lebara, 2007, for instance). However, in reality, they work within a de facto monolingual framework, offering the vast majority of services massively in and through *Spanish as the default language* or, in some cases, as the only language, with a few, unsystematic and haphazard multilingual practices, perhaps with the exception of English, a language which is offered in some services.

Thus, the telecommunications world simultaneously circulates a pro-multilingual-services rhetoric while institutionalising a Spanish-unified

258 Part 3: Sites of Resistance

market, for several reasons. The first one is that, within the private world, the pragmatic dimensions of the management of multilingualism dictate that there has to be a necessary 'economisation' of linguistic diversity (Duchêne, 2011: 102). This basically means that the languages offered shall, above all, be profitable for the company. Following this line of thought, Spanish in the private sector is constructed as an instrumental lingua franca for the entire 'Spanish-speaking condominium' which, together with global English, can cater for the vast majority of their clients (García Delgado *et al.*, 2007: 9, working for Telefónica Foundation).

Another reason for the establishment of a Spanish monolingual regime is that, again in alliance with the nation-state, the *language economists*[11] working for Spanish-based multinationals have invested massive resources in promoting Spanish as the pioneering *'lengua multiétnica, multinacional'* or *'lengua puente'* [bridge language] in order to preserve the unity of the market in what otherwise is pejoratively depicted as a messy 'tower of Babel' (García Delgado *et al.*, 2007: 11, 15, 86). For example, the Institute of Foreign Commerce of the Spanish Government (ICEX) has launched a campaign to promote Spanish as the international language of technology under the logo 'España, technology for life' (ICEX, 2010). Besides, there exist not only economic and political interests but also a tremendous cultural machinery to boost the spread of Spanish as *the* ICT language. As Del Valle and Gabriel-Stheeman (2002: 206–207) explain, for instance, Rodríguez Lafuente, the then-director of the *Instituto Cervantes* whose main aim was to consolidate the international prestige of Spanish and *'ganar la batalla de la lengua'* [to win the language battle], signed an agreement with Movistar to survey the presence of Spanish on the internet.

Obviously, within this Spanish-unified market, some companies, particularly the three main multinationals, also offer some of their services in other dominant languages, particularly but by no means systematically in *English as the global language of technology* and, to a lesser extent, French or German. I believe that English is the second code to be included in the list because it is the unquestioned language employed by thinktanks such as the influential International Telecommunication Union (ITU), the United Nations agency which sets the worldwide standards of communication and which coordinates the World Summit on the Information Society. Also, English plays a role in Spain because the Spanish state is part of the world's telecommunicative core (see Barnett, 2001), led by English-speaking countries such as the United States and the United Kingdom. And yet, it is highly remarkable that only half of the six recently launched migrant-oriented operators[12] offer English systematically in their call centres; for migrants, Spanish is the language which is always offered instead.

In this institutionalised linguistic hierarchy where Spanish clearly dominates and English, at times, serves as a 'safety net', other migrants' allochthonous codes are either token or are simply not included. When I contacted the companies, I could not find any customer services in any of the migrants' languages, not even among the six migrant-oriented operators, except for Arabic and Romanian, and these were provided occasionally and, more often than not, as an exception or as an ad hoc 'way-out' to sort out communicative problems on the spot (the migrant-oriented operator Happy Móvil, for instance, offered Arabic customer services only at the weekends at 4 pm, when the Arabic-speaking agent was available). Thus, the migrants' languages can only be found in a few uninformative mottos circulated in majority nation-state languages (for instance, they are very occasionally circulated in Urdu instead of Punjabi, or in Modern Standard Arabic instead of Tamazight), construing a fake, unrealistic, *commercial multilingualism* (Kelly-Holmes & Mautner, 2010) basically employed for marketing issues only in the written form (not as customer services languages but as the languages of advertisement). None of the informants I interviewed ever used them. Besides, these mottos are normally issued via *generic automatic translation*, which, unsurprisingly, at times renders the services non-accessible to non-literate migrant users, as illustrated in the advertisement in Figure 11.1, which is a presumably multilingual motto employed by the migrant-oriented company MundiMóvil.

Figure 11.1 The telecommunications sector's haphazard management of linguistic diversity. Advertisement by MundiMóvil
Source: http://www.mundimovil.es/

Figure 11.1 illustrates the haphazard treatment of the languages of migration by the Spanish telecommunications sector, where the motto has been translated from Spanish into Italian, English, Mandarin Chinese, Romanian, Russian, Spanish, Modern Greek, Urdu, Hindi and French by using automatic word-for-word translation, the result of which is unrealistic, simplistic and in odd non-used language, as seen in the English version: 'Calling yours never was so easy' [sic].

When I interviewed the CEO of one of the most important Catalan-based automatic translation companies working for Movistar about this lack of minority language resources and their patchy approach to them, he provided three possible explanations, presented in Example 2.

Example 2   'It's not worth the investment'

	@Location:	29 April 2009. Company's office in the Vallès Occidental.	
	@Bck:	The CEO of a Catalan leading ICT venture, after having summarised his experience in trying to assemble a Spanish–Arabic translator for the multinational Movistar, explains the possible reasons behind the lack of migrant languages in the ICT world.	
→ 1	***CEO:**	*jo crec que això lo que demostra és <la> [/] la falta de necessitat real d'això,, <no> [¿].*	
	%tra:	I think that what this demonstrates is <the> [/] the lack of a real need for this,, <right> [¿].	
2	***RES:**	*clar.*	
	%tra:	sure.	
→ 3	***CEO:**	*o la falta de preocupació pels operadors per aquest tipus de gent pues potser perquè per aquest tipus de negoci pel volum que genera és poc.*	
	%tra:	or the lack of concern about these sort of people by operators maybe because for this type of business the turnover it generates is small.	

In this example, the CEO provides three possible explanations for the companies' non-investment in migrant languages. First, he suggests that multinationals might not have a real need for them in order to keep making money off migrant customers (line 1). He also states that multinationals may not be concerned about smaller customer niches and prefer to focus on bigger migrant groups such as the Spanish-speaking Latin American market instead.

Finally, another explanation he provides is that the turnover that the non-English and non-Spanish-speaking clientele generates is not sufficient to justify investing in anything more sophisticated than generic automatic translation and multilingual advertisements (line 3).

These comments demonstrate that multilingualism, at least for this segment of the private market, is simply a *linguistic fetish* (Kelly-Holmes, 2005), a marketing leitmotif at a time when they are offering a presumably wide variety of languages which signals innovation, efficiency, competitiveness and modernity (Duchêne, 2009, 2011). This particular type of elite multilingualism reproduces the power structures of the global economic picture and does not suit the needs of those who are non-socialised in the Western multimodal culture. Overall, the digital divide, then, is in fact also a matter of a structural *language divide* observed within the private sector. This speaks of linguistic marginalisation and de-capitalisation and of the emergence of new global non-literacies.[13] In the next section, I explore the means of resisting this divide inside *locutorios*.

Mobilising Resistance: The Consolidation of an Alternative, the *Locutorios*

In this section I claim that, beyond mere ICT businesses, *locutorios* have become an alternative migrant *institution of resistance* where opportunities to overcome or subvert the established legal regimes and sociolinguistic orders emerge. In particular, I place special emphasis on the *agency* that these spaces endow migrants with and on the *language work* collectively carried out by migrant networks there to routinely bridge language divides from the periphery and outside institutional domains.

Locutorios offer access to the internet, computers, cabin calls, prepaid phone cards and top-ups, as well as photocopying, fax and money transfer services – all in one single space designed for ICT-mediated transnational communication. These ventures emerged at the turn of the century as ethnic businesses run *by* and *for* migrants in urban localities with the highest increase of migrant registrations during the first decade of the 21st century. They were set up mostly by migrant entrepreneurs who could become self-employed after having accumulated years of experience and capital as employees and after having gone through one of the main regularisation campaigns undertaken by the Spanish government in 2000, 2001 and 2005. These new venture capitalists started hiring ICT services originally provided by the formal telecommunications sector but circulated through different transnational migrant networks acting as in-group distributors, and they were later sold through the mediation of a migrant presence (the migrant *locutorio* workers). This is why, born out of transnationalism, *locutorios* are classified as 'circuit enterprises' (Solé et al., 2007).

This entrepreneurial initiative took root and, after a decade, migrant owners such as the one I followed during my fieldwork were gaining €4,500 a month from the visits of about 60–160 cabin users a day. Thus, what started as local small businesses became a striking entrepreneurial success: in the Spanish territory the number of *locutorios* went from about 800 in 1999 to more than 25,000 in 2008, according to the Spanish Association of *Locutorio* and Cybercafé Owners (Players4Players, 2008).

In fact, the increase was such that they have become key competitors for telecommunications multinationals. With the advent of *locutorios*, Movistar, for instance, had to lower the price of its international calls by a remarkable 45% (Consumer, 2004), and the rest of the multinationals also started to present their international discount plans with faked alternativeness and informality semiotics, with advertisements such as *'el locutori mòbil d'Orange'* or *'el mini-locutorio de Movistar'*, as illustrated in Figure 11.2:

Figure 11.2 The *'mini-locutorio'* by Movistar. Multinationals' competition with *locutorios* for the migrant clients' niche (photograph taken by author; Vallès Occidental, 28 November 2007)

This success can be explained by looking at the opportunities for subversion and resistance that *locutorios* provide to migrants. To start with, unlike the telecommunications sector, they offer the *social infrastructure* and the human capital which is required to access technology. For example, they subvert the dataveillance systems of the nation-state (they sell SIM-cards to the undocumented), they set up in-group regulated credit-giving networks when telephone invoices cannot be paid, and they adapt to the migrants' busy timetables and foreign time zones (*locutorios* can stay open until midnight, including at weekends).

Their success also hinges on the fact that they do not only sell technology but also distribute all sorts of other material resources which are highly required for *transnational survival*. For instance, inside *locutorios* homeless people are given access to washroom facilities, and shelter when it rains. Also, migrant networks of support there distribute food and self-manage access to informal jobs and rooms for rent from migrant hands to migrant hands.

Besides, *locutorios* are a site of *networking capital* for the gatekeeping and the re-distribution of key information such as knowledge of the host society (for instance, free legal advice on bureaucratic procedures) which migrants were formerly forced to find in more formal, top-down organised institutions (such as town councils or NGOs), and which today they self-circulate among themselves, in their own ways, and in their own space. In this sense, *locutorios* have become useful articulators of successful individual migration trajectories and transnational lives via their resistance to the various hindrances posed by mainstream society.

Moreover, *locutorios* make up for the language gaps left by the formal telecommunications system, since migrants there can take the floor and network in their own non-elite languages – those which are *not* offered by multinationals. An example of this was provided to me by Sheema, a 31-year-old informant born in Pakistan who managed to get information about Movistar's discount plans from a friend who translated the promotional material from Spanish into Urdu, on his own initiative, rendering it accessible to Urdu users, as presented in Figure 11.3. The *locutorio* worker then photocopied and distributed copies among his compatriots, circulating that information to literate members of the Pakistani local network, and resisting the 'multilingual' order of that particular company.

I also think that *locutorios* have become a major form of conducting active linguistic resistance because they provide the technoliteracy capital required to navigate the global ICT system. This is due to the fact that the migrant workers there act as *linguistic brokers* and informal mediators (Martin-Jones & Jones, 2000) for clients who are not socialised into the Western written

Figure 11.3 Leaflet with Movistar's discount plans in Urdu, translated from Spanish on a migrant's initiative and distributed in the *locutorio* (photograph taken by author; 4 September 2008)

culture, which assumes numeracy, literacy in Western alphabets (for example, the Roman script) and a command of the alphanumeric systems and the semiotic-iconic language nested in the northern hemisphere (see Chipchase, 2008; Kress & van Leeuwen, 2006[1996]). Thus, we find *locutorio* workers translating text messages from Spanish into many other languages, dialling telephone numbers for non-numerate clients who bring them in written on a piece of paper, or going far beyond merely providing ICT services by filling in seemingly unmanageable administrative forms. An instance of how this informal language mediation works to overcome cases of linguistic exclusion is provided in Example 3, which explains how, informally and rudimentarily, a *locutorio* worker enculturates one of his clients from Romania into the technoliteracy world.

Example 3   The self-provision of technoliteracy capital

> *Archid needs to check his official labour situation to make sure that he is finally registered in the Spanish Social Security, but he can't figure out how to do it online. The* locutorio *worker, his amigo 'Paki', without hesitation approaches his computer and googles* 'informe leboral.es', *which the program self-corrects into* 'quiso decir [you meant] "informe de vida laboral"'. *They both click on the*

link and get to the www.seg-social.es website, becoming post-modern learners and expert users of the search tool, which is here employed as a way to overcome non-literacy within the Western-orchestrated Spanish-only telecommunications system. (Field notes, 28 September 2008)

I believe that these *locutorio* workers have become a key segment of the emergent multilingual *word* force (Heller, 2010b) in the globalised new economy and play a crucial role in overcoming language difference and exclusion. This is, I believe, key to understanding why *locutorios* have capitalised on the collectively orchestrated migrants' resistance against structural marginalisation (particularly, linguistic marginalisation). It is this word force who, trapped within the new migrant selection agents' work regimes and an increasingly demanding clientele, with no recognition or compensation, ends up, informally, doing the multilingual job of the telecommunications sector. It is also these members of the word force who, by virtue of their communicative capital (largely undervalued both by the telecommunications sector and by their own employers), have turned these ICT ventures into truly migrant resistance institutions 'with an unrivalled force in Europe' (Adela Ros, in BBC Mundo, 2008).

Thus, I would like to finish this section by highlighting that the provision of real multilingual technoliteracy capital in a bottom-up manner is not always democratising but can also be a double-edged sword. On the one hand, it results in an alternative lucrative functional resource for the *locutorio* owners, but, on the other hand, not only the *locutorio* workers but also the clients are still left at the mercy of the present-day regimes of the private sector. Despite the fact that, for the *locutorio* users, who make the conscious choice to communicate at a *locutorio,* this is their mundane way of explicitly resisting the sociolinguistic hierarchies of the telecommunications world, this type of customer services boosts an informal market where language workers can easily go down the silent road of another type of exclusion. This has to do with unseen overwork and exploitation in migrant-regulated work-places – again, through language.

Concluding Remarks

In this article I have shown that the analysis of emerging migrant-regulated spaces organised around the ICTs *below* the radar of institutional organisations is crucial to understand their structuration and their roles within the globalised new economy. I have claimed that it is in these alternative spaces consolidated outside mainstream society and self-regulated by very active mobile-ised migrants where we can open a window into 21st-century informal transnational sites of subversion and resistance.

I have provided evidence that, through communication technology, the Spanish nation-state is making attempts at disconnecting the already unconnected migrants lacking legal status, and that it is doing so by mobilising the power it has over ICTs to act as gatekeepers of citizenship and to follow the digital trails of undocumented people. I have thus argued that in Spain the granting of citizenship is played out in the communication and information technology realm, with the help of a largely covert established linguistic regime which makes every attempt to enculturate newcomers into a Spanish-only Western literate culture.

I have also shown that, similarly, the telecommunications sector, in an interested and difficult alliance with the nation-state, actively participates in the management of migrant phenomena – or rather, of their 'unmanagement', through a series of legal boundaries, socio-economic regimes and, above all, linguistic exclusionary practices, due to the fact that its overall organisation hinges upon a market based on Spanish unity hidden behind a celebratory rhetoric on linguistic diversity.

Taking the institutional barriers that migrants face as a point of departure, I have then focused on their bottom-up *empowerment* practices by opening the doors of a *locutorio*. I have argued that the telecommunications sector, somewhat ironically, is leaving some space for *social agency* for migrants to set up their own ICT businesses while simultaneously trying to attract precisely the same economic niche. I have shown that, on being unable to understand (and thus fulfil) the migrants' real communicative needs and ICT-mediated linguistic practices, and on being forced to follow the nation-state's directives, the formal sector has approached migrant clients with much less success. It is *locutorios* that provide the crucial social infrastructure and the technoliteracy and networking capitals required for ICT access instead.

Thus, to my mind, the communicative power that migrants gain in the *locutorios* shows that, beyond mere 'service receivers' or agentless 'clients', migrants are also active consumers who engage and exert some influence on the market, not only in deciding upon their own ICT-mediated communicative practices but also on how, where and with which languages to network. Also, those who have become *locutorio* workers and entrepreneurs in turn demonstrate their capacity to self-incorporate into contemporary market regimes and sociolinguistic orders and to fully participate in the new economy in times of economic recession.

I have also highlighted that this participation, however, hinges upon the particular managerial nature of this type of business: it depends on the migrant workers' engagement with much more flexible non-mainstream and non-institutional workplaces, pointing to the fact that perhaps the informal economy, which I believe is no longer peripheral to state economies, is gaining some terrain as the realm where resistance to social exclusion can be practised. Precisely because these realms work *below* the radar of institutional organisations, I have argued that we should understand such resistance spaces as not necessarily always liberating, particularly for the *locutorio* word force who routinely bridge language gaps with no compensation or protection.

I want to conclude by stating that the migrants' subversive practices against the state and the different instances of resistance to the telecommunications system that I have presented here flag up the fact that the mobiliser of such a collective enterprise is, in fact, language. That is, the catalyst of this progressive empowerment that migrants are experiencing, by activating their mundane resistance practices, is basically the revaluing, commodification and mobilisation of their non-elite linguistic capital, put by themselves on the *locutorio*'s table. Through the *locutorio* networks, they can navigate and survive transnationally, routinely skirting the linguistic exclusion, silencing and marginalisation waiting for them in their host societies.

Acknowledgements

This project was partly funded by grants HUM2007-61864/FILO (MICINN), PIF 429-01-1/07 (UAB) and 2009 BE1 00362 (Catalan Government). The author is grateful to the C.I.E.N. research group for their support. Any shortcomings are, of course, the author's own.

Notes

(1) Original quote:
Cuando mi jefe me explota ¿Quién me escucha?,
sin papeles no hay trabajo y sin trabajo no hay papeles,
espiral extraña y España me atrapo en sus redes.
¿Qué puedo hacer? Respiro desesperanza,
malvivo en un zulo oscuro porque mi alquiler no alcanza,
acudo al locutorio a diario, ese es mi deber,
saber cómo están los míos, qué tendrán para comer.
(2) Catalonia is an autonomous region (*Comunitat Autònoma*) with its own government, the *Generalitat*. It is located between the northeastern part of the Spanish state and southern France, and it is officially bilingual in Catalan and Spanish.
(3) In Catalonia, Spanish and Catalan, for historical and political reasons, co-exist in very complex ways, the former being a dominant official language which is also the official language of the entire nation-state (and a global lingua franca) and the latter, with a long trajectory of minorisation and subordination, being a

co-official language and a *'llengua pròpia'* or 'vernacular' code (Generalitat de Catalunya, 2006).

(4) In February 2009, 51,263,388 mobile phone lines were registered in Spain, an average of 111.1 lines per 100 registered citizens – 3% more than in February 2008, when the penetration rate was of 107.8 lines per 100 users (CMT, 2009: 6–7). In Catalonia the penetration rate was even higher. In Barcelona city, for instance, there were 2.3 mobiles per household in 2008 (L'hiperbòlic, 2008: 12–13). This may explain why the telecommunications sector is trying to expand into new economic niches, particularly the migrants' niche.

(5) Original quote: 'La inmigración es en España el mercado emergente más importante'.

(6) Technoliteracy is defined as the command of a complex set of Western literacies (reading and writing competences, computer literacy, command of the ICT visual language, and so on) required to navigate the global ICT system successfully (see Area Moreira *et al.*, 2008, for further details).

(7) Original quote: '[. . .] fines indeseados, cuando no delictivos'.

(8) Original quote: 'Su preferencia inicial es un teléfono de prepago porque no requiere facilitar los datos personales ni la cuenta bancaria'.

(9) For confidentiality reasons, all names are fictitious or else not provided, in order to safeguard the informants' anonymity, as agreed with the Committee for Ethics in Animal and Human Research (CEEAH) at the Universitat Autònoma de Barcelona (File 725H). This project also takes account of the legal advice of *Col·lectiu Ronda* (http://www.cronda.com/).

(10) Interactions were transcribed following a slightly modified version of the CHILDES transcription system (see MacWhinney, 2000[1991]). In [@Bck] the background of the exchange – the participants, the context and the topic – is briefly described. In [%com] (comment) contextual information concerning the previous utterance is provided. In [%tra] (translation) free translations of the exchanges presented in the main tier uttered in languages other than English are provided (these are Spanish if the typeface is plain, or Catalan if it is in italics). All exchanges are reproduced *verbatim* (in non-standard talk) and were translated by the author.

(11) Language economy is a field of study which, broadly speaking, investigates the ways in which linguistic and economic variables influence one another (Kamwangamalu, 2008).

(12) At the time of this fieldwork these were: Happy Móvil, Lebara Móbiles, Talkout Móvil, MundiMóvil, Hong Da Mobile and Digi.mobil.

(13) I employ the term *non-literacies* by analogy with the term *multiliteracies*, coined in the 1990s by the New London Group, whose aim was to place emphasis on the importance of 'the emerging literacies associated both with the new technologies and with the multilingual composition of students in urban schools' (Cummins *et al.*, 2005: 23). Today there is no consensus on how exactly to define multiliteracies. However, it is widely agreed that an integrated command of a complex set of Western visual, auditory, iconic, digital, informational, technological and computer literacies is a precondition for global ICT navigation, in an attempt to problematise the widespread assumption that access to ICTs simply requires only 'computer' or 'digital' literacy. I also use the term *non-literacies* in the plural in alliance with Martin-Jones and Jones' critique of 'the a-social, a-historical skill/ability understanding of reading and writing' (Martin-Jones & Jones, 2000: 4).

References

Alonso, A. and Oiarzabal, P.J. (eds) (2010) *Diasporas in the New Media Age. Identity, Politics, and Community*. Reno, NE: University of Nevada Press.

Appadurai, A. (2001) Grassroots globalization and the research imagination. In A. Appadurai (ed.) *Globalization* (pp. 1–21). Durham, NC: Duke University Press.

Area Moreira, M., Gros Salvat, B. and Marzal García-Quismondo, M.A. (2008) *Alfabetizaciones y tecnologías de la información y la comunicación*. Madrid: Síntesis.

Avui (2009) 800.000 catalans no han identificat encara el mòbil, 10 November. *Tecnologia* 28. Barcelona: Hermes Comunicacions.

Barnett, G.A. (2001) A longitudinal analysis of the International Telecommunication Network, 1978–1996. *American Behavioral Scientist* 44 (19), 1638–1655.

BBC Mundo (2008) 'España: la inmigración es multimedia', BBC Mundo, 28 June. Online document, accessed 1 July 2013. http://news.bbc.co.uk/hi/spanish/business/newsid_7478000/7478177.stm

BOE (2007) LEY 25/2007, de 18 de octubre, de conservación de datos relativos a las comunicaciones electrónicas y a las redes públicas de comunicaciones. Law No. 251, Friday 19 October (pp. 42517–42523). Madrid: Gobierno de España, Ministerio de la Presidencia.

Castells, M. (2000[1996]) *The Rise of the Network Society*. Oxford: Blackwell.

Castells, M. (2009) *Communication Power*. Oxford and New York: Oxford University Press.

Castells, M., Tubella, I., Sancho, T. and Roca, M. (2007) *La transició a la societat xarxa*. Barcelona: Ariel.

Chipchase, J. (2008) Reducing illiteracy as a barrier to mobile communication. In J.E. Katz (ed.) *Handbook of Mobile Communication Studies* (pp. 79–89). Cambridge: MIT Press.

CiberP@ís (2007) El africano llama cada día, mientras que el latino lo hace en fin de semana. *El País Semanal* 477, 1–6.

CMT (2009) *Comisión del Mercado de las Telecomunicaciones. Nota mensual febrero*. Online document, accessed 1 July 2013. http://www.cmt.es/c/document_library/get_file?uuid=0ba90dbc-cd04-4b28-9c88-4eed390d547b&groupId=10138

Consumer (2004) La competencia de los locutorios obliga a Telefónica a bajar sus tarifas internacionales hasta un 45%, 28 January. Online document, accessed 1 July 2013. http://www.consumer.es/web/es/economia_domestica/2004/04/19/98817.php

Cummins, J., Bismilla, V., Cohen, S., Giampapa, F. and Leoni, L. (2005) Timelines and lifelines: Rethinking literacy instruction in multilingual classrooms. *Orbit* 36 (1), 22–26.

Del Valle, J. and Gabriel-Stheeman, L. (2002) *The Battle over Spanish Between 1800 and 2000*. London and New York: Routledge.

Duchêne, A. (2009) Marketing, management and performance: Multilingualism as commodity in a tourist call centre. *Language Policy* 8, 27–50.

Duchêne, A. (2011) Néolibéralisme, inégalités sociales et plurilinguisme: l'exploitation des ressources langagières et des locuteurs. *Langage et société* 136, 81–106.

El País (2009) ¿Usas tarjeta prepago de móvil? ¡Regístrala!, 4 March. Online document, accessed 1 July 2013. http://elpais.com/elpais/2009/03/04/actualidad/1236158228_850215.html

Extra, G., Spotti, M. and Van Avermaet, P. (eds) (2009) *Language Testing, Migration and Citizenship. Cross-National Perspectives on Integration Regimes*. London: Continuum.

García Delgado, J.L., Alonso, J.A. and Jiménez, J.C. (2007) *Economía del Español. Una Introducción*. Barcelona: Ariel; Madrid: Fundación Telefónica.

Geertz, C. (1973) *The Interpretation of Cultures: Selected Essays*. New York: Basic Books.

Generalitat de Catalunya (2006) *Estatut d'Autonomia de Catalunya*. Entitat Autònoma del Diari Oficial i de Publicacions BIGSA Industria Gràfica.

Generalitat de Catalunya (2007) Pla per la llengua i la cohesió social. Departament d'Educació, Generalitat de Catalunya. http://www.xtec.cat/lic/intro/documenta/pil. pdf.

Generalitat de Catalunya (2011) Població Estrangera. Butlletí de población estrangera i mercat de treball. Generalitat de Catalunya. Departament d'empresa i ocupació, accessed 1 July 2013. Online at: http://www20.gencat.cat/docs/observatoritreball/ Generic/Documents/Treball/Estudis/Butlleti%20de%20poblacio%20estrangera%20 i%20mercat%20de%20treball/Butllet%C3%AD%20Poblacio%20Estrangera%201t% 20trim%2011.pdf

Giddens, A. (1984) *The Constitution of Society. Outline of the Theory of Structuration.* Cambridge: Polity Press.

GSM Spain (2009) Los morosos en España superaron los 2,7 millones a cierre de 2008, 2 February. Online document, accessed 2 July 2013. http://www.gsmspain.com/foros/ h716679_Off-topic-Economia-finanzas_morosos-Espana-superaron-millones-cierre-2008.html

Harvey, D. (2003) *The New Imperialism*. Oxford and New York: Oxford University Press.

Harvey, D. (2005) *A Brief History of Neoliberalism*. Oxford and New York: Oxford University Press.

Heller, M. (2001) Undoing the macro/micro dichotomy: Ideology and categorisation in a linguistic minority school. In N. Coupland, S. Sarangi and C.N. Candlin (eds) *Sociolinguistics and Social Theory* (pp. 212–234). London: Longman.

Heller, M. (2003) Globalization, the new economy, and the commodification of language and identity. *Journal of Sociolinguistics* 7 (4): 473–492.

Heller, M. (2006[1999]) *Linguistic Minorities and Modernity: A Sociolinguistic Ethnography.* London: Continuum.

Heller, M. (2010a) *Paths to Post-nationalism. A Critical Ethnography of Language and Identity.* New York: Oxford University Press.

Heller, M. (2010b) Language as resource in the globalised new economy. In N. Coupland (ed.) *Handbook of Language and Globalization* (pp. 349–365). Oxford: Blackwell.

Howard, P.N. (2002) Network ethnography and the hypermedia organization: New media, new organizations, new methods. *New Media & Society* 4 (4), 550–574.

ICEX (2010) 'España, technology for life'. España Exportación e Inversiones. Gobierno de España. Ministerio de Economía y Competitividad, accessed 1 July 2013. Online at http:// www.spaintechnology.com/icex/cda/controller/pageGen/0,3346,1559872_6407115_641 0526_4275649,00.html

Inda, J.X. (2006) *Targeting Immigrants. Government, Technology and Ethics.* Malden, MA: Blackwell.

Kamwangamalu, N.M. (2008) Language policy, vernacular education and language economics in postcolonial Africa. In P.K.W. Tan and R. Rubdy (eds) *Language as Commodity. Global Structures, Local Marketplaces* (pp. 171–186). London and New York: Continuum.

Katz, J.E. (ed.) (2008) *Handbook of Mobile Communication Studies*. Cambridge, MA: MIT Press.

Kelly-Holmes, H. (2005) *Advertising as Multilingual Communication*. London: Palgrave Macmillan.

Kelly-Holmes, H. and Mautner, G. (eds) (2010) *Language and the Market*. London: Palgrave Macmillan.

Kress, G. and van Leeuwen, T. (2006[1996]) *Reading Images. The Grammar of Visual Design.* London and New York: Routledge.

Lebara (2007) 'Lebara Mobile partners with Vodafone to launch low cost, high quality mobile services in Spain', 13 November. Online document, accessed 1 July 2013. http://www.assets.lebara.com/medias/sys_master/8799861243934.pdf

L'hiperbòlic (2008) El telèfon mòbil supera el fix. *L'hiperbòlic* 61, 12–13. Palma: L'Hiperbòlic Edicions.

MacWhinney, B. (2000[1991]) *The CHILDES Project: Tools for Analyzing Talk.* Mahwah, NJ: Lawrence Erlbaum.

Martin-Jones, M. and Jones, K. (2000) Multilingual literacies. In M. Martin-Jones and K. Jones (eds) *Multilingual Literacies: Reading and Writing Different Worlds* (pp. 1–15). Amsterdam and Philadelphia, PA: John Benjamins.

Players4Players (2008) La asociación de Locutorios y Cíbers Españoles firma un acuerdo con Microsoft para poder salvar al sector de la crisis. Press Release No. 3094/2-11-2008, 2 November, accessed 1 July 2013. http://www.players4players.com/nota_de_prensa/3289/la-asociacion-de-locutorios-y-cibers-espanoles-firma-un-acuerdo-con-microsoft-para-poder-salvar-al-sector-de-la-crisis/

Rheingold, H. (2002) *Smart Mobs. The Next Social Revolution. Transforming Cultures and Communities in the Age of Instant Access.* Cambridge, MA: Perseus.

Robledo, J. (2008) Generación-i. La transición multicultural. *El País semanal* 6 July, accessed 1 July 2013. http://elpais.com/diario/2008/07/06/eps/1215325611_850215.html

Ros, A., González, E., Marín, A. and Sow, P. (2007) Migration and information flows: A new lens for the study of contemporary international migration. Working Paper Series No. WP07-002, accessed 1 July 2013. Online at http://openaccess.uoc.edu/webapps/o2/bitstream/10609/1274/3/ros_gonzalez_marin_sow.pdf

Sabaté i Dalmau, M. (2012a) Aportaciones de la etnografía de red al estudio de un locutorio: Hacia un cambio de paradigma metodológico. In E. Codó, A. Patiño and V. Unamuno (eds) *La sociolingüística con perspectiva etnográfica en el mundo hispano: nuevos contextos, nuevas realidades, nuevas aproximaciones.* Special Issue of *Spanish in Context* 9 (2), 191–218.

Sabaté i Dalmau, M. (2012b) 'The official language of Telefónica is English': Problematizing the construction of English as a lingua franca in the Spanish telecommunications sector. *Atlantis* 34 (1), 133–151.

Solé, C., Parella, S. and Cavalcanti, L. (2007) *L'empresariat immigrant a Espanya.* Col·lecció Estudis Socials 21. Barcelona: Fundació La Caixa.

Tan, P.K.W. and Rubdy, R. (eds) (2008) *Language as Commodity. Global Structures, Local Marketplaces.* London and New York: Continuum.

Vertovec, S. (2009) *Transnationalism.* London and New York: Routledge.

Vigers, D. and Mar-Molinero, C. (2009) Spanish language ideologies in managing immigration and citizenship. In G. Extra, M. Spotty and P. Van Avermaet (eds) *Language Testing, Migration and Citizenship. Cross-National Perspectives on Integration Regimes* (pp. 167–187). London: Continuum.

Postscript

Mike Baynham

Sociolinguistics in recent years has moved away from a position in which features of language merely correlate with features of social structure towards an understanding of the co-productive, constitutive relationship of language and social structure: forms of social organisation are brought into being, routinely enacted and indeed challenged through talk, although of course not all aspects of the social and material world can be reduced to discourse. The Spanish twenty-something in an environment with more than 50% youth unemployment, the Spanish family losing their house as they default on their mortgage, and the unemployed Greek, Portuguese or Italian graduate are not simply subject to discourses, but also to gross economic and material facts and trends that are constantly shaping their life trajectories. This is not to underplay the power of discourses as exemplified in Holly and Meinhof's contribution on the discourse of integration in Germany. Addressing such issues has brought with it theoretical, practical and political challenges. As we see in the contributions to this volume, in this environment it is often a rhetorical trick of the powerful to play the language card in ways that shift attention from more challenging and difficult-to-fix social issues of structural inequality and exclusion of which language is often an intractable part. It is also clear, however, that linguistics is not enough, perhaps sociolinguistics is not enough, as a discretely boundaried discipline to address such issues and there is a need for dialogue with social theory coming from other related disciplines – sociology, anthropology, political economy – in order to develop a rich and adequate account of the social world in which language plays its part. Conversely, given the centrality of language in social processes, we are convinced that disciplines such as sociology, anthropology, politics and political economy need the insights of sociolinguistics in order to illuminate how large-scale social processes are played out in the moment-to-moment interactions through which social life is constituted.

Developing that dialogue, as in all transdisciplinary work, is challenging: challenging in the case of language because there is a need to overcome its taken-for-grantedness and transparency in everyday understanding, a classic case of making the familiar anthropologically strange. The jury is still out on the success of this project; the world seems to keep going along certain well-defined tracks despite our analyses, a point made to me recently by Gunther Kress. Success, in any case, lies not in speaking to other sociolinguists, but is as much a political as an intellectual project, necessarily a process of building up long-term relationships with scholars in other disciplines as well as with activists, decision makers, practitioners and gatekeepers, thus making an impact on the social sciences and beyond. However, the contributions to this volume demonstrate the benefits of this social turn to understanding the linguistic issues raised by processes of migration and mobility and, by extension, point to ways that the language turn might productively influence the social sciences more broadly. Seeking a language that can influence and impact on policy and practice is a further challenge.

The role of language in the production and regulation of the social is exemplified in Parts 1 and 2 of this volume, while the contingencies of appropriation and resistance are addressed in Part 3. The use of the term 'sites' in the titles of each part points to the focus on language in institutions which is a major focus here, even though the last two contributions, those of Vigouroux and Sabaté, arguably explore what I would think of as the extra-institutional informal economy. This observation depends of course on what counts as an institution: Sabaté, for example, treats the *locutorios* as 'institutions of resistance'. We live in an age when state institutions of all sorts – health, education and welfare – are being reconstituted as businesses and of course where businesses are reconfiguring themselves as institutions, sometimes with a certain amount of irony (for example, Macdonald's Hamburger University; if you don't believe me, google it). The state offloads functions onto business and NGOs, as Codó shows us. Everywhere there is fluidity and flux. In an environment where China owns swathes of American debt and the Emirates are buying up Greece, everything is up for grabs. Across the collection we see the pervasive influence of the discourses and practices of neoliberalism as they are played out in the constitution and the remaking of these institutions, and the impact of globalisation: how there are consistent inequalities and stratifications in the way languages are valued and how they can be commodified in different ways to suit the neoliberal agenda. Martin Rojo captures this through an analysis of the capitalisation and de-capitalisation of language resources on language programmes in a Spanish secondary school. In the high-status CLIL programme, students may gain access to highly capitalisable English as a global language; in the learning Spanish programme, with its Spanish-only ideology, Moroccan Arabic has a place in local classroom interaction, but backstage and not brought into the pedagogical sequences. This theme is also evident in the contributions from Piller and Takahashi as well as Lytra, where language learning is explicitly linked to human capital enhancement. In the post-Fordist workplace, as has been frequently claimed, language is the key resource.

Much recent work to address such issues has involved deploying the theoretical tools of indexicality and scale to explore how the socially macro is invoked and played out in the interactionally micro. I have argued elsewhere that work on indexicality (in fact the etymology of the word itself) typically evokes the *pointing out* from the linguistic to the scalar social, while there is a corresponding and equally important sense in which the scalar social is *brought into* the moment of discourse. Indexicality, understood as pointing out from the linguistic to the social, only tells half the story, the other half being what Zygmunt Bauman has called the bringing in of meaning. The contributions to this volume provide many examples of this bringing of the large-scale social into the interactional moment.

Given the typical invisibility of language in social science work on issues such as migration, involving when it is found a rather restricted notion of the nature of language. It is surprising therefore how often language can be taken as a proxy for other kinds of social structuring and exclusion and thus how language solutions can be brought forward for problems that originate elsewhere. Take, for example, the foregrounding of English language competence as an issue in the wake of the London bombings. Suddenly, fluency in English is in the mouths of politicians, informing policy and hitting the headlines. Fluency in English is taken as standing (indexically) for all kinds of dimensions of social cohesion, participation and belonging. It is a bitter irony that the bombers themselves were fluent speakers of English and active social participants, playing cricket and working as teaching aides – good citizens according to all the indicators. This sudden focus positions language professionals awkwardly, since much is expected of the potential of language programmes to deliver social goods, but the nature of extra-linguistic structured inequality ensures that almost certainly they won't deliver – a double bind.

One thing that is clear from the contributions to this volume, a point particularly made by Codó, is that we are witnessing an increasingly differentiated stratification of mobile haves and underclass have-nots, whose mobility is ironically a form of 'stuck-mobility', shaped by a relative lack of ability to change their circumstances wherever they are, for example an Indian, Sri Lankan or Bangladeshi worker on a restrictive contract in Dubai or an asylum seeker waiting maybe for years for a case to be resolved. The mobility of the global business community is one thing; the mobility of an asylum seeker or an economic migrant at the lower end of the pay scale or even off it altogether is another. In a sense, everybody is going where the work is, whether it is a global businessperson juggling a Samsung and iPad in the Quantas lounge between flights on the way to the next emergent market, the financially well-padded northern European retiree on the Costa Brava, the *sans-papiers* migrant in the internet cafe in a Paris or Brussels *banlieue*, or the migrant labourer in the UAE whose working conditions recall indenture and who will be listed as 'wanted' in the newspaper if he/she breaks their contract conditions. The conditions of travel, arrival, survival and return remain at times unimaginably different and it is the job of socially committed researchers to keep this in mind and not bleach out difference with mobility as an abstraction. To that end, the contributors to this volume draw on nuanced research approaches such as linguistic ethnography and discourse analysis to get under the skin of the phenomena they are investigating.

These approaches are equally applied to an investigation of the pervasive mechanisms of neoliberalism in the workplace as in the contribution from Piller and Takahashi, on the processes of job interviewing by Roberts, and the foregrounding of communication and language skills as a marketable commodity by Allan and Lytra. The terminology says it all, not identifying *practices*, a term which speaks to the notions of social production that informs this volume, but rather *skills* which can be commodified, packaged, acquired and transferred in discrete, measurable ways. It seems that the post-Fordist language turn retains a resolutely Fordist notion of product.

The final three contributions in the volume address practical and strategic issues of agency, positioning and resistance of migrant subjects: Moyer in relation to the deployment of multilingual resources in a health care clinic, Vigouroux in relation to language choice and the accumulation of social capital in the informal economy of Congolese in Cape Town, and Sabaté in examining the *locutorios* as an unregulated space in the Spanish telecommunications market. This volume is good at evoking the lived texture of lives shaped and constrained by migration processes as well as the broad sociopolitical environment. It also turns the micro-analytical lens on the environment itself, examining the consequences of the neoliberal re-shaping of the social, the workplace, the labour market, health care and other sites and the ways these shape the language choices and subjectivities of migrants and mobile citizens. These final papers bring out the creative appropriation, *bricolage* and making do, *la débrouille* that Vigouroux points to, with which migrant subjects inhabit and make over the spaces available to them.

The institutions and institutionalised workplaces and practices examined in this volume have not so far been the focus of much sociolinguistic research because they require an understanding of broader social and economic processes and phenomena of scale, such as the pervasive influence of globalisation and neoliberalism, the understanding of which take us into interdisciplinary spaces. In this sense they exemplify the shift in sociolinguistics identified above from the correlational towards an understanding the co-productive and constitutive relationship of language and the social. As such they break new ground in critically identifying the role of language in producing and reproducing social stratification, structural inequality and exclusion.

Index